CW00525978

From *Bashes*
to *Ashes*

From *Bashes* to *Ashes*

The life of a Herefordshire
policeman & undertaker

BILL ROWLATT

FRONT COVER: Cartoon sketch by John Hawes
BACK COVER: Illustration by John Hawes

First published in November 2023

ISBN 978-1-910839-71-3

Text and photographs copyright © Bill Rowlatt, 2023.
Cartoons copyright © Gareth Philpotts, 2023.
Photographs and articles on pages 101, 171, 215, 216, 225, 233, 254 and
255 are reproduced with kind permission of the *Hereford Times*.

Designed and typeset by Logaston Press in 11 on 14 Adobe Garamond Pro.
Printed and bound in the UK.

Logaston Press is committed to printing on paper from sustainable sources.

British Library Catalogue in Publishing Data.
A CIP catalogue record for this book is available from the British Library.

CONTENTS

to

Josh, Poppy, Chloe *&* Adam

Foreword

I've had the pleasure of knowing Bill as a friend and colleague for almost two decades – first, when I was serving as an ordained Anglican priest and, more latterly, as a Celebrant (a person who officiates at funeral services). I've always found Bill to be a deeply genuine man – warm-hearted, open-minded, naturally spiritual, and with a delightfully mischievous sense of humour. All of these traits and characteristics come through his writing as you will discover when reading this marvellous memoir.

Bill's journey is a real adventure. He depicts the life of a policeman with openness and insight. You will, no doubt, find yourself thoroughly entertained and, at times, surprised by some of the hilariously shocking situations and circumstances described.

I don't think it's an exaggeration to say that Bill represents a style and era of policing that we simply don't see any more, to our great loss. Like so many public roles (among them doctors, teachers, clergy etc.) the focus has sadly been taken away from service to the people and to upholding the institution, with an ever-increasing pile of red tape and bureaucracy demanding attention.

I personally knew Bill through his years as a successful independent funeral director. His humanity shone through this aspect of his work and, I believe, enabled him to steer a course of service free from the bureaucratic clutter that haunts so many of the other professions.

So read this book with the expectation to be moved, thrilled, warmed and enriched by one of life's good guys.

Revd Mark Townsend, 2023

Preface

As you will read, for a few years now, I have been thinking about writing my autobiography but as time moves on more quickly, it has pushed me into finally doing something about it. What follows is an account of my life from my earliest childhood recollections, upbringing and education, through some stories from my two chosen careers, to the present day.

It is an English winter morning in November 2008, as I look out from my upstairs office window at my house in Eardisley, Herefordshire, watching wild birds pecking on peanuts and fat balls hanging from feeders between the willow and whitebeam tree. Everything is frosted white, eerily still and strangely beautiful. My 35-year-old son Julian just called to thank me for his birthday card as another day begins in the life of a retired local police officer, now undertaker.

Jumping ahead, I cannot believe that I started to write my autobiography and memoirs in 2008 and now, seven years later, it's already December 2015! Where did that time disappear to? They say the older you get, the quicker life passes you by, which in my experience is becoming true, so watch out everyone. In June of 2014, I was diagnosed with a tumour in my small bowel near to where it meets the duodenum. I had an endoscopy examination at the county hospital in Hereford. One of my grandsons, Josh, was with me when I was given the news. He,

God bless his heart, was so supportive and gentle. I will never forget his love and kindness, and the healing and comfort I received from his words at the time. I was so upset after being given the diagnosis, but strangely not for myself. My feelings were that I had in some way let my whole family down. The tumour was located, after coming-and-goings to my GP, after feeling a dull ache or pain near to the right side of my belly button, with bouts of more frequently-occurring vomiting. I was losing body weight and not wanting to eat. The tumour was eventually removed by a top-notch surgeon, Professor Darius Mirza, who performed his magic on me at the Queen Elizabeth Hospital in Birmingham. Darius and I got on so well that I invited him and his wife to visit Eardisley in 2017, after I'd finished a course of chemotherapy treatments. The procedure to remove the tumour involved a major operation called a whipples procedure, and I received chemotherapy treatment at the Charles Renton unit at Hereford county hospital. All of my family and friends were wonderfully supportive. I wrote the following in our village magazine:

With my heartfelt thanks

On 3 June I had an appointment for an endoscopy at the County Hospital. After the procedure I was, to say the least, shocked and shaken to the core when I was told by a very caring doctor that he had located a rare tumour at the end of my small bowel. Frightened and bewildered I then went along for numerous scans and x-rays. On the 15 July Professor Darius Mirza, a wonderful surgeon – who I had already met and had a consultation with at the Queen Elizabeth Hospital, Birmingham – rang me to ask me to present myself at casualty that day as an emergency

Preface

case at the Q.E., where he would find a bed for my admission. Five days later on 20 July the professor and his team carried out a partial whipples operation to remove the tumour, which was in an awkward location. After the operation I was told that the cancer had not spread elsewhere and was removed in its entirety. I am due to go back to the Q.E. for results and to see if chemotherapy is needed. I know I am not by any means the only local person to be diagnosed with cancer (a word right up until recently I hated to speak or hear of) and my heart goes out to everyone who has cancer. Perhaps when I am better and have more energy, I would like to start a support group for others who find themselves in this similar frightening and bewildering situation. There are too many people to thank, but I'd like to mention Gill Layton, Dick Allford and Terry Holden and everyone else who work with me, allowing my business to continue during the time it will take me to get back on my feet again.

What really amazes me has been all the love and support and offers of help from so many people. I keep using the word but I have been completely 'overwhelmed' by all the love people genuinely send from their hearts. I am so grateful to everyone, my family, friends and others I had never expected to receive cards, messages and positive thoughts from. This has helped me tremendously through a roller coaster of emotions. Thank you so much everyone.

So now I have been back at my work arranging funerals for a few months, and as someone commentated the other day, 'I see you're still upright, Bill?' I feel moved to copy in this anonymous seventeenth-century sermon called The Harvest Prayer:

Please be gentle with yourself and others.
We are all children of chance.
And none can say why some fields blossom
While others lay brown beneath the harvest sun.

Take hope that your season will come.
Share the joy of those whose season is at hand.
Care for those around you
Look past your differences.
Their dreams are no less than yours,
Their choices in life no more easily made.
And give,
Give in any way you can,
Give in every way you can.
Give whatever you possess.
Give from your heart.
To give is to love.
To withhold is to wither.
Care less for the size of your harvest
Than for how it is shared,
And your life will have meaning
And your heart will have peace.

From 2015, skip another five years to 2020, when I started to write again. Having had the pandemic and then the Ukraine war, we are certainly living in an uncertain world, and life is so different from how it used to be. Now, in 2023, the book has been written, and I hope you enjoy reading these stories.

Acknowledgements

I'd like to thank all my past colleagues in the police, sadly many of whom have now passed, and my staff, present and past, who were employed by me at Oak Tree Funeral Services for more than 20 years, who supported me during my operation and treatment for bowel cancer, through to recovery. My sincere appreciation too for all the doctors and staff at Weobley and Staunton surgeries, the John Renton unit at Hereford and Professor Darius Mirza, my surgeon at the Queen Elizabeth Hospital in Birmingham, all of whom kept me alive to write this book. I am particularly proud of the very special local community in and around Eardisley, who I had the privilege of serving as their last village policeman and their local undertaker for more than 47 years.

In particular, I'd like to thank Gareth Philpotts (cartoon sketches), John Hawes (artist), Mike Hadden (craniosacral therapist, healer and follower of Universal Sufism), Paul Davies, David and Liz from the Isle of Man, Alf and Vera from France, Jo, Colin and Tan, Rupert Winstanley, Alex Draper, Mark Townsend, Julie Collins, Jim and Julie and my grandchildren Poppy, Josh, Chloe and Adam. My brother and sisters and my son Julian. To those who have passed on: Alfie (Jo's dog), Pete, 'Herbie' Dave Bennett, Phil Wilson, Margo Dennis and my darling daughter Lucy.

Finally, my solicitor Alex Cunliffe, and Richard and Su at Logaston Press who have helped make the book come alive so professionally. Thank you to everyone.

MY FAMILY AND FIRST MEMORIES

I AM a farmer's son, one of four siblings. My parents, John Williams Rowlatt and Joan Baxter Rowlatt (née Bailey), began their farming lives at Hillend Farm – a council small-holding near Upton-on-Severn in Worcestershire – soon after they were married in 1938. I will always remember my dad saying that there was a recession in those days, when the price of farmland, with other assets and investments, tumbled and unemployment soared, and that we should never take the good times for granted, or ever forget that our economy might fail at any time. I suppose he was passing on a little piece of his wisdom from his own life's experience, as a warning that it could quite easily happen again. How wise his words have become as we are now months into a recession, not only here but seemingly worldwide – with rising unemployment and economic uncertainty. It must be worrying for so many.

My earliest childhood memory was lying in my pram in an apple orchard at Blacklaines Farm at Birdlip in Gloucestershire, which was the second farm that my mother and father bought. Dad paid £8,000 in 1946 for the 356-acre farm, with some financial support from his father, John, who had recently retired from being the first bank manager at the Upton-on-Severn branch of the Midland Bank, later known as the HSBC. My grandfather John (*pictured overleaf*) was a bombardier in the

1

First World War and served with the Royal Garrison Artillery (regiment number 104154). I have completed very little research but think he continued serving with his regiment until 1919 after that dreadful war had ended. He was wounded on active service in France, where he sustained a head injury from a shrapnel wound after he was bombed in a trench near the front line.

My grandfather, John Rowlatt

The bomb killed several of his mates. Grandfather was taken for treatment at a military hospital behind enemy lines but was quickly discharged and returned to the front line where he was reunited with his regiment to fight on. Unfortunately, I have no formal verification of this. He was presented with two First World War medals – the Victory Medal and the British War Medal – which were handed down to me and I treasure them along with the fond childhood memories I have of him. I proudly wear his war medals every year on Remembrance Day alongside my own medal, the Police Long Service and Good Conduct Medal, presented to me by the late HRH Diana, the Princess of Wales. My grandfather John was married to Muriel Elsie Rowlatt (née Williams) and census record entries show that they lived at two addresses; in Burton-on-Trent and at Great Bowden in Leicestershire. They had three sons, my father John, a farmer, Donald, who followed in my grandfather's footsteps by becoming the manager at the Midland Bank in Broadway, Worcestershire, and their youngest son, my uncle David, who worked at Cavendish House department store in Cheltenham.

I was born in a nursing home in Cheltenham and was christened at St Mary-in-Hamlet Church at Birdlip. My Christian names were going to be William Charles but as my parents carried me towards the church font, my grandfather intervened at the very last moment, persuading them to change my name to William David, as he thought I would be mercilessly teased at school with the initials W.C.! Thank you, grandfather! So, my parents, grandparents, my brother John, his twin sister Jane, my eldest sister Ann and I all lived together under the same farmhouse roof at Blacklaines Farm. It couldn't have been a very cordial existence for my mother, who they say found it difficult having to live with her in-laws as well as preparing meals and doing all the cooking and general household chores for the whole family during those early years of marriage. I was the youngest; seven years younger than the twins John and Jane and 12 years younger than my sister Ann. Shortly before dad died, when he was well into his eighties, I remember going to help my sister Jane look after him one weekend at Sibford Ferris near Banbury in Oxfordshire. An important past event must have triggered a memory in his mind, which he had to tell me about: he said to me, 'Come here, I need to tell you something!' As I drew closer to his side, he quietly and calmly announced, 'You were a mistake' – thanks dad!

Lying in a pram did I say? Well, my sister Jane decided she'd act out her adolescent motherly role one hot summer's day, when I became her baby brother victim. Mum's 1950's big black, hooded pram had four huge spoked wheels, like bicycle wheels fitted with solid rubber tyres and an old-fashioned sprung suspension system, which seem to have become fashionable again these days. I think it was a Silver Cross pram. This was my very first childhood memory. Jane wheeled me out of the house in the pram and into the orchard under the shade of an apple tree, just far enough away I suspect of being out of sight and earshot of my lovely mum. I wasn't ready to sleep, I wouldn't go to sleep and I didn't want to sleep! Neither did I want to rest or lie down! I remember it like it was yesterday – pushing myself up and forwards with every determined, physical ounce of effort which a three-year-old could muster, but Jane had other ideas. She pushed me back and down onto the pillow again and I sprang up every time, which turned into a of battle of wills. Thinking of this reminds me of a Punch and Judy performance. I was exhausted! At the age of four my second lasting memory of Blacklaines Farm was waiting patiently for the arrival of a little red Morris van, which was driven into the farmyard at a certain time on Sunday mornings. I shouted to mum when I saw the driver starting to reverse the van up to the back door. The driver got out opening up the two doors at the back to reveal rows of wooden shelves stacked high and displaying every variety of mouth-watering sweets imaginable. There was row upon row of boiled sweets inside those old-fashioned glass jars which had brightly coloured plastic screw lids, and loads of different Cadbury and Nestlé chocolate bars. This was my weekly treat which I got so excited about and was most definitely the best of my earliest childhood memories. In 1955 at the age of five, my father sold Blacklaines Farm for £22,000 before buying and moving to a smaller acreage farm at Childswickham. In between moves, my parents rented a large town flat in Cheltenham. This was so completely different from the wide-open spaces and fields which we were used to at Blacklaines. Cheltenham was where my mother grew up as a child and where I was born in a nursing home on the 21 June 1950. A comment I've made a few times is: 'The 21st of June. Ah yes, the longest day of the year, well it was for mum anyway'. I remember she shared stories with me about when she lived in Cheltenham as a little girl. She felt privileged after being placed in a position of trust by her parents in those early years. She was given her own key when they thought she was responsible enough to unlock and lock the pedestrian gate which gave her access into the beautiful, formal Clarence Square Gardens. The gardens made her feel special and loved. The gardens were private residential gardens which had an iron railing perimeter fence and only accessible by families living in the row of Georgian houses close by. The gardens were beautifully cared for and this was such a magical time and place for her during her childhood years. My grandparents' surname on my mother's side was Bailey. Granny's maiden name was Beecham. Granny had a family connection with Sir Thomas Beecham, conductor and impresario. Grandfather was James and grandmother was Gladys. My mum told me how she cherished a very close, devoted, loving relationship that she and her father had with each other. Her father was gentle, sensitive and musical, with the most fabulous tenor voice. He sang at the Cheltenham Three Choirs Festival and was a member of the St Lawrence Church choir. My mum loved him dearly, but found it difficult to show love and affection to her mother, who gave birth to an illegitimate daughter before she married. The child was later adopted. In those days it was socially unacceptable, even disgraceful and shameful, for a single girl to become pregnant and give birth outside wedlock. Apparently, my mum in her physical appearance and looks, closely resembled her illegitimate half-sister. Both of them had long auburn hair. As a child, mum would sit on her bed as my grandmother brushed her hair and repeated to her over and over again, with each brush stroke, 'I hate you, I hate you, I hate you!' because my mum reminded her mother of her illegitimate child. A spiteful and cruel case of victimisation and sadness.

Armed with a pair of large black-handled sharp metal scissors, my mum always took some satisfaction in cutting and snipping away at my hair, which I hated her doing. In those days everyone needed to save money, so it was cheaper to give your family a haircut rather than visiting the barber. Mum insisted on cutting my hair in spite of my very loud shrieks and outbursts of disapproval. I twitched, flinched and twisted my head at every opportunity to avoid contact with the big-scissors, but her stern instructions were always the same, 'Just sit still!' It wasn't easy because I'd convinced myself that she would make a mistake; miss then take a slice out of my ear, and I told her at every given opportunity. Sure enough, the day came when it happened. As bright red blood trickled from an open cut at the

Note the hairstyle! The photo to the left shows me leaning against dad's
Standard Vanguard after someone gave me a cigarette to hold!

top of my right ear, I sensed mum's instant panic and remorse knowing that she had just inflicted, although entirely accidental, such excruciating pain on her five-year-old little boy, despite my warnings. How could she? A saying mum had was: 'A little blood makes a lot of mess!' Well, this was bloody messy as well as bloody painful. Oddly, I felt some sense of relief knowing that the inevitable had happened and it was finally over and done with. I knew too that my dear mum would never want to ever attempt to cut my hair ever again.

The same day, I had my first contact with Cheltenham police. My red Raleigh tricycle which I'd left outside the flat had been stolen and I burst into floods of tears knowing that I wouldn't see it ever again. Mum suggested that we walk down the road to the local Police Station to report it missing. When we arrived, we were met by a very tall, friendly desk Sergeant who had a very large corpulence bulging over the top of his black leather belt. He said he would go round the back to check in the Police found property room. I could hardly believe my eyes when he reappeared, awkwardly bending over his belly, wheeling my bike towards me. I was thrilled to see it again and the Police were brilliant! This obviously left some lasting impressions. I couldn't wait to get it back home to the flat, and pedalled it home just as fast as my little legs could pedal, with mum struggling to keep up. Going so fast I was wobbling from side to side, and so happy I was smiling like a Cheshire cat, wearing a short-sleeved shirt, grey cotton shorts and white crepe-bandaged ear!

In 1955 'Our Father', which my brother and I sometimes called dad as a joke, purchased Mount Pleasant Farm just outside the village of Childswickham near Broadway in Worcestershire for £16,000. The farm was a 230-acre mixed arable and stock farm, with heavy clay soil. Mount Pleasant was typical of its era. The farmhouse was a large, three-storied, four-bedroomed, red-brick Victorian house with a coal-fired boiler circulating moderately warm – but never hot – water through to heavy, black cast-iron radiators. There were open fireplaces in every room. The top floor had two attic bedrooms separated by another ascending staircase from the lower floors, and were rarely used. In those days, winters were bitterly cold and it wasn't unusual to see frosted patterns on the inside of our bedroom window. Outside were deep frozen snowdrifts, and frozen water pipes in the sheds and milking parlour. I remember dad's Volkswagen Beetle being completely buried in a frozen snowdrift for a couple of weeks until we all helped him dig it out with shovels. Its engine started immediately. I also remember seeing starving wood pigeons flying around searching for scraps of food and watching them land on the tops of sprout plants to feed. But they were trapped. Their scaly feet became instantly frozen to the plants so they couldn't fly off. They were perched there until they slowly froze to death, like some biblical bird Calvary.

The warmest room in the farmhouse was the large farm-house kitchen. On the wall, mum sellotaped a big coloured map of the world so we could refer to it during school work or sometimes to settle a family debate about a particular world location. Mum endlessly prepared and cooked farmhouse meals on and in her full-sized anthracite coal-fired Aga cooker. The Aga had a plate-warming oven in the bottom left-hand corner which was kept constantly at body temperature. During lambing time, dad brought barely alive, newly-born or orphan lambs into the kitchen for mum to work her magic on. Keeping the oven door half open, mum would place a couple of the shiv-ering cold, half-dead lambs right inside the oven to warm them

8

up and save their lives, often administering a small teaspoonful of neat brandy to help them on a bit! In just a couple of hours or so, most of them recovered enough to go back outside again to be reunited with their mums, adopted by another ewe or to become bottle-fed orphans. A well-known farming trick was to skin a dead lamb, then to tie its skin around an orphan lamb so that the ewe, after identifying her dead lamb's familiar smell, would be fooled into thinking it was hers to take to, and hers to rear. Success!

Neighbouring farmers, visitors, reps and even a monk who looked after the farm animals at Broadway Abbey and monastery, who bought pigs off dad, were all invited in for food. There was always an abundance of good, fresh, wholesome food which everyone tucked into and enjoyed. Free-range eggs – either poached, fried, boiled or scrambled! Fat bacon joints which mum bought cheaply from Evesham market, paying sixpence a pound in old money or 2.5p in new money. She cooked the bacon joints slowly in a pressure cooker before pouring off the excess fat then pressed them down with a heavy weight to make the joints into one big joint which was left to cool. Thick fat bacon slices were carved off it then placed in between two deliciously thicker slices of mum's homemade wholemeal bread, layered with lashings of hot English mustard and homemade chutney. There was Aga toast, salted butter with rock cakes and fresh thick cream from dad's dairy outside. There was homemade cottage cheese, jams and super-sized large jars of peanut butter and Marmite. In the centre of the farmhouse kitchen was a big square kitchen table and chairs which gave visitors plenty of room to sit around. A regular visitor was Horace Agg who lived in Childswickham and cycled to the farm most weeks. Horace was a wonderful local character. He had a very red face and always wore a cap and waistcoat with his pocket watch on the end of a silver chain. He made all of dad's hundreds of gallons of farmhouse cider in oak barrels including plum jerkum made from red Victoria plums and rhubarb wine, which he drank quite a lot of too. He had a stutter and I remember he always used the inside of his cap to place his food on instead of using one of mum's plates. Leftovers were wrapped up in his clean handkerchief or neckerchief to take home. He used his penknife to cut in half a thick slice of the fat bacon layering it with a thick layer of hot English mustard which I don't think he'd tasted before. After taking a mouthful he said to mum, 'Mrs, th th th this mmmustard is mmmighty pppowerful!' Everyone was made to feel welcome and always had their own story to tell. They left feeling well-fed, relaxed and cheerful. Some would mention, while others would only be thinking to themselves ... did we actually see a baby lamb's front legs sticking out of Joan's Aga oven?

My parents farmed at Mount Pleasant farm for 14 years and in 1969 dad decided to semi-retire to do what he called a bit of 'dog and stick' farming. They sold the Farm for £60,000 (now worth millions) and moved to purchase their fourth and final farm – 50-acre Hollybush Farm at Longhope in Gloucestershire. Dad milked a small herd of cows, kept a flock of sheep and grew his own vegetables. Mum kept chickens and they were happy there. Geographically, they were closer to Gloucester and Ross cattle markets where dad could regularly meet up with his retired farming pals on market days to reminisce and swap farming tales over a few glasses of whisky, which was his favourite tipple. While dad's time was occupied with his dairy herd and sheep, mum continued with her beloved piano playing. She treated herself by buying a Bechstein piano and took up a childhood dream to become an artist. Mum always modestly understated her natural gift for music and art. She became an exceptionally talented artist, painting the most beautiful portraits, country scenes and still lifes using oils, acrylic paints and occasionally watercolour. At 16 she'd won a scholarship to attend Cheltenham Art College, but her parents couldn't afford to send her there. I remember her walking through the small, gently sloping fields at Hollybush Farm closely followed by her cat with her walking stick and sketchbook tucked under her arm. She would stop to sketch or paint the most exquisite wild flower scenes with beauty emanating from her soul, spilling out onto the page. She loved colour and joined various art classes to extend her knowledge and experience. I am so proud of her and we loved her dearly. I loved my father too, but differently.

MY SCHOOL, PONY AND THE FARM

IN 1957, when I was seven, my parents Jack and Joan decided to send me to boarding school at Bowbrook House School for boys in the village of Peopleton, near Pershore in Worcestershire. I cried and sobbed for my mum. It was such a young age to be separated from her and I missed her terribly. When I was older, I travelled to school by steam train from Evesham to Pershore railway stations, but, at seven, my mum used to drive me to school. Every time, I vividly remember being physically sick in exactly the same spot on the corner of a junction which was about a mile away from the school. As I got older, my school memories were a lot happier. At that age we were all expected to behave properly and to respect our elders and teachers. Our school motto was 'Manners Maketh

11

Man' and to this day I proudly value and believe in the words. We had dormitories which slept up to seven boys in each and we were individually responsible for stripping off our bedclothes every morning before breakfast and to remake them before bedtime. Our matching beds were basic, made from metal ends and sides which were bolted together in the four corners to keep them rigid. Each bed had a wire unsprung base with a thin horse hair mattress placed

Aged seven, at Browbrook House School

on top. Every morning after stripping the sheets, pillow cases and dark grey blankets off our beds, we were required to neatly fold them in a certain way then stand to attention by the side to present them for inspection. The blankets and sheets had to be folded to army standards, neither creased, crumpled nor showing anything out of place. The consequences for failing to meet this strict standard was one or more whacks on the backside with someone's slipper (usually mine because I had the largest feet) or a slap on the back of the head before being told to undo everything, and fold them all again. At bedtime we all changed into our cotton striped pyjamas, bedroom slippers and dressing gowns tied around the waist with twisted rope belts which had tassels on both ends. They looked more like something you'd keep your sitting room curtains tied back with or church bell ropes. Every morning, after washing and traipsing downstairs for breakfast, we changed into our school uniforms. Our uniforms were grey shirts, grey and maroon ties, short grey trousers worn all year round, grey jumpers and maroon school blazers *(seen here in my photo)*. We wore maroon peaked caps, with our school name and logo sewn on the breast pocket of our school blazers. At bedtime one of the teachers did the rounds by visiting the dormitories to announce 'lights out!', usually by 8 o'clock sharp, but the time varied depending on the age of the boys in the dormitory. Boarders aged from seven to fifteen years. The older we were, the later we were allowed to leave our lights on to read books, but never later than 9 o'clock. After getting ourselves ready for bed, we would walk in an orderly line down a narrow wooden staircase and into the school kitchen opposite. We helped ourselves to our hot drink of choice, made in large mugs which had already been placed out on the kitchen table. Choices included hot chocolate, Ovaltine, Horlicks and Bengers, which was my favourite. Bengers, which is no longer made, was a powder supplement added to hot milk similar to Horlicks, or we drank hot milk with biscuits. Summer and winter times were identical. There was always a large cauldron of porridge, left bubbling away all night on top of the Rayburn cooker, which was served up for breakfast the following day. From the kitchen, we walked in an orderly line cupping hands around our mugs of hot drinks to keep our hands warm, especially in winter. Then on and into the headmaster's living room. Sitting in a semi-circle, cross legged on the floor around the open fire, we said evening prayers and sang hymns accompanied on piano by the headmaster's wife. I loved these evenings. They had a homely feel, drawing my mind closer to thoughts of home and I believed in God which has stayed with me to this day. One of my favourite hymns we sang was 'The day thou gavest Lord is ended.' After this, we ascended the long wide Victorian staircase up and along the upstairs corridors and back to our individual dormitories to get into bed and wait for 'lights out'. There were mice in the dormitories, which we set traps for, taking bets on the time it would take for the first trap to be sprung. Writing this feels like a Charles Dickens novel but this is how it was and how I remember it, with nostalgia. Next morning, we lined up and filed past to have our breakfast in the school dining hall. The overnight simmering porridge, which was overcooked and lumpy, was ready to be dolloped into our individual bowls from a metal ladle. Porridge was followed by fried eggs swimming in hot fat on aluminium trays with beans, bacon, sausages and pieces of fat-saturated fried bread. It might all sound unpalatable, but I enjoyed breakfast. The headmaster's brother would always sit at one end of a long wooden dining table where he could keep an eye on us, and keep us in order. A smoothly-planed wooden plank was kept on the mantelpiece above the fireplace so that any of us who were caught slouching could be told to remove our ties and undo our top two shirt buttons. The plank was then pushed inside our shirts and down our backs vertically from the neck to waist level which forced us to sit bolt upright for the remainder of the meal. The headmaster's brother was a Scotsman who used to spread masses of salt on his porridge before pouring the milk on top – a taste I tried, but could never enjoy.

The headmaster taught us maths. I remember our class of six would be waiting for him to arrive in our classroom. Quite often, he wouldn't turn up to teach us, so we drew straws or tossed a coin to decide which one of us would be chosen to go and find him. Back then, 63 or so years ago, discipline was very strict. The headmaster was usually found in his study. I remember the day when it was my turn to find him. I went

14

along to his study which was in the main house, and knocked quietly on his door. After knocking again, I peered around the door to see that he was fast asleep in his chair. I tentatively uttered 'Sir, sir!', desperately trying not to alarm him, then cautiously walked closer towards him. There was no immediate response, so I reluctantly tapped him very gently on one shoulder. He woke up with a start and glared fiercely at me, when I said as politely as possible, 'Sir, you're late for our class, Sir'. As he stood up, I ran out of his study and all the way back to the classroom to rejoin my classmates. Some minutes later, he arrived at the classroom door, which was in one of the old wartime Nissan huts in the grounds of the school. The six of us stood up when he entered, then we all sat back down again in complete silence. If we got our sums wrong or gave the wrong answer, our punishment was a hard whack on the back of the hand with a wooden ruler or the wooden black board rubber being hurled at us through mid-air. Fortunately for us his lack of accuracy and a dodge and a duck from us, minimised nearly all chances of any direct strikes. I know all this might sound rather unbelievable but at the time, it seemed like his style of teaching was sort of normal, which of course it wasn't. One of the staff was known to have an alcohol dependency problem, so it was for this reason that I was moved from the school to attend Four Pools Secondary Modern at Evesham for a few months. Other pupils at Bowbrook were transferred by their parents to different schools. I was in a no-win situation because I ended up by being bullied at Four Pools school. Word got around that I'd been to a private boarding school. Some sadistic idiot thought up a bullying game called a 'pile on' where what felt like more than 20 kids all jumped together on top of their victim who was squidged underneath. This occurred at unsupervised break times in the school playing fields and I am amazed that no one, including myself, ended up with any broken limbs or concussion. After a short period at Four Pools school, I returned to Bowbrook. The new headmaster and his wife were Mr and Mrs Schofield who were altogether completely different from the previous regime. As a whole, these were much happier times but at one point I developed serious and painful ear infections and underwent surgery to have my adenoids removed at Evesham General Hospital, which solved the problem. In those days, ether was used as a general anaesthetic. It was poured onto a mask which knocked me out! I used to suck sweets called Victory V's, but after my operation they tasted and smelt just like ether, so they were no longer 'my fav'. After the operation I made a full recovery with no reoccurrence of any of the former excruciating ear pain or infection. The tuck shop at school was open for ten minutes every day. My parents gave me two and sixpence a week pocket money or six pence a day which is the equivalent to 2 ½ pence in today's money, allowing me to buy one bar of Cadbury's Dairy milk (sixpence), a tube of Smarties (threepence), liquorice twirls (one penny each), a Barrett's Sherbet fountain (threepence) or 15 black jacks for a penny! I ate some sweets myself, but kept the rest to take home at weekends to share with my brother and two sisters. I've asked them if they remembered this, but they have no recollection of my great sweetie sacrifice!

Dad bought me a pony from the annual pony sales at Stow on the Wold in the Cotswolds. She measured 12 hands and I named her Spangles after the square tubes of boiled sweets which were popular then. Dad told me that Spangles was broken in to go between the shafts, so she could be harnessed up to pull a small pony cart. We didn't have one on the farm but after mentioning it to me this fuelled my imagination and enthusiasm to find one. I think I was about 12 years of age when, during the school summer holidays, I cycled around visiting local farms near Childswickham asking farmers if they had any pony traps for sale. After knocking at a farmhouse door in the village of Buckland it was answered by a very kind elderly gentleman farmer whose name was Mr Hyatt. I repeated my question which I'd asked so many times before. He must have been aware of some determination on my part even at that age. He said we should go and look in a barn where he showed me exactly the right-sized pony trap that I'd been looking for. I was thrilled that it was in a dry barn, covered with straw and looking like it was in really good condition. I asked Mr Hyatt how much he wanted for it and I paid him £2 which I'd saved up from my pocket money. My brother John towed it home for me behind dad's green Morris van with both doors flung wide open at the back with me sitting precariously on the ledge, gripping tightly onto the two ends of the shafts as it was being towed along. My legs dangled down and out of the back with the soles and heels of my wellies scuffing the road as we hit speeds in excess of 45 miles an hour. At that speed the pony trap's wheels were wobbling and rattling a bit but they stayed on all the way home to the farm. In my mind's eye all it needed was a good wash and sanding down. There were a couple of surprises which I hadn't seen when I saw it in Mr Hyatt's barn. It had a beautifully curved brass rail at the front to rest the leather reins on, and a thick brass-handled door latch with brass hinges on the rear door. Using a bit of Brasso and some fine-mesh steel wool, these would all polish up a treat. It had a cast iron step for passengers to climb up into the back and two beautifully carved wooden seats on either side, providing enough space for the driver and three passengers to sit comfortably and a brass carriage lamp holder. I polished them up and sanded it all down by hand, adding a coat of clear varnish to the wood to give it extra shine. Then I found a small paintbrush and a tin of red paint to hand paint my name on the door panel at the back, adding my address: Mount Pleasant Farm. The day came when I'd sorted everything out and was ready to harness Spangles up for our maiden trip into Childswickham village. I placed her leather head collar over her head, turned it and slid it down onto her shoulders, which is where ponies and horses pull their burden. On went the rest of the harness before reversing her into the shafts to finish attaching and harnessing her to the trap. Now we were ready to leave. I climbed up the step into the back and held onto the reins to steer her and made a clicking sound before asking to her 'walk on'. I was looking forward to driving my very own pony and trap for the first time. We set off down the farm drive towards the main road where dad's wooden milk stand stood right on the corner at the junction. Every day, dad took 12-gallon aluminium churns full of full fat unpasteurised milk from the farm dairy to this point where they were collected by the milk lorry. As we set off, I realised that Spangles was reluctant to walk on more than a few yards at a time, before coming to a complete stop again. I think she had an inkling that the journey I'd planned for her involved physical effort! Unperturbed, I steered her on our way with every ounce of persuasion I could muster, turning right at the junction and onto the main road towards Childwickham village. It was hard work for both of us. I was trying all manner of encouragements to get her to move more quickly, but she only wanted to move slowly and at her own pace, obviously not wanting to leave the farm. Eventually, we arrived in the village, which was about four miles away. I steered Spangles to the right, past the Childswickham Inn which was dad's local, and on towards the parish church where years later I was married by the local vicar, Reverend Norman Haigh. After taking our tour of the village, we headed back to the farm. Nearly half a mile away from the farm, something must have triggered in her head as I noticed that she'd quickened her pace without any rein response from me, which I thought was a bit odd. About two hundred yards from the junction, I was sitting and enjoying some sunshine, intending to steer her left past the milk stand and up the farm drive. I'd never had any experience before of driving a pony and trap, only learning the knack of it by seeing dad harness up his heavy cart horse to pull the farm cart, then going with him across wet fields to feed hay to the cattle. This was much less muddy than using a farm tractor and trailer, especially in winter. Suddenly Spangles, for no obvious reason, broke into a trot, then going faster and faster into a canter which ended up in a full-speed gallop! I instinctively took to my feet, keeping my legs wide apart to maintain my balance, still clinging on to the reins. By now we were hurtling along at a seriously fast and dangerous speed which felt like we were an accident waiting to happen. I held on, tightening my grip of the reins, still trying to pull her up and slow her down, but the more I tugged the faster she went which was when it finally dawned on me that I'd lost complete control of her! At that speed we quickly drew close to the farm when Spangles of her own volition took the sharp left-hand bend galloping as fast as she could past the milk stand before racing on up the farm driveway. On the corner, I momentarily looked down to my left to see that the pony trap's wheel had narrowly missed the milk stand by a whisker as we broadsided and skidded around the corner and on up to the stable. I was thrown forwards as Spangles skidded to an abrupt standstill right outside her stable door. Her laboured breathing became almost dragon-like as she snorted and wheezed, breathing out steaming hot breath with white bubbles of snotty froth from her dilated nostrils. Beads of hot smelly sweat poured out from the pores of her skin under her coat which trickled down to the ground. I was feeling completely shocked but also incredibly relieved that we had made it home without overturning or hitting the milk stand. She knew where she wanted to be and how to get there with or without me – right outside her comfortable stable knowing there was food, water and clean straw to lie down and roll about on. The whole episode reminded me of the chariot race in Charlton Heston's Ben Hur film, which mum took me to watch at Evesham's Regal picture house, just weeks before. This was my first lucky escape!

I don't know how it happened, but dad managed to convince the school's headmaster that Spangles could be kept and stabled at Bowbrook for a while, giving me the opportunity to ride her and look after her there. One of the teaching staff owned a pure-bred white stallion and, after the two of them fell for each other, we found out that Spangles was in foal, so she was immediately expelled from school for bad behaviour and returned home to the farm! So, my life and my education began to get better now that I was back at boarding school under the new leadership of headmaster Mr Schofield. On Fridays I went home to spend weekends on the farm. My eldest sister Ann, who is 12 years older than me, followed my mum's profession by training to become a nurse at the John Radcliffe Hospital in Oxford. Mum specialised in nursing patients who were admitted to isolation wards after contracting infectious tropical diseases, not unlike the world's Corona Virus pandemic which we have today.

My brother John attended quite a few schools, ending his education at Prince Henry's Grammar School in Evesham. He was a good athlete and very competitive. John loved farming and later became a dairy farmer after attending Shuttleworth Agricultural College. I would describe father as being a bit overzealous. He often asked John to do too many farm tasks and John, who was always eager to please, did what he was asked, whereas I'd mastered the art of a bit of ducking and diving, never giving dad too much of an opportunity of cornering me. After John left school, he worked on the farm forming a business partnership with 'our father'! When I was at home I helped John with the general farm chores. Some good memories I have were hot summer harvests, loading bales of hay with pitch forks onto farm trailers then climbing up onto the top of the loads which were driven back to the farm by my brother John or Bill Griffin, who was one of two general farm labourers. After being driven back the bales were unloaded and stacked inside covered barns or built into hay stacks which were sheeted over to protect them from the weather. They say there are skills to every job. Loading and neatly stacking rectangular bales by hand onto farm trailers is one and roping off each load with hessian ropes using a knot called a half hitch to secure the load is another. As I was already on top of the loaded trailers, my job was to drop the bales off the load by throwing them down to John who was below me. Then he loaded them onto a mechanical bale elevator which carried them up into the top of the hay barn or hay stack to be stacked. Occasionally there were close misses. One bale which John hadn't seen me drop, hit him right on the top of his head which really worried me when he lay face down and motionless for at least a minute or two. After recovering, he looked up and shouted some extremely rude expletives at me ... his little brother! I promise if you're reading this John that I honestly didn't mean to do it, although you thought very differently at the time! Another incident which I got the blame for was when John and I were mucking out a cowshed for dad. After loading the muck onto a muck spreader by hand using muck forks, John drove the tractor with the loaded spreader out into a grass field to spread its load. Tractors had no cabs for protection in those days. I went with him but decided to step down off the tractor when we arrived in the field, deciding to walk by the side instead. John gripped the lever to engage the mechanism which started the muck spreader to spread. It had a moveable mechanical floor which pushed the manure backwards and onto a rotating metal spinner, so the muck was jettisoned out and over the grass. I was watching all this happening when I saw a brick hit the rotating arm. As it did, the brick shot up into the air, spinning out of control with such force. As luck had it, it just skimmed the top of John's head causing him a tiny superficial cut to his scalp, though could just as easily have killed him. John stopped the tractor and felt the top of his head which was bleeding. For some reason he thought that I had thrown something at him. He shouted at me, but it wasn't my fault. Then he stopped and jumped off the tractor to try to catch me so I ran for my life!

My sister Jane trained as a children's nanny, living with busy working families, some of whom were famous. She was employed by David Croft who was the writer of the television comedy series Dad's Army which is still my and one of the nation's favourites. Apart from Pike, I think that all the actors in the cast have since died. I remember Jane saying how much they all enjoyed creating and acting out their individual parts in the series. She also worked for the family of the late John Ogden, who was a well-known professional pianist.

At Bowbrook we played rugby, cricket, football, rounders and were taught archery. I never was too energetic about sports in general, but I tried my best. I still have my hand-written school report. The headmaster wrote in the general sports section under the games heading 'Bill enjoys a little gentle exercise!' Every day, whatever the weather we went outside into the cinder yard, wearing only a pair of blue shorts, plimsolls and white tee shirt, to do half an hour of physical exercise. Many of us suffered with chilblains, which strangely enough you seldom hear of these days. In addition to school subjects, I was taught carpentry and made a coffee table for mum and a dog kennel for dad's sheepdog Brock who was a beautiful dog with a wonderful temperament. I made my own electric guitar which I played, but after lending it to someone I never saw it again. The other farm labourer was dad's cowman Al Higginbotham. Al, his wife and their son John lived in the other farm cottage next to Bill Griffin. Al played George Formby songs on a ukulele which I was fascinated by. It gave me the incentive of wanting to learn to play. He showed me some basic chords then mum bought me a uke. I practised and practised until I progressed to playing guitar then drums, but that's another story!

I shared a dormitory at school with two school friends. Ron Basson, whose father was a senior British army officer in charge of the large military vehicle depot at Ashchurch near Tewkesbury, and Philip York-Jones, whose family ran an ice cream business from their home at Droitwich in Worcestershire, 'York-Jones Ice Cream'. I've often wondered what happened to both of them as I've not seen or heard of them since we all left school. Philip was very clever with electronics; building electronic devices which I hadn't a clue about. He became a radio ham, studying and passing some very advanced exams which was a great accomplishment at his age. I remember that he constantly suffered from a painful back injury and he reminded me of an orang-utan when I saw him hanging around suspending himself from the tops of door frames to pull and stretch his back for pain relief. We weren't allowed radios at school but we used to sneak in small crystal sets with ear pieces to tune into pop stations like the illegal Radio Caroline pirate ship which broadcast nonstop pop music 24/7 and radio Luxemburg. It was easy to hide a crystal set under the bed clothes and they worked without batteries. Another very good friend was David Ford who lived at Abbotts Moreton near Evesham. We lost contact with each other for quite a few years after leaving school until we eventually caught up again. David now lives on the Isle of Man with his wife Liz, their son Christopher who is my Godson and daughter Aimee. David's mother Jean was Manx and Liz is too. I sometimes jokingly refer to them as Davey Wavey and Lizzy Whizzy!

There were four of us who shared a dormitory together which looked directly out and along the upstairs corridor leading down a wide balustraded staircase. From our dormitory door we could clearly see to the bottom of the staircase and directly into Mr. Schofield's private lounge. At night, he always left his lounge door wide open so he could sit, relax and watch television from a comfortable armchair and at the same time listen out for any noise or disturbance coming from the upstairs dormitories after lights out. We could also clearly see his black and white television screen. With Philip's ingenuity and electronic wizardry, he assembled the most exciting electronic device, explaining

24

what we were going to do with it. He soldered together some wires and connected some other electrical components which he fitted into a box that had a mains lead and a three-pin plug. After plugging it into the mains, he switched it on. The device buzzed and glowed red. There was a dial at the front which could be switched to the right or left. Right was for 'on' and left for 'off' We took up our positions with our heads in a vertical line peeping through the gap in the dormitory door as Phillip slowly turned the dial to the 'on' position. When he did that, the headmaster's TV screen was scrambled and had squiggly lines of interference right across it, accompanied by a deafening high-pitched squeal! Philip was a genius! With split-second timing he'd pulled off the prank. We saw Mr Schofield walk up to his telly, getting more and more agitated because he was convinced that it was on the blink! Standing in front of it, he fiddled with the controls but it made no difference. By now none of us could hold back our infectious and hysterical laughter. Then Philip turned the dial back in the opposite direction and a normal picture was restored! Mr Schofield sat down again but had little respite. Philip's device was turned on again, and we saw Mr Schofield getting even more annoyed, thumping and battering the top of his TV with his clenched fist! We had to shut our dormitory door to dampen down the sounds of our hand-muffled hysterics. Philip was brilliant and our hero!

There were often schoolboy fads that everyone wanted to join in with to have fun. By now I was a school prefect which carried some responsibilities with it. Water pistols were the in thing. One dark winter's evening it was getting too rowdy and out of hand. It seemed like everyone had found and armed themselves with a water pistol and the frenzy was spreading. Many were wound up and ready for battle still wearing their school uniforms and getting drenched in the process. Everyone was running around uncontrollably outside which eventually became too much for our house master Mr Reading to get to grips with. He called me into his office giving me strict instructions to confiscate every water pistol I could lay my hands on. Boarders were hiding and crazily ambushing each other which might have ended up with someone getting hurt. 'Bill, I want you confiscate as many water pistols as you can and bring them to me', he ordered, adding, 'it's dark outside and this is all becoming beyond a joke,' I decided that I would almost do what he had asked me to do! While still carrying out my orders I had the idea of having a little fun of my own. Arming myself with two of the biggest matching pair of high velocity water pistols which I'd just confiscated, I filled them up and placed one under each arm, then continued with my quest. As a forfeit, I thought it would be funny to soak others before getting them to surrender and hand over their water weapons to me to hand in. I ran around another corner in search of my next unsuspecting victim and started laughing when I spotted a dark silhouetted figure coming towards me. With anticipation and hilarity, I let rip with both barrels giving the darkened shape a total drenching around the face and shoulders, who I hadn't immediately recognised was our housemaster Mr Reading, who had been checking on my progress!

After this, though school was an important part of my life I also looked forward to weekends and school holidays at home on the farm, and as time went on, I somehow got promoted to head boy. Recreational interests included joining the boy Scouts when I became a member of the 1st Peopleton troop, which was never a voluntary option but more of an obligatory membership. We all wore khaki brown uniforms with yet more short trousers. In charge was our troop leader Mr Bennet, who lived in a cottage close to the school near to the Bow brook by the boundary of the school playing fields. I remember Helen his daughter, who I had a crush on. Our Scout group met at Peopleton village hall, learning life skills such as first aid, laying and lighting a fire, chopping wood, cooking and how to tie different knots which have become really useful later in life. Mrs Playdon was one of our school cleaning ladies. She was a darling and lived in Peopleton village with her husband Arthur who was a retired Worcester City police officer. They were a homely, gentle and elderly couple, and I was given special dispensation to go outside the school boundaries to visit them at their home when I was about 15. Arthur usually poured me a glass of sherry to drink when I went to see them making me feel very grown up. He would reminisce by telling me stories of his police career which were riveting and were the catalyst of things to come. He fed my intrigue and enthusiasm of one day wanting to join the police. In those days the minimum height for recruits was six foot (183cm) and I was almost already that tall, so should surely grow that little bit more to meet the minimum height standard required to join as a police cadet. Worcester City police was formed in 1833. It was a small police force which had approximately 150 serving officers. Today there are 42 police forces in Scotland, England and Wales. Worcester City police's amalgamation with its neighbouring police forces of Worcestershire, Herefordshire and Shropshire constabularies took place on 17 November 1967, when it was named the West Mercia Constabulary, as it is today. A careers officer came to the school for a one-to-one consultation as in those days there was every conceivable career opportunity available, but my mind was already made up to join the police. I took five CSEs and two O-Level exams. I passed my CSE exams but failed one of my O-Levels which I later had to re-sit at Worcester Technical College. Clearly, I am no academic.

LEAVING SCHOOL AND BECOMING
A POLICE CADET

JUST before I left school, my maternal grandmother died, leaving a modest sum of money to my mum. Mum asked me if I would like to fly out with her to the Holy Land on a pilgrimage tour. I was due to leave school at the age of 16 so used

My cousin Sue Rowlatt's 21st birthday party at the Lygon Arms in Broadway, May 1966. I was 16 with my '60s Beatles hairstyle and I'd asked the band's drummer if I could have a go!

our visit to Israel and Jordan as part of my CSE course work for scripture. I still have my coursework book with postcards and references to all of the holy places we visited. I enjoyed seeing the many places mentioned in the bible and this was my first trip abroad. There was a very attractive and pretty girl, who was about my age, accompanied by her mother in the same group as us, which made the trip even more memorable. Our group attended a Christian service in the small chapel known as St John the Baptist Greek Orthodox Church on the banks of the River Jordan, where I read a bible reading and collected some water from the river in a lemonade bottle which I took home with me. Many years later, my children Julian and Lucy were both baptised in this water, which I still have nearly 57 years later, and which is still as clear as crystal.

Following our pilgrimage trip to the Holy Land, it was time to apply to join Worcester City police to become a police cadet, taking my first step towards a career in the police force, which at that time I didn't envisage would span 33 years. My application was successful and I was asked to attend a formal interview at Worcester City police station in Deansway. Mum took me to an established family gent's outfitter in Cheltenham named 'The Famous Outfitters' where I was measured for my very first three-piece suit. My dear mum came with me for my job interview, which I had just after reaching the age of 16. On arrival, we were shown into an office and introduced to Chief Inspector Hunt, who was the chief constable's chief clerk and personal assistant. I remember him so well. He was a kind, softly spoken gentleman, immaculately dressed in his Chief Inspector's uniform. He had rows of ribbons sewn on the left breast pocket of his tunic which I assume represented wartime medals awarded during the Second World War. We

Please address all letters on official matters," The Chief Constable, Worcester", and not personally

City of Worcester

TELEPHONE NO.
2 2 2 2 2 (7 LINES)
(PTE. BCH. EX.)

Eric A. Abbott
Chief Constable

REF No.
Per.Recs.(4)

P.O. Box No. 28.
City Police Office,
Worcester

25th July, 1966.

Dear Madam,

    Further to your telephone conversation with my Chief Clerk today, I have to confirm that your son has been offered an appointment as Cadet in this Force and has been asked to report for duty at 9 a.m. on Monday, 15th August, 1966.

    Accommodation has been arranged for him with Mrs. Brant, 2 Barbourne Terrace, Worcester. Mrs. Brant will be very happy for you to call on her at your convenience.

Yours faithfully,

Superintendent & D.C.C.
for Chief Constable.

Mrs. J. W. Rowlatt,
Mount Pleasant Farm,
Childswickham,
BROADWAY,
Worcs.

were then ushered through to the chief constable's office by the chief inspector where mum and I were formerly introduced to Sir Eric Abbott who was the serving chief constable. I was young, shy and rather overwhelmed by the whole occasion, but mum, who was calm and quietly supportive, helped me through the ordeal. She interjected only when she thought that I was floundering a little or when she thought I needed her support. The combination of her being there and the psychological boost of being smartly dressed in my new suit gave me the confidence to get through the interview. Then a letter arrived at the farm signed by the deputy chief constable, Superintendent Jo Davidson, stating that I was successful in my application to become a police cadet. I was measured for my first uniform and issued with two pairs of black leather police boots. Board and lodgings had already been arranged by the police with Mrs Brant at 2 Barbourne Terrace. Mrs Brant was a widow and charged me five pounds per week for five days full board and lodgings, and I knew that my dear mum was quite proud of me.

Discipline was very strict in the police as it had been for me at school and I took my new career very seriously. After three years I would be required to take an entrance exam and a physical fitness test to become eligible to join the regular force. I was a cadet in Worcester during the week but went home at weekends. Our police training officer was PC Alan Hinton, who was eventually promoted to the rank of chief inspector. Other cadets in my intake included: Robert Green, John Pratley, Keith Dyer, Terry Roberts, who became a police sergeant in his home town of Worcester (retired), Ian Johnson (retired) and Martin Stanton, the son of PC Ron Stanton who worked in the prosecutions department. Martin went on to complete his 30 years pensionable service as did Ian Johnson.

Ian was a confident and competent character who was promoted to the rank of detective chief superintendent, during which he headed investigations into many serious and notorious cases of rapes and murders throughout the force area. We were inspected daily and taught how to march to the Grenadier Guard's standard and how to properly salute senior officers and funeral processions. The rule for saluting was to 'take the longest way up and the shortest way down'. We were told how to iron straight razor-sharp creases in the front and backs of our uniform trousers and how to polish or bull our boots using only black Kiwi polish as no other polish would do. I've continued using the same polish and identical polishing skills to this day with my own shoes. To build up a mirror-like shine

Worcester City police cadet William Rowlatt aged 16, 1966 – second along, on parade during an inspection by HMI (Her Majesty's Inspector of Constabulary)

on a shoe toe cap, a small area of polish is thinly applied with a soft duster held over the index finger. Then, after applying a small amount of spit on the boot or shoe, hundreds of small circular movements are necessary to make the polish hard as it begins to shine. It's a skill you learn as you go along, making sure that just the right amount of spit and polish is applied and never too much during the whole process, then finally breathing on the toe cap and buffing it off with an even softer duster. I've spent hours upon hours bulling my drill boots to make them shine like a mirror. 'I want to see my face in them lad!' – shouted directly in my ear by drill sergeants during training, along with other sarcastic quips like, 'Am I hurting you lad? Well, I bloody should be! I'm standing on your fuc.... hair! Get it cut lad!' I detested having short hair and they knew it. This was the swinging '60s with mods, rockers, the Rolling Stones and the Beatles! I loved modern music. Some of my favourite bands were the Rolling Stones (Midnight Rambler), the Small Faces (Itchycoo Park), Them, Bad Company, Free (All Right Now). All these bands did brilliant drum fills and their songs were some of my all-time favourites; I particularly loved the bass lines in the middle. The Kinks (All Day and All of the Night) and The Who (My Generation) both had great bass lines and drums, and there were many others. A few years later I saw live performances at the NEC of John Cougar Mellencamp, Tina Turner, Eric Clapton, Mark Knopfler and Chris de Burgh, who I've seen many times since. My young grandson Josh came with me to see Chris de Burgh in concert but wasn't impressed!

As part of my training, I was required to work in all the various station departments: the photographic department; the admin office, which was the responsibility of PC Paul Major;

and the prosecutions office, headed by Sergeant W. The CID department was headed by DCI Jock Patterson and the traffic garage was the responsibility of Sergeant Ted Birch. I also attended Worcester Tech College where I continued my further education. During breaks, one of my favourite haunts in the police station was the canteen and snooker club. I became a reasonably accomplished snooker player, playing in various competitions and at venues in and around the city. The canteen was run by Mrs Whittaker, who I remember as a lovely, kind-hearted Worcester lady with a heart of gold, who could never resist wanting to feed me. Her assistant was PC Ollie Barton or 'Dick' Barton as he was affectionately nicknamed. Dick's nickname came from the famous radio character Dick Barton, Special Agent. Dick helped Mrs Whittaker with the cooking and catering, and was responsible for the day-to-day running of the police social club and the bar until his retirement. The snooker club, bar and canteen were all on the top floor of the building.

I settled into my board and lodgings, or digs as they were called, with Mrs Brant at 2 Barbourne Terrace and from there I walked to work every day. Our day began with a parade and full uniform inspection in the station's parade room by PC Alan Hinton, then we headed off to work in our various departments. As part of our training and in order to maintain physical fitness levels, we were taken swimming and played football. I also joined various local clubs and societies including Worcester's Over 18s Club at 17! One day I was working with PC Paul Major in the admin office when he asked me to go and see if the chief constable was in his office as he needed to place some paperwork onto his desk. By the side of the chief constable's office door was a button which had to be pressed before anyone was allowed to enter. Above the button was a traffic light system which had three round lights about the size of a table tennis ball. If the chief constable was sitting in his office, he would indicate his wishes to the person waiting outside by illuminating a response: 'Come in', 'Wait' or 'Busy'. Paul told me not to disturb him or to press his buzzer but just go and peep through the keyhole in his door to see if he was in or out. As I squinted with one eye looking through the keyhole, I saw Sir Eric Abbott sitting at his desk. As I watched him for a moment, he stood up and walked to the back of his office where he opened what looked like a large fitted wardrobe door which he walked inside and closed the door behind him! I thought that was rather strange and reported back to Paul. 'Oh yes, he often goes into his cupboard when he gets stressed. He locks himself inside for a couple of hours to get away from people!' I was young and gullible, believing most things I was told at that age! A couple of days later, Paul said, 'Come with me'. He took me into Sir Eric Abbotts's office and opened the large wardrobe door I'd seen at the back of the office. It wasn't a wardrobe at all but the chief constable's private, and very plush, rooms with separate library and bathroom!

At 16, I applied for my provisional motorcycle licence. Now working in the police garage I was shown how to service and repair the police Velocette LE 200 motorcycles under the supervision of Sergeant Ted Birch and Len, who was their civilian mechanic. After a few weeks, Sergeant Birch said he thought it was time for me to take my motorcycle test, so two L-plates were fixed onto one of the Velocettes. Sergeant Birch was authorised as a Ministry of Transport examiner for the driving tests of cadets and police officers who held provisional driving licences. I remember the day I took my test was a very windy day. He instructed me to do an emergency stop as soon as I saw him jump out into the road in front of me, but I hadn't a clue where or when this would happen. I circled the roads around the police station dozens of times when at last he jumped out right in front of me! On went the brakes and I successfully performed an emergency stop without running him over. After this, both L-plates got blown off the bike by a strong gust of wind and disappeared down the road, out of sight. 'Ok. That's it! You've passed Bill!' I can't deny I was more than slightly surprised, but delighted that I'd passed and could legally ride the bike back to the garage, without L-plates, which we no longer had anyway. I was authorised to ride the bikes and run errands such as collecting copies of the *Police Gazette*, which were sent by train every day from Birmingham to Worcester Foregate Street. I felt proud and responsible. No crash helmets were worn because they weren't obligatory at that time. Police officers wore their Worcester City police helmets with their distinctive silver chrome metal spike on top and I wore a peaked cap with a blue band around the middle. The Velocette LE 200 had horizontally opposed twin cylinder 200cc engines, which ran silently. Bobbies had their own patch or beat in the city centre with a list of properties they were told to check regularly. On night shifts they would rattle shop door handles making sure that the premises were secure. When it was quiet, bobbies would ride up off the street onto pavements, skilfully weaving in and out of the shop doorways rattling door handles to check if they were locked. If any door was found to be unlocked, the keyholder was called out in the middle of the night to properly secure it. Although radio communications existed between the control room, police bikes and vehicles, there were still some old-style blue police telephone boxes with a blue flashing light on the top. As radio communications improved, these were gradually phased out and removed. The blue light on the top could be activated by the police control room when they needed to speak to a bobby on foot patrol in the city centre. After seeing the blue beacon flashing, the beat bobby would hurry to the box, unlock the small door with his key and pull out the telephone handset to speak with the control room operator.

Working in the police garage had its advantages and it felt good to earn the trust of senior officers. Chief Superintendent Jo Davidson drove an instantly-recognisable shiny blue Ford Zephyr with the registration number 704 YFK. One afternoon he summoned me into his office and said, 'Here are my car keys, lad, drive to my garage and get it refuelled, will you?' I felt responsible, and even honoured, to be trusted to do this for him. After refuelling his car, I drove it back to the police station through the city centre dressed in my scruffy garage overalls. A couple of uniform bobbies spotted the registration number and without taking a good look to see who the driver was, assumed it was the chief superintendent behind the wheel and immediately stood to attention. I drove slowly past as they saluted me then flicked the V-sign back at them! Every day the chief constable drove his green 3.4-litre Jaguar from his home south of the river to the police station in Deansway. He always took exactly the same route at precisely 8.45am. Every police officer on duty in the city would be at his place, standing to attention at all of the main crossings and junctions, to salute him as he drove past, making sure that his journey was unimpeded. God forbid if any officer was absent from his post without good reason. What discipline, pride and total respect we had then, by comparison to today, and how different everything was. Having said that, it was possible for a situation to get out of hand, crossing over the line of discipline into a form of bullying.

At 17, I was sent to the Birmingham City police cadet Outward Bound Centre at Elan village in the Elan Valley in Wales for a month, being told it was for character building. There were only one or two cadets like me from police forces around the country; the majority were Birmingham City police cadets. All of us were between 16 and 18 years old. We camped under large army-style canvas tents, sleeping on wooden duck boards. One night there was torrential rain and a thunder storm and the duck boards started to float around inside our tents. There were wooden huts at the camp, which the staff slept in so they didn't have to put up with what we had to. One of the larger huts was where we prepared our food and ate our meals on wooden trestle tables, sitting on wooden benches. The camp commandant was a Birmingham City police chief inspector and other instructors were police officers from Birmingham City police. When we arrived, we were told to visit the camp barber where any hopes of keeping slick '60s hair styles were dashed! We all helped to prepare our meals by cleaning spuds and cutting up vegetables. I recall one officer taking and holding a large kitchen knife by the blade end. He took aim then threw it from shoulder height like a knife thrower. This very narrowly missed us each time he did it while we were sitting at the table. The razor-sharp knife narrowly missed the two fingers of my right hand by a couple of centimetres as the sharp end embedded itself into the trestle table, quivering like an arrow hitting its target. Although we all knew this was an accident waiting to happen, we were all too tight-lipped to say anything! Every morning we changed into our PT kits to run up and back down a very steep-sided mountain right next to the camp. We trekked for miles with thick black clouds of flies and insects following us. I don't know why, but they were always attracted to me, flying and buzzing around my head rather than anyone else's. We were transported from the camp to our walking destination points in open trailers towed by Austin Champ 4x4 vehicles, which were driven along narrow mountain roads at silly, dangerous speeds. We were taught to read ordinance survey maps and to plan route marches. One of the longest treks we did was from our base camp at Elan village to Aberystwyth, then we walked straight back again over muddy bogs and moorland. Our instructors kept a close eye on our progress through powerful

At the Birmingham City police cadet Outward Bound Centre in the Elan Valley. All our heads were shaved just after this photograph was taken, which was not a good look for me at the time. I'm the one on the far left at the back, wearing a woollen bobble hat, pulled down at the sides for protection, which mum knitted me.

binoculars at various vantage points along the route. As well as putting up with incessant insect bites, most of us suffered from blisters on our feet. We were instructed to visit sick bay each evening to have them 'dealt with'. The treatment was simple. We were told to sit down, remove our socks then raise both legs for foot examinations. Any blisters were slit open with a razor blade and dowsed with neat methylated spirits to harden them up again. I had more than my fair share of blisters. Painful or what! One of the cadets wrote a letter home to tell his parents that he was being mistreated. After receiving the letter, his parents contacted the camp. They received a letter back inviting them to visit to see for themselves how their son was being properly looked after. When his parents arrived, they were greeted and shown around the camp before being introduced to the commandant. However, just prior to their arrival, staff grabbed their son, tied him up then gagged him, placing him inside a laundry bag. They tied the open end and hauled him up inside the bag to the ceiling by a series of ropes and pulleys, just like raising a sail on a ship's mast. Included in his parents' tour of the camp was a visit to the laundry room. They were shown inside where a member of the staff said, 'this is where we store some of the rubbish we don't need!' They hadn't the slightest idea that their son was gagged and trussed up like a chicken, just above their heads in a bag. This was done to set an example to us all about what might happen if any of us had the audacity to complain to our parents or family. He was taken down and allowed to see his parents, by which time he was too frightened and disoriented to say anything, or to complain. At a briefing, an instructor asked for a couple of volunteers to help out on a local farm for a couple of days. I immediately raised my hand to volunteer but hadn't a clue what I was letting myself in for. A phrase already etched in my mind was 'never volunteer for anything', but I already had and two of us were selected. This was during sheep shearing time, so I guess it was an opportunity for the police to offer a couple of cadets from the camp to help the local farming community as unpaid labourers as a public relations gesture. I was taken to the farm with the other volunteer cadet. At sheep shearing, all the neighbouring sheep farmers came together to share the task at hand. Farmers' wives and their families busied themselves preparing and cooking a large selection of delicious food, with meats, cakes, homemade pies, Welsh cakes, jams, bread and Welsh butter etc. Sheep shearing was tough, physical, back-breaking work, after which everyone was gastronomically rewarded. At meal times, there were probably 20 farmers along with their farm labourers, who were invited from neighbouring farms. All met in the farm kitchen and were waited on and served the freshest, most wholesome Welsh farmhouse cuisine imaginable, and there was plenty of it. Everyone was so well-humoured, and we took our places next to Welsh- and English-speaking sheep farmers and labourers who we'd never met before. It was such a welcoming, memorable and happy time, and reminded me a lot of being at home. Outside, hundreds of sheep were rounded up and placed into pens ready for shearing. I was eager to show off my farm skills by wrapping and tying the fleeces as I'd learnt at home. After shearing the fleece, it's placed on the ground and tightly rolled up like a carpet, with the sides folded in, then the tail end is pulled and twisted round and round like a corkscrew. Then this is wrapped around the whole fleece and tied off to make it into a neat bundle. The tied fleeces were then placed into large hessian sacks which were hung from a beam, and trodden down by standing and jumping on top of them. When the sack was full, the top was stitched together using a wooden needle and a length of hessian string. After stitching the bags up, they were put into a stack, ready to be collected and taken to the local woollen factories. This method and tradition have probably continued for hundreds of years. Some of the farmers looked rather surprised to see how adept I was as they'd wrongly assumed that I was born and raised in Birmingham! It was at times like these, among kindred spirits, when I really appreciated my rural upbringing and my farming background. When the Outward Bound course ended, I developed a severe and intense headache which lasted for a whole week, and I stayed at home to recuperate. Mum called the doctor because she thought I had symptoms of meningitis, which thankfully it wasn't. Looking back, it was probably the culmination of complete physical and mental exhaustion from being under some duress and – dare I say – bullying, but I never told anyone at the time.

After my week recuperating at home, I was well enough to return to work at Worcester. After being seconded to the police garage and CID departments, I worked in the photographic department where I was taught to process black and white photographs of prisoners, crime scenes and serious assaults, and had visual access to historic and recent murder scenes. Nothing was held back. I saw photographs of actual crimes and violent assaults and I did the jobs I was required to do. My final attachment was in the prosecutions department. Each police force had their own prosecutions office where warrants and summonses were issued in connection with magistrates, quarter sessions and assize courts. Quarter sessions and assize courts were later abolished by the Courts Act of 1971 and replaced by Crown Courts and the Crown Prosecution Service which we have today. The CPS or Crown Prosecution Service took over from the police as the prosecutors for all criminal cases. Generally speaking, decisions to prosecute are now based on evidence from the police about whether a suspect should be charged or prosecuted, and whether or not it would be in the public's interest to do so. The other condition is that there should be a strong likelihood that a person charged would be convicted by a court. The goal posts had moved, and, in my opinion, allowed more guilty persons, who would now never be charged and therefore never convicted, to get away with criminal offences. Perhaps someone decided that the courts were getting too busy and our prisons too full?

Worcester City police prosecutions office was the responsibility of an experienced police sergeant, who rode to work every day on his Vespa scooter. Under his supervision were three PCs and two secretaries. My role included various clerical tasks and running errands. After getting to know Sergeant W, I had the impression that he was starting to regard me as trustworthy and I had not the slightest intention of disappointing him. He called me to his desk one day to ask me questions about what I'd learnt during the time I'd worked in the police garage servicing vehicles and motorbikes. 'Ok Bill, the reason I ask is that I want you to replace the throttle cable on my Vespa scooter. Do you think you can do it?' Eager to please, I enthusiastically agreed and set off to the motorcycle spares shop in the city centre to purchase a replacement scooter cable. Sergeant W gave me the money to pay for the cable and I returned to the police garage, where his scooter was parked up, and changed from my cadet's uniform into garage overalls. Armed with all the tools I needed, I set about the process of replacing the broken cable. One end was connected to the carburettor, which ran through the steering column, the other end to the twist-grip control on the scooter's handlebars. Having disconnected both ends I had the ingenious idea of wiring the end of the broken cable to the end of the new cable so it would be ever so simple to pull them through the scooter's steering column together, to then re-connect the new cable at the other end. I was already thinking how pleased with me Sergeant W would be for doing this simple little task, and how improved my mechanical skills were. Suddenly my hopes were dashed and my heart sank. The new cable had got jammed tight in the middle of the scooter's steering column. It just wouldn't budge, in spite of using some brute force to tug it through. I pulled harder. To my horror the new cable snapped. Shit! I abandoned the task and ran as fast as I could back to the motorcycle spares shop to buy another cable, which I paid for myself, so Sergeant W would be none the wiser. The same man who served me before looked rather mystified when I asked him for another identical throttle cable so soon after purchasing the first one but I didn't give him the satisfaction of an explanation. I ran back to the garage and asked Len the mechanic to help me fix it which thankfully he did. I was so relieved. Back in the office, Sergeant W asked, 'How did you get on Bill?' Clearing my throat, 'Yes, all fixed Sarg.', came my half-hearted reply. But it didn't end there. A couple of days later I think the confidence Sergeant W had in me had grown with my ability – or inability in my case – to fix things for him. He was on a roll and summoned me to his office for the second time. 'Now Bill, I want you to go to Sansome Walk, to the paint suppliers. I need a gallon tin (about 4.5 litres) of white gloss paint to finish off some painting at home. I have an account with them so you can book it to me', and he handed me the white colour code he'd written down

44

on a piece of paper. I remember that day so well because it was a scorching hot mid-summer's day and I was wearing my summer police uniform with bulled black boots, black tie and blue short-sleeved shirt. It was half-day closing with hardly any traffic or pedestrians around. I had already been assured by Sergeant W that the paint suppliers were open and decided to walk there from the police station. I went in and up to the sales counter to collect and sign for the tin of paint. On my way back along Sansome Walk I was feeling really happy about my life in general and my career. The sun was shining and I was humming a tune, confidently juggling and tossing the tin of paint up in the air and catching it again. Then to my horror I missed! Oh, shit and bloody hell! The heavy paint tin landed hitting the edge of the pavement with a dull thud right in front of me. As it hit the kerb the lid shot off and thick white gloss paint went everywhere. The entire tin emptied out and across the pavement and flowed down the side of the road. I looked down at my uniform and saw that my black tie, police shirt, black uniform trousers and shiny black boots were all splattered in thick white gloss paint. I was so embarrassed, and didn't quite know what to do next, other than to distance myself from the obvious. I turned away then went straight back to the paint suppliers to collect another tin. As I walked in, I was eyed up and down by the chaps behind the sales counter who laughed themselves silly when they realised what had happened. This time, I had insufficient money to pay for another tin so had to sign for it on Sergeant W's account. It reminds me now of a Dad's Army or Frank Spencer sketch. Carefully carrying the new tin of paint, I walked back to the police station through Worcester's busy town centre where I received some very odd stares, smiles and even laughter from various members of the public! I quickly changed into my spare uniform before taking the tin of paint upstairs to the office where I confessed to the sergeant exactly what had happened. 'So now Bill,' he said, 'two tins of paint and two new throttle cables?' But how on earth did he know about the second cable? 'You left the two new empty cable boxes in my scooter pannier!' I could only apologise. After that, I was determined to be much more attentive and to focus a lot more. I had no intention of making any more mistakes, but our lives seldom pan out like we want or expect them to, especially at that age. As police cadets we received regular career appraisals, and these were important to me, but the story didn't quite end there. A couple of weeks later, when Sergeant W's trust in me was beginning to be restored, he summoned me to his desk for the third time. 'Now Bill, I'm trusting you to take this important doctor's prescription to the chemist straight away. It's for my daughter who is ill at home and she needs it urgently.' He handed me a doctor's prescription and I headed straight to the nearest chemist in town to collect it. The pharmacist explained that I needed to wait for the medicine to be specially made up so I sat in a chair. Ten minutes or so later I saw the chemist pouring the liquid medicine into a glass bottle, which was labelled and placed in a brown paper bag. I repeated to myself over and over again, 'I will not drop this! I will not drop this!' and walked cautiously back through the busy town centre tightening my grip on the brown paper bag and holding it slightly out in front of me for maximum protection and safety. Turning right from the high street into the pedestrian passageway in Bull Entry, a child of about ten came running around the corner chased by another who ran straight into me! You can surely guess the rest? The bottle and bag flew straight out my hand, shattering into little pieces on the pavement. What should I do now? Please dear God not again! In a state of panic, I decided to return to the pharmacist to ask for another prescription. 'Sorry,' he said, 'but that was a made-up prescription which I'm not allowed to replace without another doctor's prescription.' I politely pleaded with him until eventually he relented and kindly agreed to make up another bottle which he gave to me. 'Now don't drop this one!' he jokingly said after I'd thanked him and told him how much I appreciated what he'd done for me. Sergeant W never found out and I never mentioned it to him. In spite of all the scrapes and mishaps I got myself into, Sergeant W gave me a glowing appraisal at the end of my memorable attachment with the Worcester City police prosecutions department. Another lucky escape!

As part of the Duke of Edinburgh Award scheme, I became a bell ringer. Mum's uncle's cousin, the late David Beecham, was the bell tower captain at All Saints Church in Worcester. He taught me to ring bells like my grandfather John Rowlatt had before me. I became less keen on bell ringing though after someone mentioned that if a bell stay breaks, there is nothing to stop the bell from spinning round and round out of control. Then if the ringer decides not to release the bell rope, the chances are that the ringer will disappear upwards, crashing their head on the bell tower roof. Apparently, this had already claimed the lives of many unsuspecting campanologists. I was no longer so keen after hearing this, but carried on. Sergeant W was a St John Ambulance first aid trainer and asked me to join his team. He led competitive first aid competitions between the police and the various factories and organisations in and around Worcester. The St John Ambulance was manned by volunteers, and the service pre-dates the NHS ambulance paramedics we have today. The ambulance was garaged in Deansway, close to the police and fire stations. For a while, I became a volunteer ambulance driver and attendant with the St John Ambulance crew, so I had another uniform to neatly press and iron.

I paid my landlady Mrs Brant £5 a week for my board and lodgings which I took out of my monthly wage of just over £25, which left me with practically nothing to spend. That makes me feel so old! However, mum and dad supplemented my wages by giving me pocket money and petrol money. After a time, I decided to move to less expensive lodgings, and placed a notice on the notice board at the police station to enquire if anyone knew of any lodgings. PC B was a serving Worcester City police officer and told me that his mum, who was a widow, would be interested in having me as a lodger where she lived in a small terraced house in Lansdowne Terrace. We agreed on £3 and 10 shillings per week, which left me with a weekly saving of £1 and 10 shillings (£1.50). Quite a lot of money back then. I moved into lodgings at PC B's mother's house, but soon afterwards she was sadly diagnosed with a terminal illness. I was forced to move again to my third set of lodgings, this time to number 21 Woodland Road with landlady dear Miss Hope. Miss Hope was in her seventies and was a devout Christian Methodist. She rode her moped everywhere – into town to do her shopping and to work tending people's gardens. She had the most beautiful flower and vegetable garden of her own and grew an abundance of organic vegetables. She was a plain but good cook. We got on really well together and I remember the skin on her hands being crinkled and cracked from all the manual gardening and hard graft she did for others. I always enjoyed her summer salads. One evening she had prepared a ham salad for our supper, which was garnished with all her home-grown freshly-picked salad leaves. We sat down together at the table to eat and enjoy our meal in her front room watching television. As I bit into my second mouthful, it tasted oddly bland and had a sort of chewy texture. My taste buds didn't immediately identify what part of the salad this was, so I turned my head and emptied my mouth into the palm of my hand to check it out. To my astonishment, there, amongst a partly-chewed iceberg lettuce leaf, was the biggest, fattest, shiniest, slithery live black slug I'd ever seen in my life. Miss Hope was besides herself with embarrassment and apologies and I felt really sorry for her. After that however I always gave my salads a second glance and the once-over before tucking into them. Miss Hope was the sweetest, most kind-hearted, thoughtful and true Christian lady, and I wonder what ever happened to her.

So, at this time, as I mentioned earlier, my interests included learning how to play snooker and becoming a reasonably accomplished snooker player, winning quite a few competitions against local Worcester pub and club teams. I was a competent and qualified first aider and a volunteer with the Worcester St John ambulance brigade. I was a strong swimmer with qualifications in life saving, and a campanologist with a full motorcycle licence. The police allowed me to ride police bikes up to 250cc including the Police Velocette LE 200 motorcycles or 'noddy bikes' as they were called and a two-stroke 250cc Arial Arrow police motorbike. The policewomen had the use of a Vespa police scooter, but they were a bit too embarrassed to be seen riding it, preferring instead to catch public transport, which was free of charge to any police officer on duty. Or they would ask one of the two police civilian drivers (George or Len) to drive them to their various commitments. It was George and

Len's job to chauffeur them around, as well as CID officers and senior officers. My motorcycle licence allowed me to ride civilian motorcycles of any size, as it does today. Other than picking up copies of the *Police Gazette* from Foregate Street railway station, I sometimes made longer trips to the Home Office police radio repair shop at Rubery. My mum didn't like me riding motorbikes, but I needed one to travel to and from work, as well as home to the farm at weekends. Dad bought me a brand-new Honda CD 175 with registration number KDF 55E, which was manufactured in Japan and it went like a rocket. At the age of 17, I passed my civilian car driving test which I took in Evesham. The lady examiner complimented me on my standard of driving, which I was very pleased about. This was probably due to the fact that I had bags of experience driving farm tractors and other farm vehicles from a very early age. Dad had many cars over a period of years: the earliest I remember was a Standard Vanguard (shown in the earlier photograph on page 8) followed by a Ford Cortina, Volkswagen, Ford Corsair, Triumph Herald and Vandan Plas Princess, which was the car I took my driving test in, but the one I liked most was a green 2.4-litre Jaguar with a manual gearbox. Mum often told the story of when she was washing dishes at her kitchen sink and looked out of the window onto the driveway outside to see their green Jaguar being slowly driven backwards and forwards. At first, she couldn't figure out why it was moving as it didn't appear to have a driver, but then she saw the outline of my head and a pair of eyes managing to peer over the top of the steering wheel. I was teaching myself to drive. I'm guessing I would have been about ten years old or less, but mum in her wisdom decided not to panic and left me to it. Well, we all need to learn at some point, don't we?

Not all of my early driving experiences ran so smoothly however. Dad had a Ford Thames van which had two small oval windows in the back doors. The van was normally parked round the back of the farmhouse with the keys left in the ignition. The back door of the house led into the back kitchen and a narrow staircase led from the kitchen to my bedroom. At the time, dad had a company of contractors who were installing a state-of-the-art corn drier, so that the tractors and trailers could be driven into the yard to tip their loads of corn into a deep pit to be dried. From there an electric augur would shift the grain along and up into huge metal grain storage silos. One morning I jumped into dad's van and reversed it backwards. Being young and short in stature I didn't have a clear view of anything behind and thought it was clear to reverse. Suddenly I felt a loud thump and a crashing sound behind me and slammed on the brakes. I got out to see what I'd hit as it wasn't immediately obvious. That morning an electrician who was wiring up the electrics for the grain drier had arrived at work on a brand-new, shiny, red-and-black BSA 650cc motorcycle. He lifted it onto its stand, parking it right by the edge of the deep concrete-sided grain pit. I couldn't believe what I'd done! Looking round for the object I'd hit, there it was right at the bottom. I'd accidentally reversed dad's van into the brand-new motorbike, knocking it off its stand. The bike then somersaulted down into the bottom of the deep empty pit. In sheer disbelief I shuddered and looked at it lying there. In that moment it had changed in appearance from being a shiny brand-spanking-new BSA motorcycle into something which resembled a big piece of twisted scrap metal with buckled wheels. I managed to tie one end of a piece of rope around the twisted handlebars and the other end to the back of the van and hauled it up and back out again. With no one around, I struggled to get the mangled mess back up onto its stand in its original position. I parked the van back where it was and ran up the back stairs into my bedroom to think about what I'd just done and what I was going to do. I lay on my bed, covering my ears and shutting my eyes, trying in vain to prepare myself and not think about the inevitable. After what seemed like ages, I heard from upstairs some aggressive sounding knocks at the back door, which dad answered. 'Mr Rowlatt? I want you to come and look at my bike!' Ten minutes later, dad shouted up the staircase to me in my bedroom like he already knew where I was. 'Bill, downstairs now!' I admitted straight away that it was an accident, that I was responsible and how truly sorry I was. Dad gave me the biggest telling off ever, which I deserved. The outcome was that he bought the poor chap an identical brand-new BSA 650cc motorbike to replace his other one which I had just written off. With all his faults, my dad was a very generous man and didn't hold back in making the right decision and it was never mentioned again.

One day, I was walking in uniform through the city centre when a shopkeeper summoned me into her shop where their manager had detained a suspect for theft. As a police cadet I had no authority to arrest or detain anyone, but I managed to persuade the offender to accompany me to the police station where he was arrested and dealt with by a police officer. The case went to the magistrates' court and the magistrates commended me for my actions on the day, which surprisingly ended up being printed in the *Worcester Evening News*. So not everything went wrong for me!

At the age of 17 I was enjoying a night out listening to a live band playing in an upstairs room at the Evesham Rowing Club. At about 10 o'clock some sort of a scuffle broke out right in front of me so I moved forward to take a closer look at what was going on. A young lad about my own age was on the floor receiving kicks to his head and face by an older male. I stepped between them and dragged the young lad away from his assailant and down the staircase to safety. An ambulance was called which I followed in my car to the hospital, where I discovered the unconscious lad's name was Pete Milne. He lived at Chadbury with his brother Jim and his parents Neil and Joan. At 3am I went to their house because I wanted to tell Pete's parents what had happened to him, although at the time I didn't know him or his family. I got to the front door and practised my policeman's knock ... no reply! The chances were that they were both fast asleep upstairs in bed at that time of the morning and hadn't heard me. I tried the front door, to find it was unlocked so I let myself in. I went upstairs, not knowing which bedroom was which, and opened the first bedroom door that I came to and switched on the light. Two very startled people, who were fast asleep, shot bolt upright in bed like two rabbits caught in headlights. I quickly reassured them that I wasn't an intruder but a police cadet who needed to let them know that their son Pete was admitted to hospital with serious head injuries. This was the start of a lifelong and very happy friendship with Pete's parents Joan and Neil, who were not only friends but became like second parents to me. When I was 17, dad allowed me to drive the farm Land Rover to visit Jim and Pete's home at Chadbury, where we organised parties and made our own fun. Amazingly, Neil and Joan went out on our party nights, giving us the whole run of their house. Wood Norton Manor, which was owned by the BBC, was about a mile and a half from their house. The staff and management who were trained there were provided with posh accommodation to stay in. We knew they had an outside heated swimming pool, and the good news was there was never anyone there at weekends! One Saturday night we drove into Evesham, parking the Land Rover outside Smedley's canning factory. Young female Smedley employees were provided with not-so-posh accommodation at the factory. We whistled and waited for them to meet us outside. About half a dozen of them appeared and piled into the Land Rover, then we headed off through the orchards at the back of Jim and Pete's house at around 2am in the morning. I switched off the Land Rover's lights to drive up through the trees, illuminated by moonlight, to reach the swimming pool. It was a balmy summer's night and none of us had any swimwear with us. What a surprise! We all unceremoniously stripped off and jumped in and out of the pool, laughing, splashing and generally enjoying a thoroughly naughty time, as young kids do at that age. Enjoying the company of some pretty, but completely naked, ladies seemed a totally natural thing to do. About 20 minutes later, we were surprised by something which none of us had been expecting. A night watchman appeared carrying a very bright, high-powered torch, so we all scattered and scurried away in all directions to hide and get away from him. Unfortunately, Jim was the only person the night watchman caught and recognised by torchlight. 'I know you!' he said, 'You're one of the Milne family!' I can still see the shock and horror on Jim's face as he was confronted, named and humiliated in front of everyone while standing stark naked and dripping wet! Clasping both hands in front of himself, he tried in vain to cover his manhood, making fumbled and feeble attempts to disguise his identity! Too late! We laughed, but felt so sorry for Jim too! The following day, Neil gathered the three of us together after sending Jim up to Wood Norton Manor to apologise to the management on our behalf. Neil told us off, emphasising that I could easily have lost my job as a police cadet and he was right. We took Neil's advice very seriously indeed, and were all truly sorry for our totally irresponsible behaviour. Neil ended by giving us some wise words of advice. I have never forgotten his advice, and have repeated it dozens of times over, 'Never ever shit on your own doorstep!' Sadly, both Joan and Neil have since passed away. A big thank you, Neil, for your war service too. You saved lives and risked your own life on dozens of occasions during the Second World War. You were an army captain working in undercover situations and operations, helping others to escape from Nazi-occupied territories through Spain and Gibraltar and back to England. Thank you for your bravery during the war, your fatherly love, your care towards us and for your wise words of advice. May your soul rest in heaven with Joan, and may you both rest in God's great love and eternal peace. Pete, with his brother Jim, and I became really good friends, as close as real brothers can be. We are in constant contact with each other to this day, 56 years later.

It was now time to sit my entrance exam in order to become a fully-fledged police officer. I needed to pass a medical examination and was examined by Doctor Laidlaw, the police surgeon at Barbourne Road surgery. Our training officer PC Alan Hinton was promoted to the rank of sergeant following the force's amalgamation, then to chief inspector before his eventual retirement. Alan was replaced by our new training sergeant, Sergeant M, who remained present during the written exam and which he later marked. This was a nail-biting time because if I failed the exam, it would mean three years of wasted training as a police cadet. The examination paper covered general knowledge, English and maths. I was struggling with one of the general knowledge questions, but Sergeant M spotted my dilemma. The question was – what do the letters BBBC stand for? I hadn't a clue! It would have been easier if there had been one less 'B' but, with a nudge and a wink, Sergeant M helped me to arrive at the correct answer, even though I'd never heard of it! The British Board of Boxing Control ... I'd passed!

FROM POLICE CADET TO CONSTABLE
AT HEREFORD AND ROSS-ON-WYE

A T the age of 19 I was sent to Ryton on Dunsmore Police Training Centre in Warwickshire for a 14-week residential course. We learned about all aspects of policing and police training. In those days we had to learn legal definitions off by heart and were regularly tested: 'A Constable is a citizen locally appointed and having authority under the crown for the prevention and detection of crime, the prosecution of offenders against the peace and for the maintenance of law and order'. Another was the definition of theft, which replaced the old Larceny Act laws under the Theft Act of 1968: 'A person is guilty of theft if he dishonestly appropriates property belonging to another with the

New police officers sworn in

FIVE NEW policemen and one policewoman were sworn into the West Mercia Constabulary at Worcester County Magistrates Court today.

They were: Linda Jean Hanson, aged 19, of Longwood Road, Rubery; William David Rowlatt, 19, of Childswickham, near Broadway; John Henry Garfield, 20, of Stoney Lane, Crossway Green, Stourport; John Wills, 29, of Claxton Grove, Fulham, London; John Henry Newton, 20, of St. John's Avenue, Oulton, Stone, Staffs.; John Richard Blackhurst, 22, of Symonds Yat West, Ross-on-Wye.

They were told by the chairman, Lt.-Col. Richard Wiggin: "The people of this country are proud of the police forces and the great reputation of the Police is in the keeping of every single policeman.

"I hope you will do all in your power to maintain the fine traditions of the Police and I wish you every success in your new career."

intention of permanently depriving the other of it'. I've remembered them to this day and there were over one hundred more definitions which we had to memorise. We were taught how to direct traffic, and how to march up and down the drill square endlessly to military music including Colonel Bogie. Socially, four of us formed a pop band and I played drums. It was all a bit amateurish, but we managed to entertain the other students as well as our bosses for our final end of course dinner and dance. One of the songs chosen was Heartbreak Hotel originally sung by Elvis Presley – not my favourite. On the day of our Passing Out Parade my parents attended and it was a special occasion.

News came of my first posting, which was to Hereford. My digs were in Whitecross Road – the home of M and J who had two young boys. M was expecting their third child. Their little baby girl was born when I was still in lodgings with them. M provided accommodation as well as cooked meals for me and another single policeman as and when a spare room became available. The accommodation was on a list approved by the

'Passing Out' as a police officer – I'm in the back row, fourth from the left

police. It was comfortable and we had some really good laughs together, apart from one day when M took something I'd said rather personally – telling her that I'd seen a shadow on her lip! She threw the dinner plate at me which had my supper on it and I ducked as the plate smashed against the wall behind me. My supper slid slowly down the wall marking it with gravy stains. Dare I say that this was a really close shave. I have not seen or heard from the family since 1969.

I was attached to a shift system known as 'A' scale, which was one of four shifts. Each shift had two sergeants, six constables and a police inspector working from the old police station in Gaol Street. Sergeant Bert Harding was our station sergeant. He was a north-country man and the type of policeman which many of us would still remember as Old School: traditional, solid, dependable and someone you wouldn't argue with. He was in charge of the police control room and no one questioned him nor any of his decisions. His responsibility was to deploy officers to incidents and accidents in and around the town as well as to other outlying neighbourhood beat areas, where officers still rode bicycles to patrol their beats. Bert had a particularly dry sense of humour. For many reasons we liked each other and I respected him. He took me under his wing and held my career interests at heart, always making certain that I'd submitted my reports on time to senior officers. He was friends with a police woman, Sergeant D, who was in the control room one day when Bert called her over to him. In this day and age what he said to her would be entirely inappropriate and unacceptable, but back in the '60s things were very different. Bert said to her: 'Come here D, now turn around', which she did in front of him. Then, after looking her up and down, he said, 'now turn around again, D', which she did for the second time. Then he said to her, 'D, you're the ruddy same at the front as you are at the ruddy back!' They both smiled at each other and laughed together because they knew each other well, but thankfully times have changed.

General reports were submitted on what was called an A.30 report form, which we typed out ourselves on old-fashioned Olympus typewriters in the parade room. Reports always had to be signed off with the same final paragraph: 'I am Sir, your obedient servant' then I added my signature, typing out my name, rank and collar number under it. W.D. Rowlatt. Police Constable 264. Bert or Sarg as we referred to him (we never called sergeants or senior ranks by their Christian names) had served for a very long time including previous service with Hereford City police prior to it becoming a county force in 1965. Bert was the last police sergeant to administer the birch to a juvenile offender in Hereford as punishment for their crime. This form of corporal punishment was abolished in 1948. The magistrates' court was situated in Gaol Street right next door to the police station (both are no longer there but the building remains). One day Bert took me to one side and described in detail how he'd carried out the very last birching sentence. The magistrates ordered the juvenile to receive six lashings. He was led by a constable from the court and up the steps to the police station next door, then down into the ground floor 'birching cell', as it was called. He showed me the same cell, describing how it was his duty to administer the magistrates' sentence and how he did it. The juvenile was made to drop his trousers then bend forwards to support himself by holding onto one side of the wooden cell bed where he received six lashings. The same cell was still being used by prisoners when I was there in 1969, with other cells on the first floor above. Another form of punishment was the 'cat-o-nine-tails' which fell out of use around 1870. I remember Bert saying that he never birched the same person twice!

Our shift sergeant was Sergeant Phil Noakes who was in charge of the constables on the shift. His job was to hand out and receive our paperwork and submit it to our inspector, John Clinton, whose office was upstairs. These were warrants, summonses, general reports and complaints with reported and recorded crimes, which all had to be handwritten onto a C1 crime report form. All crimes were thoroughly investigated and all members of the public who reported a crime would receive a personal visit from the police officer it was allocated to. Ranking above Inspector John Clinton was Superintendent John Keyte, who was in overall charge at Hereford. There were other sergeants and inspectors working with the other three shifts which had approximately 25 or 28 officers in total policing the city centre. These were backed up by 11 neighbourhood beat officers, CID, dog handlers, traffic officers, special constables and rural beat officers at village police stations. The other main police stations known as sub-divisions were at Ross-on-Wye, Leominster and Ledbury. These were headed by either a chief inspector or superintendent. In charge of the whole county at this particular time was Chief Superintendent Mr Peter Shaw ... How times have changed!

My 'parent constable', which all new recruits were assigned to before being allowed to work on their own, was ex-traffic bobby and Birmingham City police transferee PC Pete Foskett. Sadly, like so many others I am writing about, he is no longer with us. Pete was a very experienced officer and hugely respected by his friends and colleagues. He was a family man and a very experienced constable: he was my mentor. He taught me a great deal and I shall always be indebted to him. During our very first shift together Pete told me that he had arranged an appointment to attend the General Hospital at two o'clock. At precisely two o'clock Pete dropped me off opposite the mortuary building in our panda car, a blue and white Ford Anglia. He pointed to the mortuary door saying, 'Go through that door Bill. You're going to attend your first post mortem examination. The pathologist will meet you inside'. GULP! Talk about being dropped in at the deep end. I did what I was told and introduced myself to the pathologist who was standing alongside an elderly deceased gentleman lying uncovered and prostrate on a washable mortuary tray. He explained that the deceased had died suddenly one Sunday afternoon while digging his vegetable patch somewhere near Bromyard and continued, 'Now this may not be too pleasant for you. If you're feeling queasy, go outside into the next room. If you collapse in here on the mortuary floor then I won't help you up until I've finished my examination'. I'm not sure how much detail I should go into because some people will find it upsetting but basically a post mortem is to establish the cause of death. If a doctor or GP is unable to state the reason why a person died then he or she cannot issue a death certificate. The examination started with the removal of the top of the cranium, followed by a careful fingertip brain examination. He then opened up the rib cage after making an incision down the length of the chest and abdominal areas to examine all the body's internal organs. The heart was removed and at this point I was thinking back to my upbringing on the farm. I saw dad having to kill sick or injured animals, so to some degree this had prepared me to see a dead body. The elderly man had completed his life cycle and was there in his physical body only. My belief was and still is that someone's spiritual and physical bodies are separated after death, with their spirit going to another level or an afterlife. I continued to observe everything I was being shown, feeling a bit queasy but not collapsing. The pathologist realised that I was genuinely interested in his examination, and not about to keel over in a heap on the mortuary floor. When he examined the gentleman's heart, he placed it in the palm of his hand and pointed to a small congealed blood clot which had completely blocked one of the heart's main arteries and was obviously the cause of death. Before the body was sewn back together again, I remember the pathologist saying, 'Now if you drink plenty of Herefordshire cider, you'll never die of that!' The examination proved that the elderly gentleman died from natural causes, so no inquest and no further involvement from Her Majesty's coroner at Hereford was necessary. Little did I realise at the time that I would be present at other post mortems during my police career, including that of an alleged murder victim, after arresting a family relative on suspicion of murder.

Being a new and young 19-year-old probationary constable, word soon got out that I was a fairly adept snooker player. I was asked to represent Hereford division in the inter-divisional sports competitions of the force's three counties. In those days we were allowed a whole day to compete without any loss of pay. The snooker and darts competitions took place at Stourport-on-Severn police social club and we were allowed the use of a police vehicle to take us there and back again. I volunteered to drive, and therefore not drink, taking with me two of our best senior dart players PC Scottie Johnson, who worked at Hafod Road divisional police headquarters, and PC Fred Daniels, who was the rural beat officer at Tarrington. In those days there were never any questions asked about how much anyone was allowed to drink. The drinks flowed and a buffet provided for the whole day ... How times have changed.

Sergeant Bert Harding grew his own tomatoes and vegetables at his home in Hereford. On an early 6am–2pm shift we were paraded at 5.45am in readiness to relieve the incoming night shift, who came back in just before 6am. Sergeants Phil Noakes and Bert Harding were both present to brief us about reported incidents, crimes and locally-wanted persons etc. The briefing usually took 10 minutes or so, after which we were allocated our specific beat areas and handed enquiries to complete in the town on foot patrol or as Panda car drivers. We covered areas including beats south of the river and if required, the rural beats in villages. We were normally out and on patrol at 6am. At one briefing, Bert asked PC Mike Cowley to run an errand for him. In his north-country accent and in front of the whole shift he asked Mike, 'PC Cowley, as you know, I grow my own tomatoes', wagging his finger as he was talking to him, 'Now I want you to go out and buy me some John Innis liquid feed and don't you bloody come back without it!' Mike spent almost the whole of his shift visiting shops such as Franklyn Barnes on Commercial Road, Wyevale nursery on Kings Acre Road and as many other retail outlets he could possibly think of to get Bert's John Innis liquid feed. As our shift came to an end we returned to the station for debriefing. Mike was last in and was quietly apologetic. 'Sarg, I've tried everywhere to get your John Innis liquid feed but I couldn't find any anywhere!' Bert replied, 'You dull bugger! They don't bloody make it, that's why!'

From memory, our shift members were PCs: Mike Hopkins, who left to work at Cadbury's chocolate; Stevie Holland, who became the local beat officer at Bredenbury; Bill Turbutt, who became a fast-response traffic officer (I was best man at Bill's wedding); the late Pete Foskett, my parent constable, who retired after completing 30 years' service; Mike Cowley, who was promoted to the rank of detective chief inspector before his retirement, and then became a barrister; Robbie Kedward, who joined Hereford CID and later retired; and our two sergeants, Bert Harding and Phil Noakes.

We worked hard and conscientiously but occasionally enjoyed a bit of innocent fun if we thought we could get away with it! The May Fair visits High Town once a year when the streets are closed to traffic. Part of our police uniform issue were thick black woollen capes. They were very warm and absorbed a lot of moisture when it rained. At 4am one morning we were working a night shift and met up in High Town, bringing with us our police capes to use as mats to slide down the steep helter-skelter. At one point someone suggested we should all climb up the steep flight of steps to the very top. When we were there, we huddled together on the slide in a line, all wearing our helmets. Someone counted down '3-2-1' and, slalom-like, we were off, gaining pace and hurtling down at speed. At the bottom there were two railway workers dressed in their British Rail uniforms and caps walking to work. We all shot off the end of the helter-skelter in fits of laughter. The railway men didn't expect to be crashed into by a whole shift of policemen in uniform, knocking them over like skittles down a bowling alley! On night shifts we regularly checked shops, factories and business premises on our individual beats trying to prevent any of them from being burgled. However, if a burglary went undiscovered until after we'd finished our tour of duty we could be woken up at home and called back to the station to be questioned by the superintendent, who would check the times and places we'd written down in our pocket books to see why we hadn't noticed it.

At around 3am one bitterly cold December morning it started snowing really heavily. It was freezing cold. I was tired and wanting to sleep. I sat down on a public bench in High Town and fell fast asleep on my side with my helmet held on by the chin strap, wearing my thick police great coat and pair of black leather gloves to keep warm. After 10 minutes or so I woke up with a start to the sound of a car engine running right by my side. My coat was covered by at least two inches of thick snow. It was Sergeant Phil Noakes who had driven up as close as he could get to me in a police Morris Marina. Phil wound the driver's window down to speak with me or perhaps he was checking to see that I was still alive! I quickly brushed the snow off my uniform and stood to attention. After seeing how frozen I was, he said, 'Get in Bill', and we drove round for the remainder of our shift with cosy warm air blasting from the heater vents onto my face, legs and feet. Aah, bliss! Having completed my attachment with parent constable Pete, I was finally allowed to patrol the streets on my own and make my own decisions to do the job which I had joined up for. I was fully trained in making arrests for crime, dealing with accidents and domestic disputes and reporting people for miscellaneous offences. I'd passed my police test to drive Panda cars and personnel carriers to convey prisoners to and from court and to prisons and remand centres.

As a young constable I didn't think about promotion, just concentrating on doing the job I was doing. Some of the older police officers coming up for their retirement seemed to resent the job they had been doing for a long time, so I promised myself that I wouldn't be like them when it was my turn to retire. As with any job there were serious aspects as well as some amusing moments too. The majority of senior officers supported the lower ranks if any genuine mistakes were made. As long as they saw we had 'acted in good faith' as they put it then we didn't have much to worry about. Sometimes senior officers made mistakes too, as this next story shows!

In the summer of 1970, our shift was briefed about carrying out our duties on the day that Her Majesty the Queen was visiting Hereford. Her schedule was to meet dignitaries in the city, then to formally open a building at the College on Aylestone Hill. In that year High Town and Commercial Street were still open to traffic before being pedestrianised. We had keys for the traffic lights and could turn them on or off at all the main road junctions in the town. After turning a set of traffic lights off, a uniformed officer could step into the middle of a junction to direct traffic using hand signals, something you very rarely see, if ever, these days. My brief was to stand outside the Kerry Arms Hotel where I had a clear, unobstructed view of the roads to the front and at each side of me. These were Blueschool Street, Bath Street, Commercial Road and Commercial Street. To my left and slightly behind me was Commercial Street where I was told the royal party would travel from to go over the main junction, then along Commercial Road and up Aylestone Hill to the College where Her Majesty would be making one of her scheduled visits. My sole responsibility was to make quite certain that the royal convoy, along with its escort vehicles, travelled through the junction without any delay or encumbrance. Understandably, I was apprehensive that nothing should go wrong. I received the radio message I was expecting from the control room informing me that the royal party had left the town hall and was heading in my direction, giving me an ETA (expected time of arrival) of three minutes. After turning off the traffic lights, I stepped out into the middle of the busy junction wearing, not black leather but white cotton, gloves, which we always wore for royal visits and ceremonial occasions. True to police training practices, I used hand signals to halt the traffic until the cavalcade came into view. I could see from the expressions on the faces of car drivers and passengers that they knew the traffic was being held up for an important reason because not only was I wearing white gloves instead of a black pair but everyone it seems had read in the *Hereford Times* that Her Majesty the Queen was visiting the city. With the traffic stationary, the Queen's convoy moved towards me along Commercial Street. My written orders, which I'd read carefully, gave concise details of the Queen's cortège including the description of her vehicle and her escort vehicles. It was led by two police motorcycle outriders, followed by the Queen's limousine, two officers in a marked police fast response vehicle (armed) and finally by an unmarked police vehicle at the rear. The unmarked vehicle would be driven by a uniformed constable with a police superintendent as passenger. The superintendent was one appointed as West Mercia's most senior officer who was placed in overall charge to oversee all the security measures for the day. I was relieved that, so far, everything had gone like clockwork. The royal convoy went through the junction which I was responsible for without a problem, and I was delighted to catch a glimpse of Her Majesty for the very first time in my young career, though I saw her again on subsequent occasions. I was surprised that one important vehicle was missing from my list. The superintendent's vehicle was nowhere to be seen, so I decided to continue directing the traffic at the junction just in case he hadn't caught up for some reason or had unexpectedly been delayed. Not knowing the reason why it was absent, I dismissed any further thoughts of concern and waited for a couple of minutes before switching the traffic lights back on again and returned to stand in my original position with my arms folded. After Her Majesty's college commitment was completed, the plan was for her to travel back down Aylestone Hill when I would be required to do exactly the same again but in reverse. Just as I was beginning to feel rather pleased with how everything had happened so far, my attention was drawn to a vehicle which was noisily and persistently sounding its horn. I glanced to my left and behind me towards the direction of Commercial Street and noticed the superintendent's vehicle was stationary and stuck at the traffic lights on red. The driver sounded his horn repeatedly, desperately trying to attract my attention. They were obviously in a mad rush needing to catch up with the rest of the convoy who were now way ahead of them. I ran out into the middle of the junction stopping the traffic and signalled them through. Someone appeared to be rather angry and red faced as the car sped past me. I could make out a face at the window mouthing words which looked like, 'Thank you very f...... much!' That was rather uncalled for I thought? One of the police motorcycle outriders was PC Len Sparrow who took up the story and told me what he saw. When the cavalcade reached the college, Len was surprised to see that the superintendent's car was missing from the rear of the convoy. However, Her Majesty continued with the opening ceremony accompanied by her police protection officer and other dignitaries. The two police motorbikes were parked up at the front of the motorcade when, after a good ten minutes, the superintendent's car appeared and screeched to a standstill behind the line of stationary vehicles. Len said he saw someone who looked like he was the superintendent getting out of the car in a bit of a hurry. After rapidly walking round to the back of his vehicle, he saw him disappear so Len went to see what had happened. He saw the superintendent lying in the road in agony after tripping over the pavement and breaking his leg, so an ambulance was called which rushed him to the casualty department (A&E)! I wasn't expecting to receive another radio message quite so soon, but it came loud and clear: 'PC Rowlatt, stop the traffic! The superintendent is on his way past you to the casualty department in an ambulance'. I waved the ambulance through as it raced on past me with its blue lights flashing and sirens blaring. I wasn't sure if I should stand to attention and throw him up a salute! It turned out to be the last day of this senior officer's career, but just the beginning of mine!

My probationary period ended after two years when I was given confirmation that I was officially accepted and could continue with my career in the force. During that period, I attended various refresher training courses and ongoing career assessments. In 1971 I was married to Janette after submitting a form A.30 report requesting permission to get married, providing her full details so security checks could be made. After we married in December of that year, I was given a choice of being posted to Ross-on-Wye or Leominster police stations. As mum and dad were living and farming at Hollybush Farm, Longhope, I decided to be posted to Ross to be closer to them. We moved into our first police house in Walford Road at the junction of Tudor Rise opposite Audrey and Ken Richies, who owned and ran their own fish and chip shop known as 'Audrey's', and they became good friends. The chip shop is still open, now owned and managed by Ken and Audrey's daughter Sharron. There were two semi-detached police houses opposite the chip shop on the corner at the junction with Walford Road nicknamed 'Fort Worth!' PC Roger Firth lived with his wife and children next door to us but, sadly, Roger's wife died from a terminal illness. After she died Roger met and married his second wife. He left the force to join the fire brigade and was rapidly promoted, becoming the local fire chief at Ross fire station.

A chief inspector was in charge at Ross police station and his inspector was Mike Ovens, brother of Neville Ovens. The Ovens family were originally from Kington. Their father was a police sergeant at Kington and Neville became chief constable of Lincolnshire constabulary. After retiring from the force their father became licensee of the Talbot Inn at Kington. There were two sergeants at Ross, one was the late Johnnie Atherton who I got along extremely well with and who had a great sense of humour.

Our son Julian was born on the 30 November 1972 at the county hospital in Hereford. His was a breach birth, which was difficult and protracted. Julian suffered birth trauma and was placed in an incubator so we all went short on cuddles and hugs for a little while, but it all ended well. After Julian was born, I was completely exhausted from work and lack of sleep. The doctor on the maternity ward insisted that I take a day's sick leave, which I did. But when my boss heard that I had, he reprimanded me and I was ordered to work an additional day shift as recompense. Thankfully, times have changed!

An emergency call came in one day reporting that an elderly lady cyclist was seriously injured in a collision with a car along the Walford Road on the outskirts of town. Inspector Mike Ovens, who'd seen the message, asked me if I had ever dealt with a fatal accident before. When I told him that I hadn't, he offered to come with me just in case the accident was a fatality. When we arrived at the scene, we saw a lady's shoe in the middle of the carriageway. Inspector Ovens told me that he was almost certain that this would be a fatal accident, but how did he know? She was somebody's dear mother or a dearly-treasured grandmother perhaps? This aspect of police work was heartbreaking and families needed, and in fact had every right to expect, sensitivity and empathy from the police when they had to be told such tragic and devastating news. I never quite understood why, but it seemed like I was always on duty when any sad news had to be broken to a family or loved one and I've never forgotten any of them. The inspector and I took measurements and I drew an accurate sketch plan of the scene. Mike gave me the confidence I needed to prepare and submit my first fatal accident file. I later asked him: how did he know that this was a fatal accident even before it was confirmed? He explained that a body struck by a vehicle with fatal force often means that the footwear comes off by the sudden propulsion, and how right he was. I saw it happen at other fatal accident scenes involving cyclists and pedestrians.

I was usually the only bobby on duty when I was working an early Sunday morning shift in Ross. Some Sundays when it was quiet, I would drive from Ross in the police car to see mum and dad at Hollybush Farm. Their farm was just over the border into Gloucestershire which is a different force area. Strictly speaking I was straying across the border but the police radio reception was clear so I could maintain radio contact with our headquarters at Worcester and could respond if anything happened. I used to help dad with feeding the farm animals while mum cooked our breakfast!

During the time I was in Ross, I met Rosemary Rigby MBE, a truly remarkable lady who is the founder and owner of the

Violette Szabo Museum, which is next to Rosemary's home at Tump Lane in Wormelow. Rosemary's house was Violette's aunt and uncle's home. Violette spent a lot of her childhood years there. She was selected and trained to become a Second World War secret agent and was eventually captured, tortured and murdered by the Nazis. Like so many, she gave her life for her country. A film was made about her life called 'Carve her name with pride'. This beautiful poem was issued to Violette as the encryption code for her messages.

The life that I have
Is all that I have
And the life that I have
is yours.

The love that I have
Of the life that I have
Is yours and yours and
yours.

A sleep I shall have
A rest I shall have
Yet death will be but a
pause.

For the peace of my years
In the long green grass
Will be yours and yours
and yours.

Rosemary set up the Ross Action Group which remains active today and has raised many thousands of pounds for the Blind Association. On my days off I volunteered to drive the Ross Action Group minibus for her, taking elderly people living in residential and care homes on outings around the county. During the summer months I took them to Hollybush Farm where mum would prepare afternoon tea, sandwiches and homemade cakes in her garden, brewed with loose tea and poured from a proper teapot into proper china cups on saucers!

Most Friday and Saturday nights young testosterone-fuelled lads in Ross, who drank far too much, had battles with lads from the Forest of Dean! Fights inevitably broke out around the town and in pubs and we were there to break them up or to make arrests for various public order offences. One of the most popular meeting places was Harvey's night club at the bottom of Brook-end Street. One night I was assaulted at the club after being punched on the end of my nose which bled profusely. I arrested the person who assaulted me just before more assistance arrived. It was painful but I was thankful that it wasn't broken. After this I saw an illegally and dangerously-parked car close to the club so I wrote out a parking ticket. The vehicle was registered to a senior club staff member but what I didn't know was that the driver was friendly with one of the bosses at the station and they went on holidays together. As you can imagine, issuing the parking ticket didn't go down too well. I was called in to justify my actions, and from that day forwards I couldn't wait to be transferred somewhere else. I applied for a posting to become a rural beat station bobby. As a farmer's son I loved everything about rural farming life. Keeping law and order while living and working in a farming community really appealed to me and my heart was set on it.

Unfortunately, however, my age and experience were against me. I was 22 years old and I knew someone would say that I wasn't experienced enough to become a rural beat officer at my age. Beat officers worked most of the time on their own and unsupervised. However, I was determined to apply. A vacancy came up for the local beat bobby's job at Kingsthorne police station between Hereford and Ross, so I submitted an A.30 report requesting to be transferred there and signing it off in the usual way, 'I am, Sir, your obedient servant. W.D. Rowlatt. Police Constable 264.' After reading my application, the chief inspector called me into his office to inform me that the vacancy at Kingsthorne had already been filled, adding that, in his opinion, I wasn't suited to a position like that because of my age and lack of experience! How did I know he would say this? I wasn't surprised. What surprised me however was that, in the same breath, he contradicted himself and told me that an unexpected vacancy had occurred at the police house and beat station at Eardisley, a location I had not heard of. The house and adjoining police office had been left empty and he said I could take a police vehicle for my wife and I to go and look at it. If I agreed to being transferred, the officer in charge was sergeant 704, Ken Campbell, stationed at Kington. Ken was already in charge of six PCs as well as two officers at Weobley, one at Mansel Lacey and a new police station being built at Pembridge. The chief inspector told me that Sergeant Campbell was a very experienced police sergeant who had previously been stationed at Ross. He said that if I accepted the transfer then Sergeant Campbell would be the right person to keep a very close eye on me. I didn't argue, but neither did I agree. I later found out that Sergeant Campbell had a good reputation. His leadership and no-nonsense approach in maintaining law and order locally had earnt him the respect of the public, with his police section becoming known as 'Campbell's Kingdom'. Before retiring, Ken was awarded the British Empire Medal which he so justly deserved. May he rest in peace.

I remember feeling rather stunned and a little surprised by the chief inspector's offer to take a police vehicle for us to look at the police house and beat station at Eardisley, but that's what we did. We arrived outside after asking a local person for directions. It was located just north of the village on the A4111 to Kington and I parked the police car in the small layby opposite. It was a shivery cold January night and it was snowing again. We had no keys to let ourselves inside this rather bleak-looking, empty detached police house and office, so we breathed on the icy windows to peer inside. A good-sized garden at the front was planted with a variety of mature fruit trees with a smaller garden at the back. We decided it would provide enough space to grow vegetables and flowers and we could keep free range chickens for our own eggs. There were open fireplaces in the downstairs office, lounge and dining room and as I found out, open fireplaces in the three bedrooms upstairs. The windows were single glazed with their original metal frames. The house was built by a local builder and the village undertaker, Mr Walter Howells, during the 1950s and had no heating.

MOVING TO EARDISLEY POLICE STATION

I ACCEPTED the transfer, moving in on the 17 January 1973 when it snowed nearly every day and was bitterly cold. My new boss, Sergeant Ken Campbell, left a message to let me know that he'd ordered half a ton of house coal from local coal merchant Hedley Simcock. Before moving in, the bags of coal were delivered into a coal bunker at the back of the house. The house was previously occupied by PC Brian Reynolds and his family, and had been left empty for several months after Brian moved out. The walls and the whole house were cold and damp. That night, we slept in the lounge on our green coloured sofa in front of an open coal fire with our two-month-old son Julian in his carry cot. The following morning, we woke up to two pleasant unexpected surprises. After unlocking the back door, there was half a net of sprouts and a couple of swedes on the back doorstep which I think had been left for us as a welcoming gesture by a local farmer. I turned on the hot water tap and we had boiling hot water heated by the fire from the back boiler in the lounge which we'd kept alight all night. Hot water and vegetables! What a welcome!

I was told that PC George Barker was the first officer to occupy and move into what was then the new police station and house. George was a keen gardener and it was he who planted the fruit trees. George was followed by PC Ray Farmer, then PC Bill Button, who moved to Kington. PC Brian Herbert followed Bill, then PC Brian Reynolds before me. During his time here, Brian dealt with the tragic double drownings of two local farmer's sons, Michael Whittal and Mervyn Carter, both aged 23 years, who drowned in the River Wye on 26 May 1969. Brian's mode of transport was his police BSA Fleetstar motorcycle, which I inherited from him. Before motorcycles, PC Barker, Farmer, Button and Herbert and others before them rode bicycles to patrol Eardisley and all the other rural villages on their patch. They must have been fit!

After settling in, my first official day on duty began by meeting and introducing myself to Sergeant Ken at the police station in Market Hall Street. The chief inspector was Tony Judge at Leominster who I didn't get to meet until much later on. I was kitted out with police motorcycle boots, gloves, leathers and a corker crash helmet to ride Brian's clapped-out police BSA Fleetstar. Ken was a tall, upright, immaculately dressed and uniformed police sergeant who had an ex-forces look about him. He oozed authority and was devoted to his black and white collie dog, Hector. They were inseparable, even when Ken was taking Kington magistrates court. Hector, if he could, would sneak out from the police station office through the corridor and into the adjoining magistrates court waiting room. From there he had the knack of opening the door with the tip of his nose, then trotted into the main courtroom wagging his tail, which got everyone's attention. Then he jumped up onto the wooden court bench where Ken was sitting so he could sit as closely as he could to him with the magistrates watching on, though they turned a blind eye. Hector would wriggle his bum to get himself comfortable so both of them were directly facing the row of magistrates for the duration of the court's sitting, carrying on with the court's business and licensing applications.

Ken and his wife Wyn lived in the police sergeant's house next door to the police station. They met at Ross police station where Ken was sergeant and Wyn was a policewoman. Their son Cliff was just a little younger than me. After my initial introduction and meeting with Ken, he said that he didn't want to see me again for two weeks. The advice he gave me was to familiarise myself with my beat boundaries and to get to know as many residents, farmers and villains living on my patch as I could. The parishes and areas which I policed were Eardisley, Bollingham, Spond, Lyonshall, Almeley, Letton,

Staunton-on-Wye, Willersley, Winforton, Whitney-on-Wye and Brilley. After we moved in, local people were soon talking about the Police House being occupied again by a police officer who had replaced Brian. After this, my phone (Eardisley 322) started ringing at all times of the day and night with calls from the general public reporting various incidents, crimes and accidents etc., or sometimes local people would ring me to ask for advice. If I was out, then Janette took messages for me. It's hard to believe that in 1973 we were so young and both so young looking! They say that when police officers begin to look younger it's a sign that we're getting much older! One morning a local farmer knocked at the police house door, which was answered by Janette, and asked, 'Is your father in?'! Looking back, it isn't easy to explain how very different life was then by comparison to today, 50 years or so later, but I can try! The following are entirely my own views and opinions.

Largely speaking, I think we relied on each other and helped each other quite a lot more, which isn't to say that this doesn't happen today. The majority of local people stayed working in the local area where they were born and brought up. They knew their neighbours as well as many other people across a much wider area. Popular meeting places were animal markets, village hall socials, village fêtes, local pubs and more regularly supported Christian services of worship in local churches and chapels. There were more rural pubs around with a lot more drunkenness then. Generations of families were Christened and married in their local churches and either cremated or buried in local churchyards. Local people knew only too well who to trust and who to avoid! There was no social media, no mobile phones, no internet and no expectation of increased property prices. Many farms and rural cottages were sold off from large country estates. Some families from London and bigger cities sold their valuable business assets and houses to move here, buying such good value houses and cottages in this largely unspoilt, beautiful part of North Herefordshire and the Golden Valley. The local population started to grow much more quickly than it ever did before and with this came the need for additional housing. Circumstances like this led to the gradual change in traditional village life as we knew it, and I am thankful that I can still remember it. As changes occurred, some smaller local independent family businesses were forced to close their doors in the face of larger, cheaper competitors. People were becoming more affluent and could begin to afford to travel and fly abroad for their holidays. We began shopping in large supermarkets and at bigger retail outlets which sprang up in and around Hereford. Then, as everyone knows, joining the common market and trade with China provided us with cheaper imported goods, mobile phones and the arrival of the internet. It became possible for people to work from home rather than an office, and the majority of us started shopping online. Prior to this gradual transformation there was a strong community spirit, with a sense of pride and everyone looked out for one another. There were exceptions of course, but living life then was good, though poorer too in the material sense. But did it matter?

Local GPs worked from their surgeries at Kington, Pembridge, Eardisley, Weobley and Staunton-on-Wye with a 24 hour on-call rota system. I am a registered patient with Weobley general practice, whose doctors, nurses and staff are all fantastically committed and efficient even with all the changes and challenges which Covid brought about. In 1973 GPs held surgeries at village halls or sometimes in people's houses where patients could turn up if they needed to see and be examined by a doctor without necessarily having to make an appointment. Doctors Jack, Cleland, Lias and Reed would carry out minor surgical procedures themselves at Kington Cottage Hospital, including operations for the removal of tonsils or an appendix etc. How different to today. Most people were employed one way or another in agriculture. Unemployment was low. Many farms and estates were handed down from generation to generation and, with the development of modern farm machinery, this reduced the need to employ so many farm hands. Herefordshire was renowned for its cider orchards, fruit growing and hop picking, providing seasonal jobs not only for local labourers but for gypsy travellers who earned themselves good wages, mostly paid in cash. We often went to break up fights with gypsies in the pubs or on campsites, when they went a bit crazy after spending their wages on drink to get drunk, then fight. On the whole, families were poorer because wages were lower and luxury items, for example televisions, were much more expensive. Earning sufficient wages just to place food on the table for your family was every bread-winner's priority, and many had to scrimp and save money if they wanted to buy a washing machine or car. I was committed to my job so wanted to maintain a high standard of police public relations and, like it or not, I was beginning to become known by local people who were already making their minds up about what sort of a policeman they thought I was, or the type of policeman they wanted me to be. Their judgement of me would be determined by how I dealt with their various local complaints and incidents. The job got done, but I was always well aware of public scrutiny and being in the public eye. I didn't want to disappoint anyone, yet I could be strict or lenient based on my own assessment of a situation and not theirs.

Generally speaking, the police were and still are respected for the very difficult job they do. Back then, if any officer committed a disciplinary offence or went outside the law, they immediately lost respect and trust from the rest of us. I can honestly say that in each and every case, and there were few which I was aware of, all transgressions were thoroughly investigated and dealt with properly and efficiently. Any police officer who chose to break the rules or the law would be quietly disciplined or dismissed from the force, usually without any publicity, press or media exposure which is so prevalent today. Any and all criminal offences would result in that person being charged and dealt with by the courts in exactly the same way as everyone else was. These days it seems to me that the endless bombardment of publicity aimed at a perpetrator in a particular profession can twist public opinion into thinking that the whole of that person's profession is in some way tarnished. Regrettably, today we live in a society that fuels sensationalism and allows finger pointing, often without much evidence or truth. Sometimes good, honest, innocent people will get caught up in or can be falsely accused of something. On the other hand, there are those people who are too afraid to say anything when they know bad things have happened, . There are, they say, some police officers who shouldn't be in the job, like the recent report on the Metropolitan police. This needs to be properly and vigorously addressed. My life's experience has taught me to always trust and believe in myself and the truth. This usually flies in the face of those who are unscrupulous, and who try to make life as difficult as they can for someone else.

Thankfully we still have hard-working and dedicated professionals in our community like our district nurses for example. Back then many of them stayed and worked in the same area, whereas today I think they get switched around and have to travel further distances to where they are needed. There were more clergy who had more time to visit families, the sick and the dying, with more people traditionally attending church and chapel. There were schools with head teachers who were looked up to, as they still are, but people in those sorts of professions were allowed to simply get on with their jobs, with less internal analysis and public probing. Do people working in these professions today suffer with additional stress and anxiety because they are constantly having to justify everything they do and the decisions they make? If so, this must be very debilitating.

After my move to Eardisley police station, the very first case I dealt with was a report of criminal damage at an unoccupied house known as Ferret's Moor at Lower Welson, reported by its owner Mr Mainwaring, who was a farmer at Kingswood, Kington. When I arrived, I could see that the culprits were probably teenagers. Light switches had been smashed in rooms and plaster ripped off the walls. It was a complete mess. I saw some small-adult-sized shoe impressions in the dust on the floor and set about making local enquiries, quickly tracing three young suspects. One was under the age of criminal responsibility (11) so I invited the parents and children to attend the police station. The father of one of the suspects was a local builder and I decided to sort out an agreement with him, and the other parents, to carry out the clearing and cleaning up process themselves. They agreed to re-plaster and make good the damaged walls and to replace the broken fixtures and light fittings with new ones, all at their own expense. This was in exchange for my decision to not take any further police action, other than giving those responsible some good old-style advice and a severe reprimand. All of them, with the exception of the

11-year-old, should have appeared before a juvenile court at Kington, but I had already decided on my own course of action instead. A couple of months later, Sergeant Ken called me into his office. Like me, he knew exactly what was happening on his section and I was a little concerned about what he would say about the criminal damage incident and how I'd dealt with it by my own particular method to avoid court. I was relieved after he agreed that I had made the right decision in dealing with it like I had. Phew! In my view it was a fair decision for the three families concerned, the community, the police, Mr Mainwaring ... oh and for me too, with no paperwork needed!

When we moved here to live in Eardisley it was a thriving village community. There were two village shops, a doctor's surgery, Burgoyne's garage selling fuel and a Vauxhall franchise, Parker Kinslingbury's timber merchants, Sharples haulage, Walter Howells undertakers, Peter Preece butchers, Barclays bank, a newspaper and sweet shop, two village pubs – the Tram Inn and the New Inn, a dairy, Jim Morgan the electrician, a post office with Nora Nicholas the post mistress and a cobbler's repair shop owned and run by Dick Webb, who re-soled and re-heeled shoes and children's school shoes at very modest prices. His workshop was a wooden lean-to building with a corrugated tin roof on the end of Arboyne House. Mainly retired locals would stand and chat with Dick for hours at a time drinking mugs of tea, as he went about his shoe and leather repair work. I still had my black leather police issue boots, which he repaired for me a number of times. Dick, like so many, was a kind hearted, talented local craftsman. The village hall known as the Curzon Herrick Hall was named after the previous owners of the Eardisley farms estate and the snooker club and table were in the room above the archway entrance. Mrs Longville, who owned Lemore Manor, had a small herd of Jersey cows which her cowhand Mrs Davies looked after for her. Mrs Davies lived in Mrs Longville's bungalow along the main driveway to the house. She milked and looked after the Jersey herd and had her own milk round, delivering bottles of Jersey milk, rich homemade jersey cream and homemade, hand-patted salty butter. Eric Clarke delivered newspapers and magazines from his newspaper shop in the village and Eric's wife, Margaret, was a teacher at Eardisley Primary School. Tom Hicks was a local saw doctor who sharpened knives and mowers. He and Tom Carter, a local farmer, were just two out of dozens of local men and women who fought so bravely for their country during the Second World War. Tom Hicks was a Korean War veteran and Tom Carter shot down a German Messerschmitt plane with a field gun after disobeying orders to keep it unloaded by his senior officer. The pubs were busy and many farms made homemade cider. Cider would supplement the wages that farmers paid to their labourers.

My police office had a civil defence intercom system which was connected by phone line to the civil defence rooms located underground at Hereford police station in Gaol Street, and every month I tested the system to make sure it was functioning correctly. After turning it on at an allotted time, I listened to the password which was repeated three times. I

Hand-cranked air raid siren

My new police Mini van, which replaced the old Fleetstar motorbike

wrote the password down on a card and posted it back to the civil defence rooms. As far as I knew, these intercoms were installed and interlinked at all police, fire and ambulance stations around the country. The intercom was an early warning system to warn of an imminent Russian nuclear attack. I also had a hand-cranked siren which was stored in a wooden crate, identical to those used during the Second World War, to warn the public of imminent air raid attacks. Attached to the crate was an instruction booklet with information telling me what to do if a nuclear bomb was dropped! I periodically unboxed the siren to take it outside into the garden and test it. It could be heard miles away and I often wondered what people thought when they heard it being cranked up.

I quickly settled into my role as the village bobby, though I wasn't happy with Brian's old Fleetstar motorbike. One night I attended a poultry house fire at Staunton-on-Wye. On my way home, when it was pitch black and I was travelling at about 40 miles an hour, all the lights went out! I don't know how, but I managed to keep my balance and thankfully didn't fall off. A couple of months later the police provided me with a new blue and white police Mini van fitted with a blue flashing light on the top of an illuminated box. The box lit up 'Police' or flashed 'Police Stop' if a vehicle needed to be stopped, and there was room to carry equipment including police accident slow signs and cones etc. Sunday mornings was the day I normally set aside to clean and polish it.

I was fairly lenient when it came to laying down the law locally or booking local people, depending on the severity of the offence. It was a fine line. I never forgot that we had to live in the community too. I normally gave someone a warning or a verbal caution for something trivial. It was usually appreciated and taken far more notice of, but if the warning got ignored and the same offence repeated then the next time that person received a summons. I had a personal dislike of motorists who didn't pay their RFL (Road Fund Licence/ tax disc) or didn't insure their vehicle. In those days each vehicle had to display a current circular paper tax disc placed in the bottom left-hand corner of the vehicle's windscreen. DVLA then introduced colour changes to the disks which made it easier to identify any out-of-date tax discs. My argument was that if I had to pay to insure and tax my own car, then why shouldn't everyone else? These days, some police vehicles are fitted with electronic vehicle number plate recognition systems which immediately identify stolen, untaxed or uninsured motor vehicles, so much more current information can be sent electronically via the police national computer.

As well as local policing I became interested in the misuse of drugs, wanting to identify established associations, contacts and the networks which these people moved around in. The most available and commonly-used drug was cannabis leaf from home-grown cannabis plants, but the psychotic and psychological effects of smoking stronger imported cannabis resin from places like Afghanistan, known as Afghan black, or the Lebanon, known as Lebanese gold, was more serious. Magic mushroom or Phycobilin – now class 'A' – grew wild on unploughed pastureland, so could easily be found if you knew where they grew and could identify them. It was not an offence then to pick or possess them. It only became an arrestable offence to possess them if they were dried or prepared in some way. Freshly-picked magic mushroom are very indigestible if swallowed on their own, causing sickness and vomiting. To make them digestible, users would often mix them with honey or chop them up to add them to homemade stews or curries. LSD – Lysergic Acid Diethylamide – is a hallucinatory drug, and quite difficult to trace and identify. Illicit producers would set up small makeshift laboratories where hundreds of litres of water were required to dilute the drug to produce the exact strength. Single doses of this clear liquid drug were dispensed by a single droplet from a pipette onto small perforated squares of card, usually depicted with coloured cartoon characters of cats or dogs. As individual liquid doses dried, they became invisible to the naked eye, which was the reason they were placed onto small perforated cartoon squares so they could be divided up into single doses and distributed. These batches of cards were usually supplied through the post. The little square cartoon cards made LSD more easily identifiable during drugs raids, and each deal on each card was about the size of an aspirin. Opium, which is a class 'A' drug, was illegally imported, but rarely found or seized around here at that particular time. There were comparatively small quantities of heroin and cocaine in circulation in these rural areas too, with much larger seizures taking place in the bigger towns and cities. The most commonly-used illegal drugs seized locally at that time was LSD (class 'A'), home-grown cannabis leaf and cannabis resin (class 'B'), magic mushroom (class 'A') and amphetamines (class 'B') or 'uppers' as they were known. Heroin and cocaine are more regularly used and seized these days and in much greater quantities, because it became more cheaply and widely available almost everywhere. During my era some drug users were associated with flower-power and hippies, who started to drift here in the late 1960s and early 1970s. They were young and stood for passive resistance and non-violence. Many moved here from the London area and from other large northern cities to live their particular lifestyle in isolated, peaceful, rural locations or in old buses, communes and dilapidated cottages around Herefordshire and the Welsh border towns of Kington and Hay-on-Wye.

Local celebrities included the late Richard Booth who lived at Hay Castle and at his family home of Brynmellin, Cusop. He was later crowned as the self-styled 'King of Hay'. Richard set up the largest second-hand bookshop in Europe and book-shops sprang up everywhere in the town. He had many literary friends from Oxford and elsewhere, who he invited to stay with him and his wife, Hope, including some famous guests such as April Ashley, who I met a couple of times when she told me 'I'm the Duchess of a Ditch' (meaning Offa's Dyke). April only recently died in January 2022. Marian Faithfull, the Rolling Stones, Arnold Wesker, Duncan Fallowell, Rhona Muirhead, Arthur Scargill (Richard supported the miners unions), writer Jeremy Sandford, who was married to Nell Dunn, and two of my good friends Vera and the late Gerry Taylor who, at the time, lived at Winforton Court. In later years Richard invited former US president Bill Clinton to have lunch with him when he visited the now world-renowned Hay Festival.

The arrival and influx of the hippy fraternity became more and more noticeable as they mixed with each other after settling into their remote and isolated locations. Hay market became a popular meeting place on Thursdays. They set up stalls, selling anything and everything including their art work, free range eggs, handmade baskets and crafts. Sometimes cottages would be bought or rented for them by their wealthy parents or relatives and a few settled here, becoming parents, grandparents and great-grandparents. I recorded dossiers of suspected dealers and known drug users. I engaged in cross-border liaison with Welsh drug squad officers from the Dyfed Powys police area, as well as our own force and police forces nationally.

My dear daughter Lucy was born on 16 February 1974 at the county hospital after a high-speed drive to the hospital in my Austin 1800. We arrived at the hospital just in time for her to be born. She was born with a caul, a wax-like membrane that some babies are born with. According to ancient folklore, babies born with a caul would never drown. Both my children, Julian and Lucy, attended Eardisley Primary School under the headship of Stuart Brain, and then Weobley Comprehensive. I made a point of paying regular visits to the local primary schools on my patch. These were at Brilley, Almeley, Eardisley and Staunton-on-Wye. Brilley school has since closed. I talked to local school children about the 'Green Cross Code' and 'Stranger Danger', which were the children's safety subjects of the day. In Eardisley I took them outside to show them how to safely cross the busy A4111, then back in their classrooms they all received a signed certificate to take home, telling them they had passed. I don't remember anyone failing! I talked to them about police work and my job as a police officer. I remember one young boy putting up his hand to ask me a question: 'PC

Rowlatt, have you ever seen someone's head run over by car?'
Thankfully not! But I applauded their innocence and directness.
I made them laugh too. I showed them my special trick, which
was to stand with my back against the classroom wall wearing
my helmet. I put my thumb in my mouth and pretended to
blow. I pushed the back of my helmet against the wall, still
blowing with my thumb in my mouth, giving the illusion that
my helmet was being blown up off the top of my head, like
blowing up a balloon! Magic! All the kids loved me doing this
and they thought it was so funny. I parked the police van in the
playground and divided them into two groups. I gave one group
my personal police radio set, which was linked into the radio set
in the police van, and the other group all piled inside switching
on the headlights and the flashing blue light. There they played
being real policemen and policewomen. One day I was talking
to the whole school outside in their playground with headmaster
Stuart Brain when we heard the sound of a really noisy exhaust
from a motorbike being erratically ridden down the main road
towards us. Two young lads, who were riding it, came into view
and we all turned to see that they weren't wearing crash helmets.
To set them an example, I left the children with Stuart and leapt
into the police van. On went the blue flashing light as I drove
off in pursuit of the two law breakers! This was an opportunity
to show them the consequences of breaking the law and what a
serious business this was! My young captive audience looked on
as I disappeared in hot pursuit. As I got to know the children
and their parents, I decided to give them more of my time and
became more active with the youth in the village as they were
growing up. Some had low self-motivation or no interests other
than school, so I decided to do something about it after dealing
with this next incident.

There was a craze spreading among some Kington secondary school children for removing car badges, by prising them off the backs of cars and collecting them like trophies. One evening my phone rang. The call came from a parent who I knew in Eardisley. He'd been into his son's bedroom and caught him with a group of his school friends dishing out car badges to each other like they were playing cards. They admitted to him that they had used screwdrivers to force the badges off the cars which were parked outside the village hall at a whist drive. The parent who called me said, 'I've got them here, Bill, so I'll walk them up the road to you now at the police station'. It was pitch black and he drove his car slowly up the main road from the village with the group of lads walking in front, illuminated in his car headlights with heads held low! When they arrived, I got them to empty their pockets and place all of the badges on the police office counter. I knew a couple of them, and asked the others to give me their names and addresses, so I could inform their parents. To emphasise the sense of officialdom and to highlight the seriousness of their actions, I wrote down their names and addresses in my pocket book. They were young and upset. Fortunately for them, all of the badges which had been taken could be accounted for, so I decided to give them all a serious reprimand in my own particular style! After hearing their admissions and apologies, I concluded by giving them my reassurance that, on this occasion, this would be the end of the matter, with no further police action taken and that this was my final decision. I also gave them my assurance that none of them would face court proceedings. After hearing me say this, one of them shed tears of relief. I went to the village hall where I saw the cars were still parked with no badges on them. Standing on the stage, I announced to everyone that I had just dealt with a group of youths from the village who had admitted being responsible for removing their car badges but that I was satisfied that I'd recovered all of them so they could be replaced without loss or damage. I left them on a table at the back of the hall for everyone to collect when they left. However, this wasn't quite the end of the story! A few weeks later I received a telephone call from Inspector Peter Preece. He was prosecuting two juveniles at Kington juvenile court who were up before the magistrates for stealing car badges from cars parked at Kington, ironically on the same night that I'd reprimanded my lads in Eardisley. After adjourning the court, he said that PC Paul Kirkham had apprehended two youths for stealing badges off cars at Kington who he'd arrested, charged and summoned to court, but the parents were questioning why the group in Eardisley who were caught doing the same thing were let off? 'Have you any knowledge Bill?' the Inspector asked me. 'Er, well Sir, I'll see what I can find out!' I said. What else could I say? But the story didn't end there. Years later, the warning I'd given my lads was rewarded when they showed their loyalty and support for me. One evening I received a call from licensee Dave Harvey at the New Inn asking me to attend. A coach load of about 50 noisy, drunken Welshmen had turned up unexpectedly in his bar on an early evening pub crawl, and their rowdy behaviour was rapidly deteriorating. I changed into uniform and placed myself on duty before walking into the public bar with the intention of getting them back onto their coach to leave quietly and head back to the Valleys, but they were having none of it. I was pushed and shoved in all directions which made me feel vulnerable and scared for my own safety. In fact, I was shitting bricks! I was thinking that, if all hell let loose, a call for police assistance from Hereford would arrive too late. I hadn't noticed them but 'my lads', who I'd reprimanded years before and who were now all grown-up strong, muscular young men, happened to be out together enjoying a pint in the bar. They saw what was happening and how I was running out of steam to quell the unruly mob. The Welshmen saw and heard what happened next, which I was oblivious to. 'My lads' moved in closer together in tight formation, close behind me, then one of them, Jimmy Jenkins, tapped me on my shoulder, loudly announcing, 'Bill, we're right behind you!' This was most definitely the right moment for me to be thankful to all of them. My back-up was already there! After hearing Jim say this, my voice altered into a much more authoritative one and I succeeded in getting the Welsh mob to leave in an almost orderly manner. They got back onto the coach and were heading for home. Thanks again boys – oh sorry, men – for all your support if you are reading this! I was really grateful that you stepped in when you did.

I decided to set up a village youth club in the old wooden scout hut which was at the front of New Barns. It was an opportunity for teenagers to meet, play darts, table tennis, board games and to listen to some loud music. From the outset I insisted that I would maintain a manageable level of discipline. One of my volunteer helpers was Mark Raine, who worked at Bulmers in Hereford. The hut, which needed a few repairs and a lick of paint, hadn't been used in decades. The lads and girls all helped to redecorate it and, when it opened, it became extremely popular with local teenagers and their parents, who all supported the initiative. Those who frequented the club were mainly from the village, but there were others from Almeley and Brilley who were dropped off by their parents. We went fishing and everyone learnt to fly fish with brothers Laurie and

Pete Hutchinson. This might sound a bit harsh but if anyone misbehaved, then they would probably get a clip round the ear, but these were the days when this was expected. One night, two lads were fighting together and, after telling them to stop, one of them carried on and wouldn't back off so I gave him a kick up the backside. He ran home as fast as he could, back home to his parents. Oh dear. Perhaps I had been a bit too harsh I thought, so the following day I called in to see his mum but, before I'd even uttered a word to her, she simply said, 'I expect he deserved it!' and that was that.

I decided to take a few of the youth club members camping to Pembrokeshire via the Elan Valley, which was an area I was familiar with from when I was at the police cadet camp. The plan was to spend a couple of nights camping, but to be on the safe side I decided it might be wiser not to invite any of the girls. All the lads invited were between 14 and 16 years old. I typed out a letter to the parents of those who had expressed an interest to go. They were asked to sign the letter to agree that their son would attend entirely at his own personal risk. This was pre-health and safety legislation, but to me it made good sense. I hired a people carrier and we set off, loaded up with food, tents, fishing rods and cooking utensils. These days a DBS check would be needed, along with personal accident insurance and risk assessments etc., but back then it was just arranged with innocent simplicity. We arrived in the Elan Valley and set up camp by a beautiful lake which was brimming with brown trout just waiting to be caught and eaten, so fishing rods were assembled and a camp fire quickly lit. Soon, a couple of good-sized fat brown trout were caught, gutted and in the frying pan over an open fire when a Welsh Water bailiff appeared from nowhere! He informed me that we were illegally fishing and catching trout in an area where we were not allowed to set up camp or pitch tents for the night. I had no idea. I apologised, telling him that I was a police officer and fortunately for me he took a lenient view, but not before telling me off in front of everyone, adding that I should be a lot more responsible. The lads found this very amusing. When he had gone, we all sat around the camp fire having a few laughs and finishing our delicious illegally-poached trout before packing up and moving camp early the next morning. We travelled from there to the Pembrokeshire coast, setting up camp on Newgale beach. That evening I cottoned on to the fact that a couple of the older lads were missing from their tent and I had no idea where they were. After surmising where they might have wandered off to, I found them in the bar of a nearby pub, buying crisps and chocolate. They had also seized the opportunity to down a crafty pint just before I turned up. Who could blame them? I was young once. I pointed out that if they had been caught in the pub it would have caused very serious problems for me. They apologised, and I kept my fingers crossed that they wouldn't mention to their parents where I'd found them!

Being the rural beat officer for Eardisley was a job I really enjoyed. Financially however, police officer's wages were really low until Margaret Thatcher was elected Prime Minister in 1979. She immediately promised to award us a 50 percent pay rise, staggered over one year. This was fantastic news, though I didn't realise at the time that it was a sweetener to prepare us for the beginning of the controversial miners' strike which erupted in 1984, an event which I was to play my part in. The increase in our wages made a huge difference. Having been the Eardisley beat bobby for six years, I was seriously considering how we could possibly continue to afford bringing up a young family on what I was earning. There were lots of good aspects to my job, but these were mixed in with extremely sad events too, such as sudden deaths or dealing with road traffic accidents – these days referred to as road traffic incidents. Although the breathalyser drink-drive legislation was introduced in 1967, it took years after this for the message to sink in that drink-driving would never be tolerated. During the 1970s, when there were many more local pubs than there are now, alcohol-related accidents sometimes resulted in very serious injuries and fatalities, which were not uncommon then. Some drivers had not learnt to refrain from drinking and driving and were still prepared to take the risk, so had to accept the consequences of being positively breathalysed and disqualified from driving.

Talking of accidents, my next tale was personally embarrassing. I was working a day shift and had gone up to Brilley in the police Mini van to make enquiries and was on my way back, driving along Apostles Lane towards the main A4111 Kington road. The lane is quite narrow, with bends in places where it is impossible for two vehicles to pass without one having to give way and reverse up. I drove round a sharp left-hand bend and was shocked to see another vehicle coming straight towards me from the opposite direction. I braked as hard as I could and skidded but couldn't avoid a head-on collision with the other vehicle. I got out and saw that the bonnet of the police van was V-shaped and crumpled up, with smoke and steam billowing out from the radiator and engine compartment. I was concerned whether the driver and his lady passenger were injured, though thankfully neither of them were. The driver, who I knew, was a local farmer. He was struggling to push open his bent and buckled driver's door to get out. He said nothing to me for a couple of minutes, while weighing up the situation and looking closely at the damage caused to the police van and his pickup truck, both of which were now written-off. After eyeing me up and down a couple of times, he removed his cap, scratched his head and said, 'Goin' a bit, weren't you boy!?'

After my written-off police Mini van was replaced with a new one, I had another accident which wasn't my fault. I was out on general patrol, coming to the end of my 4pm to midnight shift, when I felt a slight shuddering sensation through the steering wheel which was getting progressively worse, so I stopped to check the van for punctures etc. Everything seemed to be ok, so I got back in and carried on driving past the two pubs in the village towards the police house and home. After driving past the Old Forge on the left, the front sub-frame dropped like a stone onto the road. I was forcefully thrown forwards, and lost complete control of the steering. I couldn't believe it when I saw that the front offside wheel of the police van had come off and was bouncing down the middle of the main road towards Kington. At that moment an Austin Allegro came round the corner from the opposite direction, with the wheel heading straight towards it. It hit the windscreen, bounced off and changed direction. Now it was bouncing back towards me like Barnes Wallis's wartime bomb! As I saw it coming closer, I crouched down and tightly tucked myself in under the steering column for protection. The wheel narrowly missed hitting the police van and bounced over Robert and Mary Preece's garden wall at the bungalow, flattening most of Mary's flowerbeds. A young, rather shocked and puzzled driver got out of her Allegro to ask me what had happened. What could I say, other than 'The wheel came off!' After radioing headquarters at Worcester for assistance, the police van was trailered back to the police garage in Hereford. The following day, my phone didn't stop ringing with calls from senior officers at Leominster, Hereford and headquarters wanting to know the circumstances of the accident, because any unroadworthy police vehicle would have legal implications for the chief constable. The cause was metal fatigue. After almost making it home, I think this should be added to my list of lucky escapes!

One very warm Sunday summer's day, we had a glut of ripening fruit on the fruit trees in the front garden that PC George Barker had planted. Opposite the police house was a small layby where I sometimes parked instead of parking in the police drive. There were eaters, russets and Bramley cooking apples, with deliciously ripe red, yellow and greengage plums. I had an idea to set up a fruit stall in the layby where my two small children, Julian and Lucy, could sell the fruit to earn some pocket money. It was my weekend off, so I hammered together a few offcuts and planks of wood to make a stall, then both of them sat patiently behind it with a pot of loose change and boxes of the ripe fruit to sell. I could see the children through the lounge window, so could keep a safe eye on them. I had

another idea of placing two POLICE SLOW signs on either side of their stall, which would help to slow the traffic down a bit and encourage potential customers to stop! Lots of people pulled up in their cars to buy the fruit, and some were amused by the police signs, asking questions and taking photos. On reflection it was probably a step too far! Sales soon started to outstrip supply when I had to pick more fruit to keep up with demand. During a quieter period, I went back into the house for a mug of tea, leaving Julian and Lucy outside enjoying playing shop-keepers. From the house I saw another customer pulling up alongside their stall in a red Ford Escort. The driver wound his window down to talk to them, and I realised this wasn't a normal customer! I saw the driver was wearing a police uniform with three silver pips on his epaulettes! Oh my gosh! This was the chief inspector from Leominster, who had driven past and couldn't help seeing the police slow signs I'd put out. Shortly afterwards he drove off again. After making sure the coast was clear, I rushed outside and folded up the signs to put them away and asked Julian what he'd said. 'He asked where you were, dad, so I told him you were on a weekend off!' I wasn't sure if that would help me or not! I was surely going to be held to task for setting up a fruit stall outside the police station, and for the entirely inappropriate use of two police slow signs. However, I think the situation was too bizarre for the chief inspector to deal with, and I didn't hear another word. Another lucky escape!?

I have always been interested in the history of farm machinery and decided to tinker with a couple of old engines, which I'd bought from local farmers, and I got them running again. Somehow this reached the ears of Tony Boyce, a local reporter, who decided to take a photo and write about it in the *Evening News* (overleaf).

I purchased the 5/6 horse-power Bamford open crank oil engine from the late Mr John Bufton at Llanedry Farm, Brilley. The engine started on petrol then switched over to TVO (tractor vaporising oil) when it got hot. It used to power Mr Bufton's corn mill, which fed his farm animals during the Second World War. I knew Mr Bufton had fond memories of it being used, and I promised him that I wouldn't sell it after buying it from him for five pounds. I restored and painted it and took a photo for Mr Bufton which he kept on his mantelpiece. The engine, which is still in my ownership, is on loan to the Waterworks Museum – Hereford, where it can be seen working on the museum's steam open days.

As police wages were so low, I worked on local farms hauling bales during harvest time to supplement my wages. Each year I earnt just enough to take my family away on holiday. We usually headed for Solva in Pembrokeshire, New Quay in west Wales or to Bracklesham Bay in West Sussex, where friends Neil and Joan Milne moved to from Evesham after Neil suffered poor health. Their seaside house was in a beautiful spot close to the sea front. Bill and Shan Kinch, who were antique dealers in Eardisley, owned a new, large luxury touring caravan, which they generously allowed me to borrow from them to tow behind my car. Before moving to Eardisley, I owned a vintage Norton Dominator twin cylinder 500cc motorbike which I had plans to restore, but, because I wasn't paid a lot, I made the reluctant decision to sell it to buy some extras for the children. I was young, physically fit and very familiar with driving farm tractors and operating farm machinery. Earning a little extra cash made a lot of difference and, as a family, it meant that we could get away on holiday for a couple of weeks each year. Police officers weren't allowed to earn additional money,

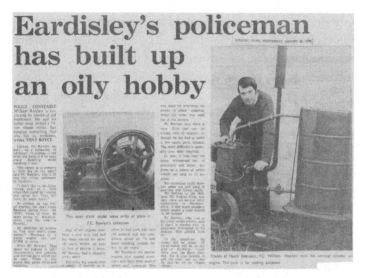

Tinkering with old engines. I restored the 5/6 horse-power Bamford open crank oil engine (left) and it now lives at the Waterworks Museum in Hereford.

run a business or have a second job, but I enjoyed farm work, which came naturally to me, and putting my family first was worth the risks. I worked for farmers Geoff Glyn-Jones of New House Farm, Almeley; the Matthews family at Spond; Andrew Cameron at Letton Court; Val and Tom Stephens at Wootton Farm; and for Neil Ewart at Upper Welson.

One Sunday lunchtime, I was digging over the vegetable patch in our front garden when I heard a clattering sound coming from a motorbike being ridden down the main road from Kington. A 125cc motorcycle came into view, with its engine rattling and banging like a bag of nails. It slowed down, then came to a complete standstill, conking out outside the police station. A young man got off the bike, removed his helmet and looked down despondently at the broken engine. I went over to introduce myself to him. He told me he was an Aberystwyth University student studying for his degree. I asked him where he was heading; the university had started their summer recess and he was on his way to his parents' home in Devon. Devon!? I suggested telephoning them so they could pick him up, but he said neither of them drove and there was no one else he could contact for help. As it was near to lunchtime, I invited him in to share lunch with us, which was already cooked and ready to serve. He accepted the invitation, and we agreed it was a good opportunity to discuss his predicament. When we were finishing our meal, the police phone rang, which wasn't unusual even on Sundays. It was local farmer Geoff Glyn-Jones from New House Farm at Almeley. 'Hello Bill, is there any chance you could come over? I've just baled some hay and could do with a hand to get them in,' adding that the forecast was rain … 'Do you know anyone who could come along with you to give you a hand?' Talk about coincidences! 'Hang on Geoff,' I said, placing the phone down to ask our lunch guest if he was interested in coming with me to earn some cash, which I suggested could be put towards the repairs to his bike. Enthusiastically he jumped at the suggestion. After filling our bellies with roast Herefordshire beef, homemade horseradish sauce and all the trimmings, followed by generous helpings of homemade apple pie and cream, we drove over to Geoff and Carey's farm at Almeley. Never having laboured on a farm before, my friend took to the task really well. I showed him how to pitch bales up onto a trailer with pitch forks (or pykles). It was physically hard graft and a completely new experience for him, totally in contrast to his academic life. We sweated and chatted as we worked alongside each other. Maybe this was an insight into how local farming and rural policing were inextricably linked. I invited John to stay at the police house for two more nights to continue bale bumping with me for three more days. Eardisley had a second-hand motorcycle sales and repair shop at the Malt House. Years before, there were different businesses that traded from there. Jack Hales ran a garage, servicing and repairing vehicles. John Hales sold second-hand Land Rovers. Roy King had a shop selling pet food and plants. Alan Wilding set up his business manufacturing bespoke carpets and rugs, and Lez Penning ran a recording studio where many famous bands from across the country came to record their chart songs. We set off wheeling John's broken motorbike into the village for them to look at but the engine was beyond repair. My university student friend had earned himself sufficient cash to buy a second-hand 125cc motorbike as a replacement. After thanking me, we said goodbye and he set off to ride his new second-hand bike all the way back to his parents' house in Devon, but not before I asked him to promise that he wouldn't write a letter of thanks to the chief constable or mention me, or anything about his stay at Eardisley police station! Hopefully, after his second attempt to get home, he arrived safely but I never knew as I never heard from him again. Often circumstances like this just happened, which was all part of living life as a rural beat officer – one which I enjoyed tremendously.

Another request for help came when master of the foxhounds Neil Ewart telephoned me. Neil lived at Upper Welson Farm. 'Bill, are you working today?' I wasn't sure why he was asking me. 'Yes, I'm on a day shift, Neil,' came my reply. 'Oh, damn it!' he said. 'Why?' I asked. 'Well, I've got an articulated lorry arriving from Birmingham. It'll be here at lunchtime. I've sold some bales of hay, and Harry could do with a hand to load them.' Harry was Neil's farm manager who lived at Almeley. 'OK,' I said, 'I'll take my lunch break and I'll be up with you at one o'clock.' I took my wellies and a pair of overalls to change into and drove, in uniform, up to the farm in the police Mini van. The articulated lorry and driver were already there. I parked the police van in the farmyard, leaving the police radio on maximum volume so I could hear any messages I needed to respond to if headquarters tried to contact me (my call sign was Echo Mike 56). The lorry driver was struggling to figure it all out when he saw me arrive and change out of uniform into a pair of overalls and wellies before helping Harry to load the lorry. Harry started up the bale elevator and the lorry was loaded in exactly one hour. At the back of my mind, I knew there might always be someone who would drop me in it, so, if it happened, I would say that I was loading the lorry as a favour during my lunch break. As the driver was roping off the load, Harry shook hands with me to say thank you. After changing back into my uniform, he asked me to reverse the police van up to a large pile of logs. He opened up the back doors and threw dozens of dry, ready-to-burn logs into the back of the van. By the time he had finished, the van was overloaded. The back doors wouldn't shut properly so I tied them together with a piece of string to stop any logs flying out on the journey home to the police house. I drove slowly from the farm with the police van at nearly a 45-degree angle from the weight of the logs inside. Those were the times and those were the days!

I was bathing our son Julian, who was about three, when I saw his face had turned a scarlet red colour. His whole body shook as he went into some sort of fit and he stopped breathing. Instinctively I rushed downstairs cuddling and cradling him in my arms to go outside for fresh air. I gave him very gentle mouth to mouth resuscitation, which my police first-aid training had taught me to do for someone so young. After moments and thank God, a miracle happened and his little chest started to rise and fall indicating that he'd started breathing again. With his eyes rolling, he urgently needed hospital treatment. We called '999' and an ambulance arrived at the police house quite quickly, and I went with Julian at full speed to the county hospital in Hereford. I didn't know at the time that my old shift 'A' scale was working a day shift. As the ambulance reached the city boundary along Kings Acre Road, we were met by a police fast-response vehicle, which took up the lead in front of the ambulance to escort us at full speed through the town's busy junctions and traffic lights to the hospital. At a couple of junctions, I spotted two of my old colleagues; they were standing in the middle of the road holding up the traffic to wave us through. I later found out that my old shift was sent a radio message telling them that it was my son in the ambulance. Everyone pulled out all the stops, and did everything they could to help. Julian's diagnosis was a cerebral convulsion brought on by a sudden high temperature, which was successfully treated by our family GP, John Davies, from Weobley surgery. I wanted to write about this because I am still enormously grateful to the late Doctor John, and to all of my police colleagues who were around at that time to help. To this day, I have such admiration for their resourcefulness and quick-thinking. I feel so thankful for the services we receive from doctors, nurses and all our NHS staff who work tirelessly, giving so much of themselves, and who go out of their way to help others. I know there are some flaws in the system, but generally we are still very fortunate in comparison to other countries. These memories and those acts of kindness have stayed with me to this day. I will always remember them, and be entirely grateful and proud for what everyone did. Thank you.

MUM AND DAD

I N the early '80s our family received some devastating news.
Our lovely mum visited her GP after suffering from stomach
problems and a lack of physical energy. Following tests and
X-rays, mum was diagnosed with cancer of the colon and
needed a surgical procedure to remove a tumour. This was
followed by radiotherapy treatment. Mum hated the thought
of being physically 'messed about with' as she put it. I guess
this might have been due to the fact that she worked as a nurse,
or maybe something to do with her being quite sensitive and
shy by nature. As a family, all of us supported her but none of
us had any idea of the eventual outcome or what her prognosis
was. We didn't know how long she would survive. Mum felt
that she had to help herself recover too, rather than only relying
on medical treatment. She heard and read about the Bristol
Cancer Help Centre which was opened by Prince Charles.
At the time, they offered a new and radical approach which
achieved some very positive results for the treatment of cancer.
A book was written by Doctor Rosy Thomson who worked
at the clinic entitled *Loving Medicine* (ISBN 0-946551-49-9).
Writing in her book, she describes her patients' experiences and
their transformation through the holistic treatment of cancer.
Each chapter is dedicated to a group of patients, all of whom
gave permission to be written about in the book. Chapter
three is about mum and I love these words by her GP Doctor
Parsons who begins, 'It is certainly gratifying that this gifted
and charming lady has survived so long and there is no doubt
of the tremendous physiological help she has derived from the
Cancer Help Centre'. She continues, 'discovering that Joan

was not just alive but beaming!' She tells my father, 'Jack, this is nothing short of a miracle!' Mum consistently followed the Bristol diet sheets, eating organic, vegetarian food with dad growing most of the vegetables she needed in their garden. Dad grew an abundance of organic carrots which were put through a juicing machine, as organic carrot juice was believed to combat residual cancer cells. Mum also received counselling at Bristol to overcome the hurtful memories of her feuding parents and the constant abuse she received from her mother as a child, such as when her mother told her that no one would ever love her. She also received spiritual healing, which was an incredible experience for her, and something which I recognise and occasionally practise.

Mum wrote these words about healing:

Often I notice that new patients at Bristol (Cancer clinic) are unsure or bewildered at the thought of spiritual healing. There is no need to feel afraid of a 'poor performance'. All that is needed is to relax and let yourself receive the love (in whatever form it is given) that is offered by the healer – not enquiring how or what – keeping thought receptive. Trying to let the looming thoughts of the healer flow over and through you triggers off a reaction –expanding spirituality and uplifting the inner self to heights unknown before. As spirituality grows, so then physicality recedes, thus strengthening the power of the healing. As love is given by the healer, and received by the patient, the whole fuses into one spiritual experience thus lifting and expanding the awareness of the souls of both with an ever-increasing outreach and love for the whole

world. In this truly wonderful progress of mind, error
and sickness fall into second place, and to those uplifted
souls, no longer exist for those precious moments of Truth.
Afterwards, both are enriched and the sense of wellbeing
holds in its hands the healing that was first intended.
Thus, in one tiny episode of time, the good in the world is
increased and the error diminished. Not only do we benefit
our own being and spiritual growth but expand others
too – reaching far beyond and above our own limited
understanding.

During the course of treatments, mum, if she could, helped
others who found themselves in similar distressing circumstances. In her own peaceful, reassuring way, she comforted,
loved and supported as many people as she could and some
who she had never met from countries abroad who telephoned
her or wrote to her. In 1984 dad retired from his 'dog and stick'
farming at Hollybush Farm which went under the hammer.
My sister Jane and her husband, Brian Holliday, lived in
one of the school houses provided by the Quaker school at
Sibford Ferris in Oxfordshire, where Brian taught and was
head of Geography and Economics. Jane and Brian bought
a charming period terraced cottage known as Anne's Cot at
Sibford for mum and dad to move into. Jane and Brian became
their devoted carers, taking care of their general welfare as
our parents slipped into their twilight years. They say that
farmers never retire. The school buildings and grounds were
surrounded by two unfenced fields which dad, who seldom
missed any opportunity even at his age, negotiated with the
school governors to allow him to put up livestock fences and
graze his flock of sheep. This became an idyllic situation and

a sort of gradual slowing down for them as they entered old age, yet maintaining their varied interests. Mum continued with her art work and playing the piano. She would sit during winter evenings by the log fire cutting out coloured felt patterns of mice which she hand-stitched together, making dozens of these little fellas which were sold for the blind association charity. Dad chatted with the locals and to school children who persistently asked him questions about his sheep, with his thumb stick in one hand and sheepdog Ben by his side.

Writing about the past reaches deep into my inner self, bringing to the surface some really strong emotional feelings, sometimes these are painful and I didn't realise they would affect me quite so much. I've been asking myself the question: why did I decide to write my memories down, with some associated stories of two careers? There will be some local interest perhaps, but this is a narrative of my life with my own personal memories, interesting or otherwise. I've been thinking about my family ancestors too. How did they cope with all the changes they experienced in their lives and the heartache of living relatively recently through two World Wars? So, this is my life's story, written for posterity, and gifted to the treasured memories I have of my very dearest and most loved daughter Lucy, my son Julian, his wife Amanda and to my four very extra-special grandchildren, Josh, Poppy, Chloe and Adam. Bless you all!

Now came another difficult time in our lives. Our dear mum was diagnosed with a secondary tumour and was operated on at the John Radcliffe Hospital at Oxford. Her local GP – the late Doctor Sue Heath – was so caring and committed to her job. Like so many others, I am certain that mum was regarded as a special person in Sue's life too. Mum had a wonderful friend,

Heather, who was a local healer living with her husband and family in Sibford. Heather visited mum at the cottage to give her spiritual strength and healing, which helped her to relax. Eventually the cancer spread. Mum never wanted to leave this life anywhere other than from her home at Anne's Cot. I took a week off work to stay with her shortly before she died, giving my help and to be close to her. A few things stuck in my mind as we talked. I remember making a cup of tea in a proper cup and saucer for her. Mum took a sip and said, 'You always make tea, just as I like it!' I remember too her sitting on the edge of her bed where she looked down at her now-frail legs and said, 'You'll never believe it, but I had the most fabulous legs as a young tennis player!' and I gave her a gentle kiss in the middle of her forehead. My week's leave ended and I went back to work the same day. At about ten o'clock that evening the phone rang at Kington Police Station and I answered it. It was my sister Jane who said, 'You'd better return tonight. Mum isn't expected to last long now.' I was given additional time off work and drove back to Anne's Cot the same night. I knew that Dad, my brother John, my two sisters Ann and Jane and Heather were all with mum at the cottage. I remember driving back feeling so cross and agitated because I didn't want mum to die without me being with her, and I drove as fast but as safely as I could to get there quickly. When I arrived at the cottage, the door opened and I was greeted by dear Heather. I don't know how it happened but Heather knew exactly what I was thinking on my way there and without me saying a word, she calmly said, 'Don't worry Bill, Mum's been waiting for you'. Shortly after, mum passed away very peacefully as we were all sitting around her bedside and it was such a wonderful privilege to be there when it happened. I wanted to relieve my family of any further emotional stress so I organised calling the undertaker Mr Humphreys, and helped him do what was needed. It wasn't until he left that I broke down in floods of tears in front of my dear brother John who comforted me. Mum died on 8 December 1991 aged 77 years. My dad continued to live into old age. By chance, the cottage next door to Anne's Cot came up for sale, which he bought and moved into. Brian retired from teaching at Sibford School, then he and Jane moved into Anne's Cot, with Dad living next door. As a family, we were all so grateful to Jane and Brian for the endless time and commitment they unselfishly gave to mum and dad. Dad became progressively less independent and physically less mobile. Eventually he moved into a local care home, where he died on 25 May 1999, aged 88 years, after a well-lived life of farming.

RURAL POLICING — THINGS THAT HAPPENED

I WAS churchwarden for the first time at St Mary Magdalene Church in Eardisley. Stuart Braine was headmaster at Eardisley Primary School, which my two children Julian and Lucy attended. The Reverend David Lowe succeeded the dear Reverend Frank Wilford (who retired, then went to live in a flat with his wife May, which was owned by Sir John and Lady Cotterell at the Garnons Estate at Byford), then the Reverend Ken Newbon succeeded David Lowe. In 1979 the children's TV programme, Blue Peter, launched their nationwide appeal to raise money for starving children and families in war torn Cambodia. It was called the 'Cambodian Blue Peter Appeal' and I thought of an idea to raise publicity and extra funds.

My idea was for a few of us to do a sponsored fast, drinking only water and sleeping in the church bell tower from Friday until Sunday night. The idea seemed to capture the imagination of local people and the media so Stuart Braine, Steve Hatcher, the late Doctor Brian Beach and I took up the challenge. The *Hereford Times*, local press and television reported the event and followed our progress.

Our fundraising fast, pictured on the roof of Eardisley Church. Clockwise from top: me in my sheepskin coat (with hair!), the late Doctor Brian Beach, Steve Hatcher, Stuart Brain

Our fundraising event was a resounding success. It caught people's imagination and drew local people closer together. We raised somewhere in the region of £1,290 which, at that time, was a lot of money and a tremendously good result (equivalent to about £8,500 now). This included the proceeds of a bring-and-buy stall, which the school children, parents and grandparents set up in the church lychgate. The physical effects of fasting were interesting too: our hearing and our sight became more acute. We were all extremely hungry by 6 o'clock on Sunday evening, when a cold buffet was arranged at the Police House. My first flavoursome mouthful of food was intensely mouth-watering. We repeated the event all over again just two years later when, on that occasion, Reverend Ken Newbon replaced Doctor Brian Beach.

Brian and his wife, Doctor Helen Beach, were held in such high regard. As well as a caring husband and wife team, they were senior partners at the Weobley and Staunton Surgeries. Brian was my GP and in those days I smoked cigarettes and an occasional cigar. One winter I developed flu symptoms and a rasping cough. After visiting the bathroom, I was alarmed to see that I'd coughed up blood, so made an appointment see Brian, who booked me in for a chest X-ray. He didn't mince his words: 'You've either ruptured a tiny blood vessel in your lung from your constant cough as a cigarette smoker or you have lung cancer. I should give them up if I were you, Bill'. I did, and didn't need to be told a second time.

One afternoon Brian phoned me from his surgery at Staunton-on-Wye to report that he had prescribed some strong medication to a patient, handing him the full bottle of tablets. 'One to be taken twice every day' were the instructions on the label. 'He's swallowed the lot, Bill, and washed them down with a few gulps of whisky from a bottle he'd hidden in his jacket pocket. He's left the surgery now and has started walking towards his home at Bredwardine. Just thought I should let you know, Bill!' Thanks Brian! I carried out a check on Brian's patient to find out that he was previously known by the police and nicknamed 'Big Jim'. He was a tall, muscular well-built chap, who had a propensity towards violence when drinking! Police records showed that the last time he was arrested, it took six bobbies to detain him. He'd robbed the fruit machine in the bar at the Swan Inn at Letton, which he didn't let go of during the arrest. After knowing this, I decided on a plan of action which was essentially to do nothing. I stayed by the police station telephone knowing that it would start to ring at some point and I called the duty inspector at Hereford police station to place them on standby. I received about half a dozen calls or so from the general public who reported seeing a large man twirling and hopping around on one leg in circles like a circus acrobat, then skipping along the grass verge at the side of the main road at Staunton. Without moving away from the phone, I continued monitoring his movements from the calls I was receiving, plotting his progress and the route he had chosen to get home. The last call I received was just before midnight: 'There's a man acting peculiarly on Bredwardine bridge. He's thrown an empty whisky bottle over into the river and he isn't wearing any trousers or pants!' Why wasn't I surprised? A bottle of Brian's pills washed down with a bottle of whisky! I rang for reinforcements and called in on my neighbour Peter Preece to ask if he would come with me and watch my back. Peter and I arrived at the house where the man had been staying and saw that the front door had been ripped off its hinges. Then a violent free-for-all took place when he was arrested with the help of colleagues and taken to Hereford. I never did find out what medication Brian gave him, and Brian didn't say. You were a brilliant doctor and friend, Brian, and admired and looked up to by so many who knew you. May God give you his eternal love and peace.

The relationship between the police and the public was generally speaking a very good one, and I wanted to play my part in maintaining the status quo. I decided which offences to book people for, and which less serious offences they could be cautioned for. Soon after the car badge incident, it became force policy for all first-time young offenders to be cautioned by a senior officer for a crime. This meant that I no longer had the discretion to caution them myself. Formal cautions, given by senior officers, were officially documented so they could be referred to (like previous convictions) in magistrates courts. Any juvenile who received a police caution, but subsequently re-offended, would be charged to appear at court. At about this time, the late Inspector George Bastable was a senior officer at Leominster. George transferred to Leominster subdivision after spending a large part of his police service as a detective with the Midland serious crime squad, where he was working at the sharp end of policing. He was vastly experienced in dealing with and investigating very serious violent crimes and armed robberies etc., during which he learnt some rather well-rehearsed interview techniques. At the end of his attachment with the serious crime squad, George transferred to Leominster as a uniformed police inspector, which was no doubt much less demanding and stressful for him. He moved to live in Leominster with his wife and family until his retirement. George administered verbal cautions to many juvenile offenders. When it was a juvenile I'd dealt with, he used to drive from Leominster to Eardisley police station in his own car, sometimes accompanied by his wife for company. I always tried to arrange juvenile cautions to take place on a Sunday when it was normally quieter. George and I always wore our best police uniforms to give a good impression. Before George began, the parent(s) were asked to sign a document giving their consent for their son or daughter to receive an official police caution from George. If they failed to turn up on time or refused to sign (which no one ever did!), then the offender would be summoned to appear before a juvenile court and lost any right to be cautioned. I would describe George's style of cautioning as unique, effective and skilful. On every occasion, I knew his patter and what he would say to them. The parents were allowed to sit, but their young son or daughter was told to stand. George started off by saying, 'If it hadn't been for PC Rowlatt here then this matter would have far more serious consequences for you and your family, so you have a lot to thank him for!' This immediately showed me in a good light, particularly if I needed to deal with the same family again at a later date. Then George would focus and move closer to the young offender saying things like how corrupt and dishonest they were to even think of committing the crime in the first place. 'What on earth came over you?' he would ask them, then 'Why did you do it?' or 'What on earth were you thinking of?' Then came his cringeworthy crunch line! 'The fact is that you're nothing but a liar and a common little thief!' These final, deeply-offensive and demoralising words were always the straw which nearly broke the camel's back! It even made me want to cower! Parents who had been sitting patiently expecting George to give words of advice were now listening to their son or daughter receiving a full character assassination! The parent(s) could hardly contain themselves. It rattled them and I could see them thinking to themselves, 'You can't say that!' 'How dare you?' or 'Who the bloody hell does he think he is?' George always took them to the very edge, nearly tipping them over the top, which stretched and tested their patience with him. Then, just at the point when they were about to explode and retaliate, he added another question, 'Now, would you really like to know what's even worse and so much more serious than anything you've done already?' After saying this, there were puzzled expressions on their faces! Pausing and with split-second timing, George said, 'Well ... I'll tell you! What's far worse than anything you've done already is that you've let your parents down really badly!' The parent(s), who had got themselves all worked up and were so cross with George, immediately changed their allegiance and in that moment had altered their opinion of him! You could see them thinking how right George was and it was definitely their young son or daughter's fault that they were there, placing them in this embarrassing position. It showed everything in a completely different light. Parent(s) left my office thanking George and wanting to shake hands with him! Just before his retirement George told me how much he enjoyed coming to administer cautions at my police station, and he once said, 'Afterwards Bill, you made my wife and I feel so welcome because you always invited us in for some of your elderflower wine and homemade Welsh cakes!' May you rest in peace George. You were a good senior officer who I and many others had the good fortune of working with. We respected you. It was such a privilege to have known you and may you rest in God's eternal love and light. Thanks, George, for being you.

HRH Princess Margaret's visit took place in May 1980 when she visited the Grange in Leominster to unveil a plaque. She was flown in by the Queen's Wessex helicopter which landed on the grassed area outside the Grange and adjacent to the Priory Church. Just before it landed there were the usual stringent security checks. This is difficult to believe, but a senior officer in charge spotted two people on the roof of the Priory Church near to the bell tower. He radioed in to the police control room to enquire who they were? Back came the reply, which we all heard, 'They're campanologists, Sir!' He sent a message straight back to control, 'Well get them down, they've got no right to be camping up there!' One evening a buffet was arranged at the police station in Ryelands Road when George was introducing a senior officer to the town's dignitaries. As each of them lined up to shake hands, George introduced them to him individually. 'Sir,' he said, 'This is the mayor and his wife'. The officer shook hands with them then said, 'Good evening, Mr Mayor and Mrs Mayor, very pleased to meet you both!' George's face was a picture!

I had two specific roles for the day: to assist the Queen's flight pilot to guard Princess Margaret's helicopter; then, in the afternoon, to take up a traffic point at the T-junction outside the Monument Inn at Kingsland, where Princess Margaret's cavalcade would travel through to get to another commitment. The Wessex helicopter stayed in the grounds at the Grange for the duration of Princess Margaret's visit, in case of any threats or security breaches so she could be quickly flown out again. I was enjoying sitting in her helicopter's plush red seats talking to the pilot, who offered me one of her boiled sweets from a tin. I asked him how Princess Margaret usually reacted when she got back to the helicopter. He said she always sat down, relaxed, kicked off her shoes and unwrapped a sweet from the tin. Later on, I was driven by Inspector W to my point at the T-junction, right outside the Monument Inn pub opposite the rugby club. For reasons known only to himself, this particular uniformed inspector never referred to any of us by our names, referring to us only as 'officer'. I got out of the police car, as he said, 'Now wait here, officer, until you receive a radio message from me telling you to stop all the traffic to wave the royal party through!' I knew that I had well over an hour to wait before Princess Margaret was due to arrive when I heard a noise, 'Psst', then another 'Psst, Psst', and I looked around. It was the landlady of the Monument Inn pub who was standing by her kitchen door, trying to attract my attention. She asked if I was there to stop the traffic for Princess Margaret, and I said that I was but that she wasn't due for another hour. Then she asked if I would like a coffee, so I said 'thank you' and walked through a side gate and into the kitchen. After ten minutes or so, I'd just finished a mug of coffee when I was surprised to see Inspector W was back again in the police car, looking for me. 'Shit!' He was checking where I was. I ran as fast as I could from the kitchen and leapt over a metal fence back onto the road on the other side. What I didn't see when I jumped over the railings was that the posts had razor-sharp spiky tops! One of them completely ripped and tore down the middle of my uniform trouser leg from top to bottom, from the crotch down!! Thankfully, Inspector W hadn't noticed because he was so cross with me and demanded to know where I had disappeared to. I said that the landlady had kindly invited me inside for a coffee. He was furious with me! 'I dropped you off at your point here. Now stay there, officer!' he ordered. He revved up the engine and drove off again, as the land-lady went back inside, locking her kitchen door. I was in a dilemma and in desperate need of a needle and thread, but I was riveted to the spot in case the inspector came back again to look for me. I practised standing to attention and folding the two frayed edges of my right uniform trouser leg together but I couldn't completely hide the gap, which showed some bare leg and thigh in between. I was dreading the arrival of Princess Margaret's cavalcade, which eventually arrived and drove slowly past me. I could only hope that none of my bare bits were seen as I stood awkwardly to attention at an uneven keel and saluted her! What was it with me and royal visits?

One afternoon I was off duty at home, when a knock came at the police house door. I answered it wearing casual clothing. After checking that I was the local bobby, a man introduced himself to me as Captain Barnsley. 'I'm a helicopter pilot and I'm here to report a very serious incident,' he told me, so I pointed to my office door then walked back inside to unlock the door and let him in. He was carrying an Ordinance Survey map, which he unfolded on the police counter, and explained that he had been spraying potato crops from a helicopter on land belonging to Bulmer's at a place called Quebb. Quebb was about three miles from the police station in a location I was familiar with. Pointing to the map, he marked the exact spot and house, circling it in pencil. Captain Barnsley said, 'Each time I turn the aircraft around to fly over the top, a man comes out of the house armed with a rifle which he aims and fires at me. It's happened a couple of times and it looks like he's trying to shoot the aircraft down.' I asked if he had heard shots or the sound of a gun being fired but he said he couldn't hear because of the excessive noise from inside the cockpit. I knew the house was lived in by Arthur Gibson, although someone else could have been culpable so I formulated a plan of action with the captain, which gave me time to change into uniform and rendezvous at the location at a precise time. 'I'll get as close as I can to the back door of the house', I told him, 'Then I'd like you to take the same flight path over the top of the house as you've done previously. If it happens again, I'll apprehend the person firing at you'. I drove up to Quebb, parking the police van on the grass verge a suitable distance away. After walking down the lane, I hid near the back door of the house by the garden vegetable patch. At the precise time agreed, I heard the sound of the helicopter approaching and was surprised at what happened next. Not only did Captain Barnsley fly over the top of the house, but he momentarily hovered over the middle of the roof, then skilfully lowered the height of the aircraft so the skids were just touching the ridge tiles! An angry middle-aged man ran out through the door, looking skyward, swearing and shouting at it and taking aim with the rifle, so running forwards I rugby tackled him to the ground. Thankfully, he lost grip of the weapon so it was lying on the ground a reasonably safe distance away. It was Arthur. The weapon, which for all intents and purposes looked like a real rifle, had a stock, action, trigger and barrel made from a piece of water pipe. Dusting ourselves off, I asked Arthur if we could go inside and talk about what had happened over a cup of tea. Arthur complained about the noise and disturbance he'd suffered from the helicopter flying over his house, and he'd seen some overspray coming from the spray booms drifting across onto his organic vegetable patch. He had a point. I submitted my report, which was returned NFA (No Further Action) necessary. After the incident, I used to call by and see Arthur and his wife Olivia and we became friends. Shortly after writing this story, I rang Arthur to ask him if he minded me writing about the incident in my book and he was delighted that I had. Two weeks or so later, Arthur sadly passed away and I feel privileged to mention him here. Arthur, you were an engineer; eccentric, clever and intelligent. Not only did you make the rifle look so real but you designed and manufactured Quebb woodburning stoves, which were far ahead of their time, and also built your own full-sized working windmill at Leinthall Starkes without planning permission! May you rest in peace Arthur.

I knew so little about the Latvian community who lived on my patch at a large house known as Nieuport House at Almeley, which was owned by Herefordshire Council. Before the Latvian community moved there to live, it was previously used as a TB sanatorium. Nieuport House was the Latvian spelling, but it reverted to Newport House after it was closed and sold off by the council in the late 1990s, becoming privately owned. During the time the Latvian community lived there, Latvian-born Mrs Veperis was their house manager. She lived with her Latvian husband in what was called the Doctors House, which was in the large grounds near the main house. From 1939 Latvia was occupied by the Soviet Union, followed by Nazi Germany 1941–44, then the Soviet Union from 1944 until their independence was won in 1991. So much sadness and oppression permeated Latvia during the Second World War. Thousands were killed and young men were being sent to Germany to be illegally conscripted into the German army. Fleeing as refugees, many Latvians left behind their families, their jobs and their businesses to live in our country, as well as other countries around the world, including America. I visited Nieuport House for a variety of official reasons, and the residents were quiet, shy and reserved people. The first time I visited I was in uniform, driving up their drive in a police vehicle to reach the main house. This was when I saw the first signs of fear. A small group was outside taking a recreational stroll when I noticed that I was being watched intently, but at the last moment and to avoid eye contact, the group turned their heads away and looked down, directly at the ground, and I later found out why. My uniform reminded them of the horrific acts of persecution and aggression, which they and their families suffered in Latvia. I remember how really sad and eerie this felt, similar in a way to the images we have all seen in films or on television of the Second World War German concentration camps, where the Jews were persecuted and murdered. After seeing their reaction, I wanted to reach out to them and be trusted, rather than mistrusted, which, if this could be achieved, would take time and patience. From that day forwards I made an effort to visit Nieuport House as often as I could, trying to allay some of their indoctrinated fear. Mrs Veperis spoke reasonably good English. To reach her office on the ground floor in the main house, I had to walk across the hallway, passing residents who I knew were fearful and didn't speak any English. I always acknowledged them when I passed with a simple but friendly 'hello' and a smile. It was slow progress but, in time, they were becoming a little less wary of my presence. I can't explain why, but it was really important to me that they felt liberated and protected and not feel threatened by me or my uniform.

Their community was almost entirely self-sufficient. They grew large quantities of vegetables in their kitchen gardens, which they ate, pickled and preserved along with fruit from the orchards. Two Latvian cooks catered for everyone. One of them, who I knew only as Pete, was a former captain in the Latvian army and spoke broken English. I spent many happy and entertaining hours sitting and talking with him in the large kitchen, listening to his stories about how life was in Latvia and his service in the Latvian army. His favourite tipple was a Polish spirit, which he always insisted I shared with him, but only a few nips! I was on duty! Many of them suffered from mental health problems and depression caused by the trauma of fleeing from Latvia and leaving their families behind. There were elderly single men, single women and married couples who were grandparents and great-grandparents who had families they would never see again. The men slept in single beds in their single rooms in the old stable block in the yard, while others occupied the larger main bedrooms in the house. All of them left Latvia very suddenly amid so much fear and bringing with them very few of their personal possessions.

Tragically, some took their own lives by overdosing with their prescribed medication, by hanging or by drowning themselves in nearby Upcott pool. It was part of my job to deal with their bodies with the local undertaker, and to attend the inquests at Hereford. Generally, the Latvians preferred burial to cremation, and many are buried in the lower right-hand section of Almeley's churchyard where headstones mark the graves with Latvian names and inscriptions. If you visit, then please take a moment to say a prayer for them or just take a moment for reflection and thought.

In time, their trust in me slowly improved although, as you would expect, some remained dreadfully suspicious of any authority and uniforms. Their annual celebrations took place around my birthday during the summer solstice between the 21 and 23 June. Latvian families from other communities around the UK travelled to Nieuport House. They camped out, lit fires, cooked food, sang traditional Latvian songs, danced, drank and generally celebrated. Being such a thoughtful and generous people, they always invited everyone living in Almeley to share and join in with their celebrations.

Late one afternoon Mrs Veperis telephoned me at the police station to ask if I would call and see her at seven o'clock that evening. I hadn't asked her why. I was on duty and arrived in uniform a tad late, at a quarter past seven. Mrs Veperis, rather hurriedly I thought, beckoned me to follow her into the main banqueting hall. As we entered the large room, I saw that it had been decorated with balloons and brightly coloured flags and bunting. Long trestle tables were placed end-to-end, covered by table cloths and laden with masses of Latvian food and drink. Dozens of Latvian hosts, some who I recognised, had been patiently sitting and waiting for me to arrive. Mrs Veperis led me to a chair which was at the head of the table. Everyone stood up, which completely took me by surprise as she announced that I was their guest of honour. This was a kind gesture and completely unexpected. I found out later that it is Latvian tradition to offer food and friendship as a thank you for someone. In this case, me, for just doing my job, which I always tried to do in a non-authoritative way for fear of upsetting or reminding them of their tortured history. It was a special evening amongst warm and friendly people who were just beginning to melt away from their initial fear of 'the man in a uniform'! This honestly meant such a lot to me.

Another memorable incident occurred after I was told to attend Leominster police station by the chief inspector, who instructed me to work there for the remainder of my shift. There was a very serious ongoing incident which began in the Ross area. A vicar had been abducted by a man who had taken him hostage and had stolen his car. The car was later seen and stopped by PC Derek Morris, stationed at Presteigne, after he'd seen it being driven through his area. The suspect evaded arrest but, with bravery and determination, Derek tackled him. The man armed himself with a fencing post then turned on Derek, leaving him seriously injured, including a broken leg. After getting back into the stolen car with his hostage, the suspect drove off again towards Knighton. I was in the communications room when I overheard a conversation between the chief inspector and force headquarters, who were discussing details of the pursuit. The pursuit had crossed over our force borders into Wales so the decision was made to call in our police helicopter to assist Dyfed Powys Police with an aerial search. Interrupting his call, the chief inspector held the telephone to one side. Turning to me he asked, 'How well do you know the Knighton area?' In a split second my response was, 'Like the back of my hand, Sir!' which I have to admit was a bit more than a slight exaggeration. I was not only keen to be involved in the ongoing search and capture, but there was the added attraction of a ride in the police helicopter! I hot-footed it to Shobdon airfield where I met the helicopter pilot, who had already landed and refuelled. What I didn't know was that it was a two-seater aircraft in police livery with a civilian pilot. The pilot handed me a pile of Ordinance Survey maps before we climbed into the aircraft, clipped on our safety harnesses and adjusted our headset volumes so we had clear communication with each other. Then, before I knew it, we were airborne! Quite quickly after taking off, the helicopter hovered in the sky like a bird of prey before the pilot announced, 'OK Bill. You're in charge, now where do you want me to fly and what do you want me to do next?' I hadn't anticipated the question, which flummoxed me, and I refrained from saying, 'Just do what you normally do!' I knew that the pursuit had shifted further north towards the Knighton area, which was where we were now heading. En route, I made several attempts to contact police headquarters via the force radio to receive current updates, but for some reason the higher our altitude, the less clear the radio's reception was. Every few miles I asked the pilot to drop down to 'hedge hop' as I tried to communicate, but without success. In what seemed like no time at all and without any clear audible radio contact or instructions we hovered slowly over a place where we saw houses below. It dawned on me that we were flying above Llandrindod Wells now, searching for a suitable, safe landing site to make radio contact from the ground. Below us, I saw a couple of police dogs with their handlers and some police vehicles driving around, but I didn't know the reason why they were there. Then a large open area of school playing fields came into view where I asked the pilot to land. After landing, I saw PC Micky Doolan driving towards me in a fast response vehicle. He wound his window down and said, 'Bill, that was fantastic! Just like a proper film set!' I hadn't a clue what he was talking about, then he continued, 'After we stopped the car and chased the suspect, he ran and broke into someone's house over there. We all dived in to arrest him when you were hovering directly over the top of the house! Well done!' Needless to say, I was not only lost, but lost for words too!

I knew many, if not nearly all, inhabitants in Eardisley, and made it my business to introduce myself to anyone who moved in to live on my patch. I would, if I could, knock at their door to introduce myself. Responses were understandably varied. Most were supportive, but a minority wanted to know why I had called, and were defensive. For those who weren't so welcoming, I explained that I lived in the village and if for example they needed an electrician or a plumber in an emergency, then I was probably their quickest and most useful contact, adding that they could ring me at the police station at any time for advice. This was usually sufficient to satisfy their curiosity, and mine.

The village had a slaughter house, which was accessed from the Almeley Road, where the Eastfields estate was built after the abattoir's closure. When the abattoir was still in business, I was amused that the lady who lived in a bungalow opposite renamed it 'Lambkins' in protest!

TAKING A POT SHOT –
GIVING EVIDENCE AT COURT

O NE Sunday morning at about 11 o'clock, I called in at Leominster police station to deliver the despatches from Kington. I was in the communications room when a '999' call was received and answered by Shelagh, one of the communications room staff. Also in the communications room was the duty inspector, Inspector Ron Davies. The call came in from a lorry tanker driver who was pumping out animal waste fluids from the underground storage tanks near the abattoir's entrance. The driver reported that a man had approached him carrying a loaded revolver, telling him that the noise from the tanker was disturbing his sleep and to immediately stop what he was doing or he would shoot him! In order to convince the driver that he was being completely serious, the man pointed the gun and, taking careful aim, shot at him! The bullet went straight between his legs, narrowly missing him, and ricocheted off the drive. With total shock and disbelief, the driver looked down between his legs and saw that the bullet had taken a chunk of concrete out of the drive. The inspector instructed me to call out our police tactical firearms unit until I explained that I thought I might know who was responsible and that if he and I went over to Eardisley together, then there would be no need for any further police reinforcements or an armed response team. Ron took me at my word, reluctantly agreeing. I've not forgotten his words, which were repeated to me quite a few times as we hurriedly made our way over to Eardisley, 'Bill, are you sure you know what you're doing!?'

I drove, as we both blue-lighted it over to Eardisley. By the time we arrived, the public bar at the New Inn was packed

128

'Sir, meet the Major. A pillar of society'

with local Sunday lunchtime drinkers as I drew up and parked outside. Ron said, 'This is a pub, Bill. Why have we stopped here?' The answer I gave was intended to reassure him, but I think it had the opposite effect. 'Well Sir, I think the chap with the revolver will be in the bar having a few whiskies.' Then came the all-too-familiar question, 'Bill, are you sure you know what you're doing!?' We walked into the crowded bar with the inspector following me. Customers turned and looked at us, trying to figure out why I was with a police inspector, guessing that something potentially serious must be happening. A dapper elderly gentleman, dressed in a tweed suit and wearing a shirt and tie, spotted me from the bar and walked over to us. He reached out his hand for me to shake and said, 'Bill. How are you? Good to see you again. God bless you!' It was exactly who I was expecting to see in the bar, retired army Major Rees Jones, who lived in a rented room at the pub. 'Major, could we have a quiet word with you please?' I said. 'Yes of course dear boy, God bless you!' I suggested that we go through to a room at the back, where we wouldn't be disturbed and our conversation would be private. As we walked past the bar, the Major took a gulp of whisky from a cut glass tumbler, emptying it, and stubbed out a half-smoked Capstan full-strength cigarette into the ashtray. I ushered him towards the door and the three of us entered the room to sit down together.

All this time the inspector said nothing, but I could see that he was apprehensive, keeping a close eye on me but an even closer eye on the Major! I opened up our conversation to talk about the rather delicate, but extremely serious, incident of the lorry driver being shot at. When I was talking to him, the Major slowly reached towards the side pocket of his tweed jacket with the open palm of his right hand, a bit like a cowboy gunslinger would do! Thinking that the gun was in the pocket, Inspector Ron caught my eye and nervously muttered, 'Bill, Bill!' to get my attention. The Major heard him too. After sliding his hand deeper into the side pocket, he reached in, slowly pulling out a packet of cigarettes. With a grin on his face, the Major said, 'Just my cigarettes, Inspector!' as Ron breathed a deep sigh of relief. I already knew the Major well enough to know that he was never a threat to us, and mercifully my hunch that it was him was correct. We discussed everything in detail after he admitted that he'd got a bit annoyed with the tanker driver for waking him up, and had shot at him with his Second World War army revolver, adding, 'But only as a warning, Bill,' in an effort to reason with me and to lessen the consequences of his actions. We followed the Major upstairs to his rented room, where I slid my hand under the single bed, feeling for and pulling out a rather rusty Second World War army strong box, which contained several rounds of live ammunition, gun cleaning equipment and the Major's Webley

'Oh no, Bill dear boy, bless you! I don't actually shoot them'

army issue service revolver which was still loaded. After taking possession of everything, we amicably shook hands and left the Major in the bar to enjoy the rest of his day with friends, drinking his whisky and smoking his Capstan full-strength cigarettes. Major Rees Jones was a highly-decorated officer who had a distinguished army war service record. He received numerous awards for his leadership and bravery in action. He was an extremely kind, intelligent and well-educated gentle-man whose judgement, shall we say, went a little awry! I had respect for him and submitted my report about the incident, which was returned NFA (No Further Action necessary). God bless you too, Major!

At around this time, I became interested in gathering information about the misuse of illegal drugs, and the identities of those who were supplying and using them. With the flower-power of the 1960s, illegal drugs were becoming more commonplace, but nothing in comparison to the gargantuan amounts circulating in society these days. The interaction I had with people living on my patch as their local bobby was important. In addition to investigating and making arrests for crime, I was beginning to identify previously-unknown individuals who were drug dealing, as well as users across Herefordshire and over the border into Wales. This became more relevant later on in my career.

All local cases went before the magistrates sitting at Kington magistrates court in Market Hall Street, next to the police station. During the 1970s, the local chairman of the magistrates was Doctor Logan Jack who was a local GP at Kington Surgery and resided at Huntington Court. Other magistrates were: Mrs Julia Green from The Whittern at Lyonshall; Mr Frank Smith of The Leen Farm, Pembridge; Mr David Hill, who was bank manager at the HSBC bank in Kington; Mr Harold Davies, a farmer at Castle Farm, Eardisley; Mrs Joyce Banbury of Field Cottage, Lower Welson, Eardisley; May Willford, wife of Reverend Frank Willford from Eardisley rectory; Mrs Pat Parker of Weston, Pembridge; and Mr Peter Johnson of Kington. Pat Sloane was the magistrate's clerk and a solicitor with Vaughan and Davies solicitors in Duke Street. Mrs Ethel Grigg from Cannonford Avenue, Eardisley, was the magistrate's clerk's clerk. Mr Bob Jenkins, who lived and ran a bookshop in Duke Street, was court reporter for the *Hereford Times* and the *Mid Wales*

Journal newspapers. My boss, Sergeant Ken Campbell, presented cases at the magistrates' court, together with the local licensing extensions and applications for licensed bars at local functions. When a 'not guilty' plea was entered, a solicitor for the defence was appointed with a prosecution solicitor to argue their case. If local magistrates considered a case was too serious for them to determine, or a longer prison sentence needed to be imposed (more than six months), then they would 'commit' the case to the Crown Court, which was held at the Shirehall at Hereford. Kington magistrates court was finally closed in January 1989, and all cases were transferred to Leominster and Hereford. Leominster magistrates court was then also closed soon after.

I went to interview one of the magistrates I've named as he was involved in a traffic accident, which was clearly his fault. While driving, he pulled out of a road junction into the path of another vehicle. After interviewing him, I reported him for the offence of 'driving without due care and attention', under Section 3 of the Road Traffic Act. The day his case came up at Kington magistrates court, he was sitting on the bench hearing and determining other cases. I was there because I wasn't sure if he would enter a guilty or not guilty plea. A not guilty plea would require me to give evidence. When the case came up, the three magistrates shuffled around to change places. The magistrate in question became the defendant and walked across to sit in the dock. From there, he stood up as Pat Sloane read out the charge, to which he pleaded guilty. He received a fine and an endorsement (now points) on his driving licence from his other two magistrate colleagues, no doubt feeling a little awkward and embarrassed!

I always felt a bit of nervous apprehension when I was required to attend court after a defendant pleaded not guilty to a charge, but at the same time I enjoyed the mind games and challenges of facing a defence barrister or solicitor under cross-examination. Most cases at the magistrates' court were defended by a solicitor, and by a barrister at Crown Court. My fear was being asked a question I couldn't answer or the introduction of some new evidence, of which I had no previous knowledge, but that never happened. I could usually guess whether a defendant I'd dealt with would be pleading guilty or not guilty. There were never any of my cases where I thought that the defendant was innocent, even though the outcome sometimes ended in a not guilty verdict. Not guilty verdicts were usually returned after some clever barrister or solicitor had argued their case on a point of law, or when the confidence of some well-meaning prosecution witness had been shaken by some clever cross-examining questions.

I remember two defended cases I gave evidence at; one was at Kington magistrates court and the other at Hereford Crown Court. The defendant at Kington magistrates court was a young woman driver, who was summoned to appear after she was involved in a very straightforward case of driving her car without due care and attention. For reasons of speed or lack of concentration, she'd driven her car round a sharp left-hand bend at Lyonshall then drifted across the centre white line onto the wrong side of the road, colliding with a box-sided lorry travelling in the opposite direction. When I arrived, I saw that a narrow horizontal aluminium strip attached to the side of the lorry had pierced her windscreen, going straight through to the back of her driver's seat, embedding itself underneath her left armpit, trapping her and narrowly missing her heart. The fire brigade freed her. Thankfully she was uninjured and extremely lucky to be alive. As she was a clergyman's daughter, I wondered if there had been some divine intervention going on. I sent the only deflated tyre on her car for forensic examination. This would determine if the tyre deflation was a contributory cause or not. The report came back stating that it was not the cause of the accident and was post-collision deflation. Before the case started, I was told that the driver and her family had engaged the services of an extremely expensive top London barrister, who had travelled all the way from London to Kington to defend her case. I stepped into the witness box to give my evidence and to be cross-examined by him. The barrister went to great lengths to convince the magistrates that I had not completed my accident investigations thoroughly. Firstly, he inferred that his client's tyre, which was deflated at the scene, was the cause of the accident, but I could refute this as I'd sent it away to be forensically examined and could prove otherwise. He repeatedly told the magistrates that his client was most certainly 'not guilty' of the careless driving charge. When cross-examining me, he repeatedly implied that she was not guilty and was totally innocent of the charge. 'Did she protest her innocence at all times when you interviewed her, officer?' I had to agree. I was already thinking ahead, trying to work out his defence strategy until eventually, after repeating again that his client was 'not guilty' and 'innocent' of the offence he asked, 'Is she, officer?' I agreed. 'So, you agree do you, that my client is innocent?' 'Yes Sir', I replied. 'So, will you explain to this court why she is here today?' 'Well Sir', I paused before replying, 'Because, in law, everyone is innocent until proven guilty.' The magistrates looked across at each other and were slightly amused, before retiring and returning within minutes to announce a guilty verdict!

Another defended Crown Court case I dealt with was at Hereford. The case involved a very serious assault, after two men had been drinking miles away from their home town of Kington. After ordering a taxi to take them home, they promised to pay their fare when they arrived at Kington. The taxi driver was unaware that they had hidden a baseball bat under a coat on the back seat of his taxi. When they were nearly home, the taxi driver was forced to stop. One of the passengers viciously assaulted the driver with the baseball bat, causing him serious head injuries and the men ran off. I was called to the scene to make enquiries, and seized the baseball bat which was left behind. The driver was rushed to hospital. After establishing who the suspect was, I traced and arrested him for GBH (grievous bodily harm). We always carried a pocket book with us to record conversations with suspects, known as contemporaneous notes. When giving evidence at court we were allowed to produce our pocket books with the barrister's permission so we could read from our notes to refresh our memories. After the suspect's arrest, I'd written down the details, including his name, address, time and his reply after caution. Then I asked him for his signature in my pocket book which he scribbled down. After his detention was authorised by the custody sergeant at Hereford, the prisoner was too drunk to be interviewed until he had sobered up the following day so PC Bob Hughes and I made our way back to Kington. Before going off duty, I checked the contemporaneous notes which I'd written down in my pocket book and noticed that the prisoner's real name didn't match his signature. Unable to decipher the signature, I asked Bob for his opinion. 'He's signed himself as Willie Mays,' Bob said. 'Who the heck is Willie Mays?' I asked. 'The famous American baseball player!' Bob explained.

Weeks later, the defendant pleaded not guilty and I was summoned to attend Hereford Crown Court to give evidence in the case. In court, led by the judge, barristers for the prosecution and defence, the jury and witnesses were all present, with the exception of the taxi driver who was too ill to attend court. I stepped into the witness box, took the oath and was led through my evidence, initially by the prosecution barrister. Then it was the turn of the defence barrister to cross-examine me. The barrister questioned me about my handwritten contemporaneous notes made on the night of his client's arrest. 'And this is a true record of the conversation you had with my client on the night you arrested him?' he asked. 'Yes Sir.' 'And did he sign your pocket book, officer, after you had completed your notes?' 'Well, Sir, not exactly', I responded. After pondering over my reply, he asked with a degree of sarcasm, 'What do you mean officer, not exactly?' 'Well, Sir, he signed his name ...' then it was my turn to pause, flicking through the pages in my pocket book to find the signature on the correct page, I replied decisively, ... 'He signed himself Willie Mays, the famous American baseball player!' At that point the judge intervened. Lowering his glasses, looking down and across at me in the witness box he said, 'Officer, you really shouldn't have said what you have just said, but you've said it now and I must address the members of the Jury accordingly. "Members of the Jury"', he began, and continued by asking them to completely ignore what I had just said, but how could they? I'd already said it, and it was true. In a manner of speaking, the defendant had sealed his own fate. The outcome was that the jury found the defendant guilty and he received a prison sentence.

BRICK THROUGH THE WINDOW –
KEEPING ONE JUMP AHEAD

ONE Sunday morning just before Christmas my phone rang. It was Mrs Barrett who lived at Great Oak Cottage, along the Woodseaves Road. She reported to me that a man had hurled a brick through her lounge window and he was still hanging around outside. After reassuring her that I would respond as quickly as I could, I changed into uniform and raced up to see her. When I arrived, I saw a man in his mid-seventies lying down on the grass verge opposite her cottage suffering from exhaustion. I questioned him and he admitted that he was responsible for throwing the brick and breaking her window. Arthur was his name and he told me that he was hungry, having only recently been released from Gloucester prison, where he'd spent most of his institutionalised adult life behind bars. Because of the extensive list of his previous convictions and having only recently been released, the magistrates at Kington had no alternative but to sentence him for a further six months prison term to be served at Gloucester prison, which was the only prison he'd ever been inside. This was exactly what he wanted, and was precisely the reason he'd thrown the brick so he could be back inside just in time for Christmas. He told me that each Christmas he was allowed to dress up as Father Christmas and hand out presents to his fellow inmates. In prison he was warm and well fed. Arthur and I 'clicked' and got along really well with each other. He was no threat to me, which was why I was allowed to take him on my own in the police van to Gloucester prison, to serve his sentence.

Before we left, I called at the village shop in Eardisley to buy Arthur enough tobacco and cigarette papers to last him for the whole term of his prison sentence. I rang my brother John, who was a dairy farmer at Shotts Farm, Staunton, near Gloucester, to check if he was at home, and to drop in on him on our way to the prison. We arrived at the farm where John had prepared mountains of cheese and onion sandwiches, jars of pickled onions and crisps for us to enjoy with a few glasses of his homemade cider for Arthur. A couple of hours or so quickly passed before it suddenly dawned on me that time was running out to deliver my prisoner to HMP Gloucester! After arriving and parking the police van in front of the two main prison gates, I got out and knocked on the reinforced side reception door. I stood directly in front of an eye level sliding hatch, which was slowly raised, as were the two eyebrows of a male prison officer standing on the inside. Peering out at me he asked me for some identification. 'Prisoner escort from Kington!' I announced. 'Where the bloody hell have you been?' was his response. 'We were expecting you two bloody hours ago!' I heard the clatter of keys, which I later noticed were part of a bunch of keys on a long chain attached to his belt. After unlocking and opening the door, he ushered us through into the small prison reception area. I handed over the warrant and my prisoner. I emptied out Arthur's tobacco, cigarette papers and a couple of his personal possessions from a zip-fastened plastic bag onto the counter, which were all checked and signed for. After a formal pat down to check that my prisoner had no other possessions on his person, it was now time for me to take leave of my slightly inebriated friend, but not before the prison officer commented that he'd never received a prisoner from the police before smelling of alcohol and tipsy! With slightly slurred speech Arthur said, 'Bill, I've had a great time. I've never been treated so kindly by any other policeman before.' And he meant it. Perhaps Arthur's life had been a lottery for him. I knew little about him, but I knew deep down he was a good man. As the prison officer unlocked the door again to allow me to leave, he knowingly smiled at both of us which was when I felt some relief knowing that Arthur was back on his home territory again, where he wanted to be just before Christmas, and where I knew he would be looked after. Months later I was shocked and saddened when I read in the *Hereford Times* that Arthur had been found dead, living a homeless existence in Hereford. I respected Arthur but never really knew him and have never forgotten him since. May his soul rest in the most secure and peaceful place for him in heaven, with God's freedom and love.

This next story was my attempt to stay one step ahead, with a bit of ducking and diving, shall we say. PC Jim Curtis was an experienced officer stationed at Kington who was fast approaching retirement age. The most senior officer in charge at Hereford, and for the whole of the division, had earnt himself a bit of a reputation for his strict discipline and correctness. Like many of his subordinates, I tried to keep well out of his line of fire. On this particular day, Jim and I were both working a day shift together at Kington. Jim loved eating raw mushrooms. After he'd finished his mug of tea and munched his way through a quarter-pound bag, he said he was off to Hereford police station to drop off an urgent dispatch. 'I'll come with you Jim,' I said. It was fashionable then to have long hair and sideboards, which I had. As a uniformed officer, however, I have to admit that I was pushing the boundaries of my appearance to the limit or even further. In other words, my bushy sideboards and hair were far too long. Jim and I set off from Kington, parking the police vehicle in the main police station car park at Bath Street, Hereford. Jim's advice was for me to stay behind in the vehicle, 'Just in case we bump into you-know-who. He'd go nuts if he saw you with your hair like that Bill!' Choosing to ignore Jim's sound advice, I insisted on going with him into the police building via the back door, to minimise the chances of us bumping into 'the bear', which was his nickname! As we turned the corner, I was shocked to see the very person in question walking towards us accompanied by an immaculately-dressed, high-ranking, uniformed army officer. Their conversation immediately ceased as they both clapped eyes on me, giving me a couple of cold, piercing stares, full of obvious disapproval, which ran straight through me. Passing them, Jim and I saluted in unison, making me feel like I was taking the micky, but not intentionally so. I could see that 'the bear' was extremely displeased and annoyed by my general appearance, so Jim and I scurried away from Hereford to return to the relative comfort-zone at Kington. I walked into the police station to hear the phone ringing and answered it. 'Mr …'s secretary here, is that you PC Rowlatt?' Oh my gosh! I just knew what his secretary was going to say next. 'He would like to see you in his office right now, so please make your way back to Hereford police station.' Time for a spot of quick thinking I thought to myself, and I rang Ethel Gregg's daughter, Linda Davies, who was the local hairdresser. Luckily for me, she was at home and picked up her phone. 'Could you fit me in for a haircut please, Linda?' I asked. 'Yes of course, Bill, when would you like it cut?' 'Er, well straight away if you could, please Linda?' I raced from Kington to Linda's address in Eardisley, confessing to her that I was in a spot of bother with the boss and needed my hair cut in double quick time. I had another neatly pressed uniform at home and a pair of very shiny black polished boots for special occasions and by heck this was one hell of a special occasion! After getting my hair cut, I hurriedly changed into my best uniform and drove as quickly as I could back to Hereford police station. Even though I say it myself, this time I was immaculately turned out. I stood outside 'the bear's' office and took a couple of deep breaths then tapped nervously on his office door and in a loud, bellowing voice I heard him shout, 'COME IN!' He was expecting me. Standing to attention, I threw him up a military style salute. 'You wanted to see me, Sir?' I announced. A complete transformation in my appearance had taken place since he'd seen me a little more than an hour or so before. This was beyond comprehension. I was impeccably turned out, with short regulation-length hair, shiny black boots and neatly-pressed uniform. It was a complete shock to his system. After eyeing me up and down a few times in sheer disbelief, his face turned bright crimson. He'd been completely outwitted, and oh how annoyed he was with me. I glanced over his desk to see that he had my personal file open in front of him. I stayed standing to attention while he flicked through every page, struggling to find a reason to explain why he had called me back to see him from Kington, 20 miles away. Needless to say, I was extremely relieved when I was awkwardly dismissed from his lair!

One summer, just as the corn was ripening, local farmer Andrew Cameron telephoned me to report that about half a dozen goats, normally tethered in woodland at Brobury, had slipped their collars. Andrew said, 'Bill, they've all broken loose and are hoovering my corn, so I've taken them back to tether them up again. Can you find out who they belong to?' The following day Andrew was back on the phone. 'Bill, those bloody goats have broken loose and are hoovering my corn again!' In the meantime, I'd made enquiries and found out very little other than the owner lived somewhere in the Leominster area. Andrew continued, 'Just letting you know, I've taken them and loosed them out up at Brilley!' Oh dear.

I was on a weekend off when it happened, and Jim was on duty at Kington covering both his and my patch. He telephoned me at Eardisley police station early on Friday evening.

'Brilley Mountain, I've found it! Lovely hedges and gardens up there!'

'Bill, there's an infestation of goats up at the top of Brilley mountain, they're causing havoc up there! The phone hasn't stopped ringing from members of the public. They've wrecked fences and trampled all over people's gardens chewing off their roses and plants. What do you know about them?' 'Absolutely nothing, Jim,' I replied. 'Bloody liar!' was his response. I explained that I thought the owner lived somewhere in the Leominster area, but that was all I had found out. On Sunday morning a pickup truck pulled up outside Eardisley police station. In the back were several goats, all bleating and peering out inquisitively. The driver said he'd found them and herded them up from people's gardens at Brilley! After scratching and shaking his head, he commented, 'I know they keep getting out, but I can't think how they got all the way up there'. After that, I received no more 'hoovering' complaints from Andrew. Weeks later, I heard from unofficial sources that they had travelled even further away to distant pastures new ... in Dorset!

Police work involved dealing with some very tragic incidents too, such as a fatal traffic accident which I attended. A family were on their way to Wales to spend their summer holiday together, travelling in two vehicles, one following the other. Mum and dad were in the lead vehicle, with the other car driven by their daughter, her partner in the front passenger seat. At a junction, the lead vehicle pulled across the road safely, closely followed by the second vehicle driven by their daughter. A heavy goods lorry collided with the side of her car, causing her to be fatally injured and trapped inside, while her passenger escaped uninjured. Like so many accidents, these were devastating circumstances for the whole family, their lives changed forever in that one split-second of time and fate. Bravely, her family stayed with her the whole time, while the emergency services did their work to release the body. My heart went out to all of them, and I did everything I could possibly do to comfort and console them. What happened next was beyond belief, had I not witnessed it myself. A car pulled up near to the crashed vehicle and a young male driver jumped out holding a camera. In front of everyone, he ran over to the flattened car and started taking close-up photos. In those days, cameras were non-digital and had a cassette film cartridge inside them. I was completely incensed by what he did. How anyone could think about doing what he did was beyond comprehension. I saw him about to get back into his car and ran across to him to ask what the hell he thought he was doing? I couldn't help myself, I snatched the camera and opened it to remove the film. Throwing the film on the ground, I stamped all over it, breaking it up into little pieces beneath my boot, then I gave the camera back to him, shouting at him to leave. I was aware that I'd acted entirely inappropriately, and I was out of order reacting as I did, but

I just couldn't and wouldn't allow that to happen. Later on, I saw the superintendent and admitted to him what I'd done, and to the disciplinary offences I was guilty of, even before any complaint was received, which it never was. All common decency and respect were completely absent and I will never understand that person's mentality. My mum used to say that we sometimes live our hell on earth, and this was exactly how everything felt that day.

On a lighter note, we received a call from a well-known, highly-experienced local GP at Kington surgery, who wanted the police to assist him and the duty psychiatrist from the county hospital's Stonebow unit, to go with them to a house where they wanted to admit a patient to the Stonebow unit under the provisions of the Mental Health Act. At the house, Doctor P held a large syringe primed with a strong cocktail of muscle relaxant and sedatives, which he was poised ready to inject into the thigh of their patient, if the patient decided to fight or play up. The injection would render the patient instantly drowsy and compliant. Following some lengthy negotiations, no amount of discussion could entice their patient to go voluntarily with them to hospital.

What followed was a free-for-all, with arms and legs flying everywhere. During the mayhem, Dr P who was feeling rather pleased with himself shouted out to everyone, 'Ok. I've done it! Injection in!' The Stonebow psychiatrist looked up at him sheepishly, then calmly

'OK. I've done it! Injection in!'

capitulated, 'Doctor, you've injected me, not the patient!' His demeanour changed so quickly, like he was someone else who had all the characteristics of a floppy rag doll!

For weeks, the fire brigade in the village were receiving a string of fictitious 999 emergency calls. All of them had to be treated as genuine calls until they were attended and found to be false. The local fire crew and myself were getting pretty annoyed and fed up with them, as often the police and fire brigade would attend to emergency calls simultaneously. I decided to pay a visit to the brigade's headquarters in Worcester to investigate the calls and liaise with their chief fire officer, as I'd asked him to keep copies of the voice recordings of the caller. After copying them onto a cassette recorder, I went home and listened to them repeatedly. It sounded like the same person making the calls, although the male caller tried to disguise his voice by using different accents and voices. After listening to the recordings, it dawned on me that I thought I knew who the person was, and I took the recordings to Eardisley's sub-fire officer, the late Ken Townsend, for us to listen to together. After confirming my suspicions, I now had a suspect, but one I knew very little about. What I didn't understand were his reasons for wanting to make the calls, or what he had to gain from them, until Ken enlightened me. The suspect had only recently joined up as a retained firefighter, which I was unaware of. Firefighters in Eardisley were, and still are, part-time, retained and highly-trained firefighters, who do a tremendously professional job and are paid by 'the shout', as they call it. So the suspect, if I could prove he was responsible, stood to gain financially from the call-outs. The more frequently they were called out, the more payments he would receive, so a picture was emerging. Proving it would be challenging though, so I rang for some advice from

the detective inspector at Leominster CID, informing him of
the enquiries and the progress I'd made. 'Ok, go ahead and
arrest him and bring him over to us so the detective sergeant
and I can interview him for you', were my instructions. I have
to admit that I felt a little bit miffed that I wasn't going to
be allowed to take part in the interviewing process myself,
especially as I'd already done most of the leg-work. However, I
did as I was told and arrested the suspect one Sunday morning
at his home. After explaining the reasons for his arrest and
cautioning him, he denied his involvement. When we arrived
at Leominster police station he was placed in a cell, and later
transferred to an interview room. I rang the canteen upstairs to
inform them that he was ready to be interviewed. They entered
the interview room and I was told to leave. More than half
an hour had passed when the DS rang to speak to me in the
canteen, where I was patiently waiting for a result. He told me
that the suspect had not admitted to the offences and wanted
me to sit with him in the interview room, while they took a
coffee break. I took my suspect a cup of tea and some biscuits
before sitting down with him. Our conversation covered a
variety of topics including his family and friends etc., other
than the reason why I had arrested him, then unexpectedly he
said, 'Bill, I don't like the attitude of those other two! I'll tell
you, but I won't tell them! I admit making all the calls and I'm
really sorry.' We went into greater detail, confirming the times,
the locations and where he'd made the emergency calls from.
To make a call he'd gone into the bar at the Tram Inn and
ordered a pint. When the landlord was busy serving drinks,
he walked through to the pub toilets, passing the landlord's
private lounge, where he knew the phone was, to make a '999'
call. When he returned to the bar and finished his drink, his

fire brigade pager would activate and no one was any the wiser when he ran out to respond to the emergency. I recorded a statement from him under caution and telephoned the DI in the canteen to inform him. 'Er, Sir, he's made a full confession and I've recorded a written statement from him under caution.' The DI and the DS were not at all happy, after he'd given them the run-around before deciding to admit everything to me and not them. The matter was thus resolved and dealt with by the court, and this incident only goes to show that it's often the way we treat people which is important.

DICK'S TRANSFER TO KINGTON — ARRESTS, POACHERS AND PIGS AS PETS

IN 1980, PC Dick Allford was transferred from Hereford to Kington police station. He was allowed to visit the police station in Market Hall Street in a police vehicle to meet, for the first time, the sergeant, other colleagues and myself. I would describe our impressions of Dick's first visit as dramatic and amusing. When he arrived, he failed to judge the distance between the police vehicle and the court house wall and so scraped the police car right down one side, which meant that he had to be immediately suspended from driving vehicles for the next six weeks until he could take a re-test. Dick and I worked together for several years as colleagues and friends, and it would be impossible to write down all the seriously funny stories we shared, but I'll mention one or two!

Dick had absolutely no ambition for promotion to the rank of sergeant, but the chief superintendent made it quite clear to everyone that he wanted as many unqualified officers as possible to study and sit for their sergeant's exam. This gave me an idea! The sergeant's promotion examinations were held at the Shirehall in Hereford every November. After reading the chief superintendent's memorandum, a couple of us decided to type out a fictitious A.30 report from Dick requesting to apply to sit his sergeant's examination. After copying his signature, we signed it: PC629 R. Allford and submitted it. Months passed, during which we had forgotten all about the forgery, when one day Dick opened up an official-looking envelope which was addressed to him. Inside was a typed memorandum stating that he should report to the Shirehall in Hereford on the 1 November to sit his sergeant's exam. 'Hey Billy, I think they've made a mistake!' Dick innocently protested, then he telephoned the training office to withdraw. 'We have an A.30 report here signed by you,' they said, followed by, 'Anyway it's too late to withdraw. You have to attend.' 'But I've done absolutely no revision!' Dick pleaded with the person on the other end of the phone, which fell on deaf ears. Being a bit too optimistic, and adopting an attitude of 'I'll show em!' Dick did a bit of quick revision before dutifully attending to sit the exam at the Shirehall. Two weeks later he opened up another official-looking envelope and pulled out the letter inside. Stamped right across it in black, bold capital letters was the word FAIL, accompanied by some bitterly disappointing percentage results! Dick had spectacularly underachieved in each of the three examination papers: Crime, Traffic and General Police Duties. As if that wasn't enough, stapled to his results was a letter signed by the chief superintendent requesting that he made an appointment to see him. With such abysmal results, Dick was reprimanded for his total lack of preparation and for not taking the sergeants exam seriously enough! ... Sorry Dick!

After discussing how poorly police officers were paid by comparison to other workers in the public sector, Dick and I came up with the idea of earning ourselves a bit of extra cash by buying six pigs and fattening them up to sell them on as porkers. We needed to keep our mini pork-rearing enterprise 'hush hush' as we didn't want it to reach the ears of any senior officers at Hereford or headquarters. We weren't officially allowed to have another job or any business interests, so it might be risky. My brother John kept pigs and sows on his farm, so Dick and I decided we would share the costs of buying and fattening up six weaner pigs, just as soon as we could find a suitable building to rear them in. We knew there was a disused barn near to the roundabout at Kington, next to Turnpike Cottage where the late Ray Dawson and his family lived. The barn belonged to local farmer Edward Mayglothling, who agreed that we could use his barn for our pigs. The barn, which hadn't been used in decades, had a curved, corrugated tin roof and a door inside which was tied together with bits of what's known locally as 'Radnor belt' (string to hold your trousers up!). We patched up the leaky roof and repaired the latch bolt on the wobbly door. We bought bales of wheat straw for their bedding and borrowed an old galvanised pig trough for their food and slops. As an added bonus, Edward generously offered the use of his building without charge. John delivered six healthy weaner pigs in his stock trailer, and we let them out into their comfortable new pigsty. We took it in turns to feed them on all sorts of grub, including pig weaner meal which we bought from J & P Turner at the Mill, mixed in with stale left-over cakes, buns and stale bread from Hussey's bakery and Jane's Parlour in the town. This all got washed down with gallons of left-over beer and larger slops, donated to us by some publicans in the town, which would otherwise have been tipped down the drain, and our piglets settled into their new habitat. We had fun raising and feeding them, but keeping the news of our 'piggy' enterprise from senior ranks might be difficult. In fact, the pigs were talked about in the town, which put a few smiles on people's faces. Sergeant Ken Campbell had retired, so Dick and I decided it might be wiser not to mention to his successor anything about our six four-legged pets!

Weeks passed as they rapidly gained weight on their high carbohydrate, protein and alcohol diet! We took it in turns to feed them twice a day depending on which one of us was on duty at the time. One afternoon, Dick and I were working together on the late shift at Kington when the sergeant called us into his office. 'I've heard you two are keeping pigs,' he said. 'Well, if I catch either of you feeding them on duty, you'll be for it!' That evening, their normal feeding time came and went, but we knew that the sergeant had left and gone home after finishing his shift, which left us on our own until ten o'clock. We just had to take the risk and feed them, because it was already well past their feeding time. Dick and I prepared a swift plan of action, which was to drive up to the barn under the cover of darkness in the police car and fill up the two black plastic buckets by mixing in the pig meal, bread, cakes and beer. When we got there, they were ravenously hungry, squealing their heads off and running around with the excitement of being fed. I shone my torch, reaching over to undo the bolt on the door so Dick could step in with one bucket in each hand to empty them into the trough. Our uniforms had a whistle and chain looped into the top breast pocket of our police tunics. As Dick stepped in, his whistle chain got caught round the door bolt so he couldn't move. The pigs ran round him plunging their heads and snouts into the two full buckets of food, spilling it everywhere and gobbling up as much as they could snaffle. The pigs almost knocked Dick over, but with his whistle chain snagged around the bolt, he was anchored to the spot. I went into rapturous hysterical laughter, which made me worse than useless in trying to free him. Dick held on to the buckets, with one leg half in and half out of the pig pen, shouting at me, 'Billy, Billy, help me, I'm stuck!' which made me cry with laughter. Eventually, I untangled him so he could tip what was left inside the buckets into the pig trough, then we hurried back to the police car.

Dick said, 'Billy, I'm in shock!' so we went to the Royal George Inn at Lyonshall to get Dick a brandy, which is good for shock! We were welcomed by the landlord, the late John and his wife Elaine Allen, 'What have you two been up to?' they asked, and they started to laugh as we told them our story, sponging off as much of the pig mess and snot from Dick's uniform trousers as we could. Then a radio message came through

'Ok Dick, back your car up. They're ready to load!'

to report to Inspector Pete Dew in the canteen at Leominster police station. When we got there, he made us two mugs of coffee and we sat down to talk. I thought it strange when he started sniffing the air a couple of times where Dick was sitting, then he said, 'Dick, you smell like pig shit!'

The pigs grew into porkers and needed to be taken to Peter Preece's slaughterhouse in Eardisley. Dick owned a red Ford Escort estate so we dropped the back seats, filled it with clean straw and loaded them in one by one! By the time we got to Eardisley there was pig shit everywhere, all over the upholstery and windows, which were steamed up! Dick spent weeks trying to get rid of the piggy smells inside until eventually he gave up, and was forced into part-exchanging his car for a more fragrant-smelling vehicle.

One Sunday afternoon, retired army Major Philip Verdin, who was a local landowner and farmer at the Buttas Farm, Canon Pyon, called the police to report that he had seen poachers on his farmland with dogs, hare coursing. I attended on my own, where I met the Major and his son James. I was amazed to see 13 men hunting with dogs, chasing and killing hares in a field. The three of us managed to stop them from what they were doing, and got them to gather round. All of them were from south Wales. It is an offence to poach hares and, after recording their 13 names and addresses in my pocket book, I reported them for summons. All pleaded guilty with the exception of one, who appeared at the county magistrates court at the Shirehall in Hereford and pleaded not guilty. His defence was that it wasn't him present on the day, but someone else who must have falsely given his name and address. Major Philip was the next witness to be called into the witness box to give his evidence and be cross-examined by the defendant's defence solicitor. Major Philip always wore an eye patch over one eye after he was injured during an army exercise, when his eye had to be surgically removed. The solicitor asked him how good was his eyesight in his good eye, inferring that he had wrongly identified his client, who was in the dock. 'Major, with only one eye and your eyesight as it is, you definitely can't positively identify my client who you see here in this court room as the same person you saw on the day, can you? I suggest that your eyesight isn't as good as it should be.' The Major was insistently defiant: his eyesight was good enough to win the war on D-day, and it was just as sharp then as it is now. The magistrates found all 13 guilty. Major Philip was awarded the Military Cross for outstanding service during the war. He served with the Royal Dragoon Guards and was awarded an OBE.

Dick and I were on duty together at Kington when we spotted a yellow three-wheeled Reliant van parked in Church Road by the war memorial. The van looked just like the vehicle driven by Delboy from the TV comedy series Only Fools and Horses, so we decided to speak with the driver and search it. In the back was an Aladdin's cave of every conceivable power tool and electrical equipment, all brand new and in their original packaging with the price labels left on them. I arrested the driver on suspicion of theft, and took him to the police station. After unloading his van, we searched his house and garden shed where we found even more new stolen goods locked away, which he was selling at local car boot sales. All of them were stolen from shops and stores in Hereford, Kington, Presteigne, Knighton and Leominster. After the case was dealt with, it took me a couple of weeks to list and return all of the stolen property to the owners. As I was returning some items to a hardware shop in Knighton, I happened to glance through McCartney's estate agent's window, where I saw a small, quaint, end-of-terrace cottage advertised for sale. It was named Ivy Cottage and was at Beguildy, which was a place and area I'd never heard of. Buying our first house was not as straightforward as this might suggest. As a family we were living in the police house at Eardisley, which was rent-free and maintained by the police. At the same time, we were becoming a nation of homeowners, and it seemed sensible to think about buying our own property, which would most likely increase in value. On the other hand, by buying a house and living in it, it would mean the loss of my rural beat officer's posting at Eardisley, where I really loved the job, and to which I was totally committed. If I left Eardisley, I might be posted anywhere, even back to Hereford on shifts, or to another division that I would be completely unfamiliar with.

IVY COTTAGE AT BEGUILDY

IVY Cottage was advertised for £12,500, so Janette, myself and our two small children, Julian and Lucy, took ourselves off to Beguildy to look at it. The cottage was located right next to the churchyard of St Michael's Church. In fact, the kitchen wall was built deep into the side of the churchyard with the bedroom windows overlooking the graves and headstones outside. It needed lots of TLC and a full restoration programme, including damp course, new doors, walls re-plastering and re-plumbing. The cottage was several hundred years old, with a large, open stone fireplace in the front room, which, when we stepped inside it, we could look up and see out to the open sky above. My thinking was to arrange a mortgage to buy the cottage, but by some means stay living in the police house in Eardisley. Then I had the idea that, if I could restore the cottage, it could be rented out for holiday lets, which would pay for the monthly mortgage instalments and we wouldn't need to move. I went to the Halifax Building Society to arrange for the loan. The decision was made and Ivy Cottage was ours!

At the time, Len Lewis was landlord of the Tram Inn in Eardisley. We got along well together, although the combination of local bobby and local licensee was not seen as a good mix, especially when it came to local complaints. Occasionally, wives complained to the police after their husbands arrived home from a pub in the middle of the night, worse for drink, making it difficult for me because it was my responsibility to crack down on after-hours drinking and to maintain the licensing laws. If I didn't sort it out then I would soon have some inspector or chief inspector on my back. Most licensees on my patch locked their doors at 11 o'clock closing time, but then, as everyone knew, most of them illegally continued to serve drinks to a few of their 'friends' after hours in what was known as a 'lock in'. They used to say that a pint after hours tasted much better! I gave all of my licensees a reasonable degree of leniency when it came to after-hours drinking, but this changed if any licensee took advantage, such as noisy patrons slamming car doors or too many after-hours drinkers, who were blatantly flaunting the law by staying behind, and which nearly always attracted complaints. We had to visit pubs at least once a month, entering the time and date of the visit in the pub register, which was checked and signed by a police inspector or rank above. The Tram Inn and police station being in the same village felt like they were a bit too close for comfort, but then Len and I had a mutual understanding and respect for each other's professions and positions.

A few years before, Len and his father Ken owned K. Lewis and Son, which was a builders and funeral business at Kington. After their business was closed, Len took over as licensee at the Tram Inn, which was owned by Ansell's Brewery. Len and his wife Gill ran the pub together, but were later divorced. Before this happened, Len and I visited Ivy cottage as often as we could to start with the restoration work. We uncovered some beautiful old oak beam lintels above the doors and windows, which were left exposed. The large open fireplace had a huge oak beam above it but when it was lit, it bellowed smoke out into the room. I will never know how previous generations lived there without getting smoked out. To overcome the problem, we sealed the chimney off on the inside above the beam and installed a log burning stove and flue. No more smoke. Although there was no central heating, the little log burner threw out so much heat that it comfortably warmed up the kitchen, and warm air was drawn up the staircase and into the two small bedrooms above. When the log burner was lit, it effectively warmed the whole cottage. Local people told me that it had once been lived in by a lady who single-handedly raised 14 of her children, and milked a house cow which grazed in the field opposite. With Len's know-how and my fetching-and-carrying skills, we soon made the little place homely and habitable again.

Janette and I advertised Ivy Cottage for holiday lets in medical journals and church magazines. Consequently, we had quite a few doctors, dentists and clergy staying, including a bishop (I think from memory he was the bishop of Liverpool, but can't be certain), who sent us a thank you card after he and his wife said how much they enjoyed such a wonderful and relaxing holiday there. We hadn't noticed the table cloth was missing until they returned it freshly laundered, after spilling a whole bottle of red wine over it. When no one was renting it, we spent time there ourselves, meeting local people who became friends and acquaintances, including the late Tony and Beryl Greenwell (whose funerals I arranged and directed) and their family, who ran the Radnorshire Arms and the Edwards family from the village shop. In these current, difficult times both businesses have remained open.

Like me, there was a local bobby stationed at Beguildy. PC Bill Pewtress and his wife Millie had two daughters and lived at the police house with Bill's handsome liver and white spaniel dog 'Dash', who was spoilt. Bill was a born-and-bred country person, and a shooting man. You would often see him carrying his shotgun under his arm, with faithful gun dog Dash at his side, walking over fields, shooting rabbits and pheasants, which he gave away or sold to the locals. There is a lovely walk on the top of Beacon Hill. Go up the lane opposite the pub, passing Ivy Cottage and the church on your right. This leads right up to the top. The hill has beautiful, panoramic views across what was formerly known as the county of Radnorshire and is well worth visiting. Bill, who was originally from Moorhampton near Weobley, was a rabbit catcher by profession before he joined the police. As well as snaring and selling rabbits and game birds in Hereford, he placed others on the train at Moorhampton railway station (Weobley), which were taken to Birmingham and sold in local markets and at butcher's shops. Bill's initial mode of police transport at Beguildy was a DMW motorcycle, which, like mine, was later replaced in the 1970s by a police Mini van. He had a brilliant, sharp sense of humour, and was well-known and respected among the predominantly law-abiding farming community. He was popular too with his police colleagues at Knighton. The chief constable (J.R.

Jones) of the Dyfed Powys constabulary would call in at rural Beguildy police station for a cuppa with Bill and Millie, knowing that he would always receive a very warm welcome. When the sergeant wasn't around, Bill would regularly give lifts home on the back of his police motorbike to stranded young people who had drunk a bit too much after leaving the local dances in Knighton. They rode pillion, sitting uncomfortably on the top of the police radio pack where the pillion seat was. Sometimes Bill worked at Knighton police station, where he and colleagues would play practical jokes on each other as well as on the police sergeant. Sergeant Astley was issued with a brand-new pair of size nine black, leather police boots, which he locked inside his locker the night before for safe-keeping. Bill and his colleagues managed to secretly swap them for an identical size twelve! The next day, Sergeant Astley took the boots out of his locker and tried them on, walking round in front of everyone. He looked down at the boots and said in his deep Welsh accent, 'Bill, I think they've made a mistake! I will have to send these boots back. They are far too big for me!'

Beguildy was and is a very friendly but small rural community. The primary school was open at the time, but later it was closed and then demolished in 2023 to make way for houses. Prime Minister Margaret Thatcher was passing through one day when she saw children playing in the playground. She informed her aides that she wanted to stop and pay an impromptu visit to them, which surprised and delighted the staff and pupils. The school had an outside swimming pool, which all local residents were allowed to swim in, including ourselves. Just before Bill's retirement from the force, he and Millie purchased the police house at Beguildy, which was being closed and sold off, just like hundreds of other police houses and stations, across the country. After he retired, Bill and Millie sold it and moved to live in a bungalow at Bearcroft in Weobley. Bill continued with his country pursuits well into his retirement years, spending a lot of his time as a beater on the local farms and estates around Weobley. Bill and Millie were so well-known and are fondly remembered around Beguildy and Weobley. When Bill and Millie sadly passed away, I was responsible for arranging and directing their funerals. Thank you for the good times we shared together, and may you both rest in God's eternal love and peace.

DRUGS SQUAD

I N 1981, after building up comprehensive dossiers on illegal drugs activity, I was given the opportunity to join the force's drugs squad as a detective constable, working in plain clothes on undercover deployments and executing drug warrants. I worked alone or with a team of detectives to seize and execute warrants, with the aim of reducing supplies of as many illegal and illicit drugs as possible. This was our common goal, as well as identifying and prosecuting unscrupulous dealers, who profiteered from their sale and supply. I realise this was just a drop in the ocean and wouldn't change the world, but doing something beats doing nothing. I worked with drugs squad detectives based in Hereford and elsewhere, and teamed up with a drugs detective who lived at Madley. The areas we were mainly responsible for were across all of rural Herefordshire within the sub-divisions of Leominster and Ross.

One of the courses I attended was a residential drugs familiarisation course at Welwyn Garden City, where we were taught and trained in all aspects of the misuse of drugs legislation. We went on informative site visits, including a tour of the Roche pharmaceutical factory and to an engineering company which converted British-manufactured vehicles, such as Range Rovers, into reinforced bulletproof vehicles for VIPs, such as the Prime Minister and our security forces. The vehicles were also used by foreign diplomats as well as being exported to other countries. We received lectures from all kinds of drug experts, including an American drugs enforcement officer who was specially flown in. We were given comprehensive training on how to conduct drug searches, and were shown some not-so-obvious places where drugs could be concealed, for example inside drilled holes in the tops of doors. We were taught how to deal with anyone who was suspected of swallowing drugs to evade arrest, and the potential dangers and risks associated with their actions. The Misuse of Drugs Act legislation was hammered into us, along with how to deal with and prepare for drug searches and how to preserve evidence. We were shown videos and photographs of actual cases of extreme suffering inflicted upon victims of all age groups, which I can only describe as pure evil. I have never forgotten these appalling images and writing about them is a vivid reminder. The real-life cases were horrific beyond all comprehension, and devoid of all human decency. My stomach churns over even today as I am reminded of them, especially cases involving young victims – children and babies – which I have never managed to totally eradicate from my mind. Cases highlighted in the media recently show how some reports of child abuse and cruelty are overlooked for a variety of reasons – staff shortages, incorrect assessments, departmental cutbacks or just by someone turning a blind eye – so cases never get properly investigated, which I consider indefensible.

We were shown how quickly surveillance equipment could be set up to covertly film and eavesdrop on conversations inside houses and buildings. I saw photos taken from space of people bobbing about on boats and ships, and this was way back in 1981, so with modern techniques this must surely be even more sophisticated. Our course ended with a meal at one of the finest Chinese restaurants in Soho. Walking through Soho's red-light district with a group of all-male, young detectives to reach the restaurant was an experience in itself. I was not only thankful to be in their company, but also relieved that they were only ravenous for food!

I shared a small office at Ross police station with my drugs squad colleague, visiting periodically to submit reports and to occasionally meet with senior officers. He and I worked together or separately, depending on the type of enquiry we were involved in. Sometimes we were called in to Hereford to assist officers there. For several weeks, a small group of us travelled to Shrewsbury every day from Hereford on an observational and intelligence-gathering task, which culminated in a successful drugs raid and seizure taking place close to the town centre.

Herefordshire (West Mercia police) borders Powys (Dyfed Powys police), and they remain two separate police forces today. We shared information with each other's drug squads and with special branch. There were times when I teamed up with a drug detective (H) from Llandrindod Wells for our mutual benefit. Drug dealers zigzagged over our force boundaries so information was exchanged back-and-forth. When following a suspect's vehicle in unmarked West Mercia vehicles into Powys, we would radio through to their headquarters the make and registration numbers of our vehicles so we wouldn't get pulled over by them. One evening, 'H' asked me to assist him with an

undercover operation at an isolated farmhouse and outbuild-
ings near Builth Wells. Wearing dark clothing and blackened
faces, we arrived in an unmarked police vehicle, parking
it on the side of a lane where we cut down bracken to cover
and hide it. We walked to our destination and hid in an old
timber-framed barn where we set up an observation point and
placed our equipment on hay bales. Crouching down, we were
in the perfect position to observe a large drugs party gathering
directly in front of us. The equipment we carried were cameras
and infrared night scopes to magnify and illuminate people's
profiles, borrowed from the SAS camp. Their equipment was
far superior to ours. At around 4am, just as I was thinking how
vulnerable we were and what might happen if our cover was
blown, we were joined by an unexpected visitor. We assumed
he was local, and intrigued by what was going on. He crept
in from behind us and squatted down between myself and
'H', so the three of us were all in a line looking ahead, almost
rubbing shoulders with each other. He had no idea that he'd
sandwiched himself between two officers keeping undercover

obs! We were frozen to the spot,
and forced ourselves to keep totally
silent, not wanting to even breathe
in case he should see us and scream.
Eventually, after 15 minutes or so, the
man, who fortunately never looked
to his left or right, reversed himself
back out and disappeared.

One bitterly cold winter's evening,
I'd applied for a warrant to search a
flat in Llewellin Road, Kington, for
evidence of a criminal offence known

In the drugs squad as
a detective constable,
working in plain clothes

as abstracting electricity. After going in, I woke the suspect who was fast asleep in his chair, surrounded by electric fires which were all switched on. Not one fire, not two, but five of them! The flat was as hot as a furnace, so we turned them off, leaving all the doors and windows wide open for it to cool down. Using adapters, the suspect had plugged in all five electric fires into one end of a long piece of ordinary three-core electric cable. He'd threaded the other end through the kitchen window to the outside, then scaled the street lamp to wire it in without any consideration for his own or anyone else's health and safety!

I dealt with a case where several burglaries were committed in Kington by the same person, who was charged and appeared before the Crown Court after entering his plea. The court, for some reason, granted conditional bail for him to appear back at the Crown Court for sentencing. Not unsurprisingly, he didn't appear and a warrant was issued for his arrest. After checking known local addresses, I realised that he'd gone to ground and asked around for some help to trace him. A couple of days later, a result came back. I was told that he'd moved from Kington to far-away Pembrokeshire, where he was living in a small caravan in a potato field somewhere close to St Davids with his Alsatian dog, so I rang St Davids police station. The phone was answered by one of the local Welsh bobbies who introduced himself to me as PC G. 'PC G speaking, can I help you?' I introduced myself and told him who I was looking for, but that the information I had was, to say the least, a bit sparse. In fact, it was a complete long shot. In his broad Welsh Pembrokeshire accent PC G said, 'Yep, I know exactly where he is, boy. You come on down here and I'll take you to the field where he is in the caravan!' This was amazing! Here was a local bobby who kept one ear to the ground, with vast amounts of local knowledge though he never wrote any of it down. I arranged to meet PC G at St Davids police station the following day. On the way, I drove through Solva, which is a small Welsh harbour and fishing village where my family regularly holidayed, usually staying in a cottage or caravan near to the sea. I would tow a small fishing boat behind my car from Eardisley, which we launched off the quay at Solva. We spent such happy times there, having so much fun catching mackerel, gurnard, sea bass and rock salmon (or, as local Welsh fishermen called them, 'snot gobblers'!). Sharky was Solva's harbour master and a great local character.

Everyone knew PC G, and there wasn't much that happened locally that he didn't get to know about. Unfortunately, I think these old-style policing methods have long since gone now. True to his word, we drove to an isolated farm near St Davids, miles from anywhere, up a long farm track and into an open potato field where a small two-berth caravan came into view. As we approached on foot, I heard the dog barking and snarling menacingly from inside. We hammered on the caravan door, but received no immediate response. PC G and I looked knowingly at each other before starting to rock the small caravan from side-to-side to check for occupants. The caravan door was immediately flung open as the occupant appeared in the doorway, clutching both sides of the door frame to stop himself from falling over. Then I arrested my prisoner, not for the first time. On our way back from St Davids we stopped at the Ship Inn in Solva for a bacon butty and a mug of tea in the back bar with my prisoner still handcuffed, then made our way back home to Herefordshire. How times have changed!

In general, we were allowed a free hand to investigate drugs enquiries in the way we saw fit, which sometimes involved taking personal risks. One night, under the cover of darkness, two of us were searching for a cannabis plantation in a rural location we were tipped off about, when our presence disturbed two dogs, which started to bark. A crazy individual appeared from his cottage carrying a double-barrelled shotgun. He unleashed his dogs to search for us, so we ran for it through a corn field, diving for cover! As we lay there, I felt my heart pounding rapidly deep inside my chest. I genuinely thought we might get shot. We lay on the ground, motionless and in complete silence, until eventually the guy with the gun gave up his search and called his dogs off to go back inside! This was most definitely another lucky escape!

Mentioning the shotgun reminds me of the time I was a probationary constable aged 19. I was asked to help a very experienced Hereford detective – the late Tony Barnes – arrest a man living in a caravan at the caravan park by the new bridge in Hereford. Tony said, 'Bill, the chap I want to arrest will be inside, but I know he's got a shotgun. I'll knock on the door and shout "police". We'll both stand back on either side of the door, just in case!' I did exactly what I was told, and Tony did just what he said he would do. The door practically got blown off its hinges from the inside by a shot fired from a single-barrelled shotgun. We quickly pounced and tackled the prisoner to the ground. Thankfully, Tony had done his homework, which probably saved our lives or stopped us from being seriously injured. I know that the job carries high risks, particularly with so much media coverage recently about knife attacks, and with shootings and murders on the increase.

Drugs squad investigations involved positions of trust and as long as we achieved some reasonably good results, senior ranks would generally let us get on with the job. Hours, days and weeks were spent carrying out painstakingly long covert observations before a drugs raid was struck, hopefully always with the element of surprise. Not such a pleasant task, however, was to look through black plastic rubbish bags, which sometimes provided valuable clues and evidence. With due diligence and preparation, searches were usually positive so that controlled drugs could be seized to prevent their further distribution and misuse. We all knew that each job was just the tip of the iceberg, but it was what we did. I am not qualified to write about the reasons why some people misuse drugs or alcohol, but they say it's an attempt to change their lives, to make life more tolerable or to deflect the mind from some deep-seated personal problem or mental health issue. Heroin is a harsh drug, incredibly difficult to remove from the body's endless cycle of dependency. Dangerous too for the user, because it is often cut and other substances added to make deals worth more before being resold. In my time, a variety of substances were known to be added, such as crushed aspirin or Polyfilla! I knew a male person who, with his female partner, were heroin addicts. They would help each other to inject heroin into themselves until one time it went badly wrong when after injecting her she tragically died in his arms. After this he stopped using heroin and turned informant and helped us. The substitute and treatment for heroin addiction has, for many years, been methadone, available on prescription from the NHS. More recently, a revolutionary drug called Buvidal is being prescribed to addicts with monthly injections. Reports suggest that heroin addicts are beginning to lead near-normal lives without needing to commit daily crime to finance their addiction to heroin, which sounds like a very positive step forward. We all know how addictive alcohol is, and that it kills people. It doesn't make any sense that the stuff is glamorised. There are many choices of drugs, both legal and illegal, available in society and they are all so darn cheap. Depending on the circumstances and the quantity, the consequences of being found in possession seem to be a lot less severe nowadays, and are often dealt with by a police caution. Lack of police resources must make a difference. It also seems that the chances of being searched depends on which part of the country we live in. The dreadful consequences, however, remain exactly the same as they always were. Catastrophic for individuals, families, relationships, health and more. Drugs and alcohol figure hugely in our society. But why is seeing someone get legless regarded as funny, when there are nearly 10,000 alcohol-related deaths each year? Social media too takes such a stronghold with some young people who can feel peer pressure to experiment with drugs. Now I'll step down from my soap box!

I visited a hippy commune, which was located just on our side of Herefordshire/ Powys border, where I had an arrest warrant to execute. At about midday, I drove down the driveway to an isolated farmhouse where I had information that the person named in the warrant lived. At the commune were a few old, broken-down abandoned vehicles, including a couple of large yellow high-mileage GPO (General Post Office) lorries, which got sold off at local car auctions and were ideal for hippy families and their children to live and travel around in. Most had log burners installed in them for the winter months. When I arrived, no one was there, so I took the opportunity of looking around and searching through abandoned vehicles. I opened up the two back doors of the first GPO lorry I came to and was surprised to see that I'd woken up a giant of a guy, who sat bolt upright in bed when he heard the doors open. He was sleeping on the biggest handmade wooden bed I'd ever seen which stretched the whole width of the lorry. For a minute or so we said absolutely nothing to each other, exchanging fixed stares for words. He turned out to be the person I was looking for, and occasionally we still bump into each other today, 42 years later!

Search warrants were signed by one of our local magistrates. When we needed to apply for one, we phoned one of them, arranging to see them at home. May Willford, who was our vicar's wife, and Joyce Banbury, who lived at the Field Cottage, Lower Welson, were two local magistrates who were usually at home and available to sign warrants at short notice. After arranging to meet one of them, the warrant first needed to be authorised by someone of the rank of police superintendent or higher. Warrants were typed out and attached to another document known as an 'information' and I always took a copy of the New Testament bible along with me. Before signing a warrant, we had to swear an oath on the bible like we were in court in front of the magistrate: 'I swear by Almighty God that the evidence I give shall be the truth, the whole truth and nothing but the truth'. Then we confidentially gave them the grounds for the search warrant, with our reasons and suspicions for why a search was necessary. I have to mention that no local magistrate ever refused to sign. This was the one occasion when hearsay evidence was allowed to be given outside normal court proceedings. Their signature was usually followed by a few words of encouragement, 'Good luck, Bill!'

I organised a drugs search warrant in the Brilley area. After obtaining the search warrant, I met colleagues and Sergeant John Moss for briefing, then entered the house by force to begin searching. During the search, I remember coming across an ordinary-looking Cadbury's chocolate biscuit tin, which I picked up to look inside. Neatly packed inside was a home-made bomb with explosives, wires and a detonator sticking out, primed and ready to explode. I very carefully placed the tin back onto the floor and got everyone to evacuate the building, then summoned the army bomb disposal team from Hereford, which arrived quickly. The bomb squad officer in charge decided that the device was too unstable to take it anywhere other than into a nearby field at the back of the house, where it was blown up by a controlled explosion. I'd obviously never expected to find a bomb, and had no idea why it was assembled inside a biscuit tin, other than there was a probability it was meant for some unsuspecting recipient. I was relieved this wasn't me.

I achieved satisfaction from investigating drug offences, optimistically hoping that, during this relatively infinitesimal period in time, everything we did was worthwhile, and might have helped someone, somewhere in the greater scheme of things.

UNIFORM DUTY

A FTER a year or so, I moved back into uniformed duties, and in 1983 police forces were continuing to sell off urban and rural police houses around the country. There was a semi-detached police house in Back Lane, Weobley, which had not been lived in for months and which was categorised as 'surplus to police requirements': this meant that any serving officer, who did not already own their own house, was invited to apply to buy it, so we did. I had now been stationed at Eardisley for 10 years, and I wanted to continue working in the area, though this was not guaranteed. My application to buy the police house was approved, but we still owned Ivy Cottage in Beguildy, which needed to be sold in order to finance our move to Weobley. Jacksons Estate Agents in Leominster placed the cottage on the market for £17,950, which was the same price as the police were asking for the Weobley house, and our mortgage was easily transferable. After looking around Ivy Cottage, Roger and Joy Butcher, who were licensees at the Swan Hotel in Kington, fell in love with it and bought it.

In 1983 we moved into what was formerly known as 'Number 2 Police House, Back Lane, Weobley'. We renamed it 'Littlebrook' because of the small stream which ran through the front garden. At that same time, it was a relief to be told

Ivy Cottage could grow on you!

IVY COTTAGE, Beguildy, Nr. Knighton, Powys occupies a pleasant position in the lovely rural hamlet of Beguildy, a charming stone rendered semi detached cottage offering well appointed two bedroomed accommodation with attractive features, including exposed stone walls, oak beams and floors.

Constructed with stone rendering under a slate roof, this attractive semi detached cottage affords modernised accommodation with exposed stone walls, oak beams and floors. The accommodation briefly comprises: lobby, lounge with feature stone fireplace incorporating a wood burner, kitchen, bathroom, 2 bedrooms, cellar/store shed.

Outside there is a cellar/store shed about 10' x 6' and flower borders to the front and side of the property.

Price: £17,950 freehold to include carpets as fitted or laid. Agents: Jacksons, Tel. Leominster 2363.

that I would be posted to nearby Kington police station, where I already knew many local people, which would make policing a lot easier than if I'd been posted elsewhere. Julian and Lucy attended Weobley Comprehensive School to continue their education after leaving Eardisley Primary School. Julian went on to Hereford Sixth Form College and achieved some outstanding

A-level results, then to Leeds University, where he met his wife-to-be, Amanda, who became a teacher. Julian received a civil engineering degree, later changing occupations to become a loss adjuster though, at one point, he started up his own business as a stone-mason, which was named Herefordshire Headstones. My daughter Lucy attended Worcester University where she qualified as a mental

Lucy, Julian and Bill in front of 'Littlebrook' in Weobley

health nurse (RMN) and, after a short spell working at a hospital, she became employed as a manager for a private company in Worcester helping clients with their mental health issues. Sadly, Lucy became increasingly unwell in her young life and career, eventually having to leave her job. I have four grandchildren – Chloe and Adam, who are Julian and Amanda's children, and Josh and Poppy, who are Lucy's children. I am immensely proud of each and all of them for their individual achievements, and love them dearly.

MINERS' STRIKE

THE outbreak of the miners' strike was in 1984 when Margaret Thatcher was Prime Minister. Both Dick and I were among officers sent from our division to join officers from other divisions in West Mercia. Police officers were drafted in from forces around the country to police the strike, which was led by the left-wing miner's union representative, Arthur Scargill. There were approximately 10,000 striking miners, and 5,000 police officers deployed. Orgreave colliery was notorious for being the most troublesome colliery, where most of the disruption and violence was focused for the duration of the strike. Dick and I were fully trained in methods of crowd control. We had reinforced plastic shields and were issued with extendable 'casco' metal batons for our protection. Training sessions showed us how to extinguish flames from Molotov cocktail petrol attacks which was scary! Other projectiles included pots of paint which immediately obscured clear vision through the riot shields we stood behind. We were also told to expect other projectiles filled with excrement and urine which was an unpleasant thought! Our police training was disciplined and thorough. Our protective clothing, which was issued to all officers, included leather boots, flame-proof suits, gloves, riot helmets with visors and neck protectors. All-in-all, we were reassured and prepared as much as we could be by the very high standard of protective clothing, training and equipment given to us.

Every week we were transported by coach from Hereford to the Yorkshire coal mines, then transferred into Ford Transit personnel carriers fitted with steel-mesh hinged shields, which could be quickly dropped down over the windscreens when trouble threatened. At night, we were billeted in all sorts of different buildings and venues, such as army camps, RAF hangers and even a miner's holiday camp, similar to Butlins. When we arrived in Yorkshire, the police organisation was impressive and efficient. Highly-skilled, high-visibility police motorcycle outriders rode their powerful machines to meet us at pre-designated road junctions where they'd join us with sometimes 100 or 200 police transits and coaches containing police forces from around the country, all in one long convoy. It was an imposing and deliberate police presence. We were there for the long-haul; for weeks, which ran into months. We were regularly placed on standby duties during the daytime, held in Ford Transits all cooped up together, a dozen of us in each vehicle with a sergeant in charge of each crew. You can imagine the card games, the banter, the humour, the occasional arguments and with some unmentionable anonymous body odours wafting around inside.

Being on standby, we were sometimes blue-lighted to where trouble was brewing and we donned our riot gear from our kit bags en route like firemen do when attending a shout. Each transit crew had one person trained in first aid, like I was. At the start of each day, we were offered a full English breakfast and during the day we received a bag of sandwiches with crisps, a piece of fruit, a chocolate bar and numerous cans of coke as well as coffee and tea. At night, a further cooked meal was available and served up to anyone who was still hungry. A lot of the sandwiches got wasted and were thrown away in rubbish bins. If a suitable, friendly exchange occurred between ourselves and a group of miners, which happened occasionally, then we would offer them our sandwiches. Some took them, but others told us in no uncertain terms to 'F*** off!'

One afternoon, we were in our transit with 11 other crew members and a sergeant. Fifteen more police transits and their crews were parked bumper-to-bumper in front of us in a semi-circle on a piece of waste ground, surrounded by trees and vegetation. It reminded me of a '60s cowboy film when early American settlers strategically parked their horse-drawn wagons in a circle to protect themselves from attacks by Indians. I was sitting in the furthest-back seat, by the two back doors. During a moment of reflection, it occurred to me just how many dozens of leftover sandwiches were being thrown away every single day, and today was no exception. I thought how incredibly wasteful this now-regular occurrence was. Surely some of mother nature's wildlife – birds or foxes – could benefit from them, rather than them going to landfill. I gathered up handfuls of the leftovers from the other transit teams, and carried them in boxes back to my seat. I opened the rear doors and emptied them in a pile on the ground, so no one would see them or be any the wiser. No more waste. But no sooner had I done this than our convoy received a radio message to say we were being urgently deployed. In no time at all, we were on the move with the convoy's 'blues and two's' activated. Suddenly, a tall, smartly-dressed uniformed police superintendent stepped out in front of our convoy to halt its progress. I feared the worse! He'd spotted my gift to mother nature! Oh Shit! He strode in our direction and stepped up into our transit, shouting, 'Which stupid prat dumped all those bloody sandwiches at the back of your transit?' I felt sorry for the sergeant at the front, who had absolutely no idea what the hell he was talking about! I stood up to confess all as heads turned and looked at me. 'It was me, Sir!' I said, followed by laughter and rounds of applause, which temporarily ceased when the superintendent shouted at me again for clarification, What the f*** did you do that for?' 'I wanted to feed the birds, Sir!' came my reply. 'Clear them up!' he shouted, and abruptly left to the sounds of even more laughter and applause. Because we were responding to an emergency, I quickly unlocked the back doors and scooped them back up inside before continuing on to our assignment. I hated waste and continued to dispose of the sandwiches by a less obvious drip-feed method! I hate waste or throwing food away, and to this day I always throw any leftover food for birds on my lawn.

Inevitably, the miners dispute caused a lot of ill-feeling and friction between union members, as well as the NUM and the government of the day. It changed forever the lives of miners and their families, who were so proud of their jobs and their family traditions which had been passed down through the generations. In a manner of speaking, this was a political fight and we were pawns in the middle. I was interested to hear that the country could never be held to ransom if essential power supplies got cut off because electricity could be fed in from France and the rest of Europe by huge undersea power cables. At the time, there was much cheaper coal being imported from countries like Poland, and millions of tons of our coal stock-piled at the pit heads, camouflaged by grass. I have no idea if these snippets of information were true, but I saw for myself the tons of coal reserves covered over by grass.

It was always a welcome relief to come home again, nearly every weekend, travelling down from the top of Fromes Hill by coach and seeing the beautiful, rolling Herefordshire country-side in front of me. I always heaved a big sigh of relief at this point to see wonderful mature oak trees coming into view, and Hereford cattle herds grazing in small patchwork green fields on the landscape. It was such a special spot for me as it always reminded me how lucky I was to be nearly home! Historically, Herefordshire farmers handed down their farms from genera-tion to generation, providing continuity of jobs, and it dawned on me that this was similar to the Yorkshire miners who were so proudly fighting against change, and so desperately trying to hold on to their family traditions as miners, and of course to their jobs.

My position as first-aider was put to good use early one evening when we were billeted at a huge RAF hanger near Leeds. After taking a shower, Dick helped himself to a Max Pac plastic coffee cup which he filled to the top with boiling hot water from the kettle, stirring in the coffee granules and milk powder with a plastic spoon. Dressed only in a pair of underpants, he was sitting on the end of his bed holding the plastic cup in one hand (not a pretty sight!) The plastic cup suddenly slipped through his fingers and the entire scalding-hot contents spilt over his bare leg. Dick jumped up like a jack-in-the-box and I could see that the skin at the top of his leg was beginning to turn a pinkish-red colour. Tongue-in-cheek, I said, 'Dick, you've scalded your leg! As this week's official first-aider, I must take immediate appropriate action and get you to the casualty department (A & E)!' 'Come with me please!' After putting on a shirt and a pair of tracksuit bottoms, we got into a police transit and I drove at full speed, with blue lights flashing and sirens blaring, all through the built-up area until we reached Leeds General Hospital. When we arrived, we were greeted by a medical reception team of five nurses and two doctors standing in a line waiting to receive us. Spotting I was carrying a first aid kit, one doctor asked me, 'Has your patient been injured on the picket line?' 'Oh no, Doctor,' I explained, 'He's just spilt a cup of hot coffee over his leg!' The police control room had telephoned ahead of us to tell them to expect an officer who was injured, but didn't mention how! After applying some cream to Dick's leg, we left casualty with both doctors and nurses in fits of laughter!

The misery and uncertainty continued for the striking miners and their families, and, like dozens of times before, we were placed on standby duties, parked up in our Ford Transit personnel carriers, just waiting and waiting. One day our unit received a shout, and we were on our way to the colliery most talked-about as being violent – Orgreave. My stomach churned as we donned our protective gear on the move. Without a word being said, we were all aware that our moods had changed. Everyone was silent. This was serious stuff, and I imagined for a moment how it must have felt to be transported to the front line of a war zone. On arrival, I saw the litter, the mayhem, the dirt and sticky, squelchy deep mud. We were waved through dozens of lines of mounted police, policemen on foot and dog handlers, then on through the main colliery gates past hundreds of jeering, sneering and confrontational miners. In a flash, we were ordered to bail out of our transits to face hundreds of turbulent, aggressive strikers in ordered formation behind our protective shields, now doing in real life what we were trained to do. It was confrontational hell! All sorts of objects were being hurled at us, including some projectiles which might have been loaded with all the nasty stuff we were told to expect during training. Where would this stupidity and hatred all end, I was thinking to myself, and have to admit I was shitting bricks! After what seemed like a shorter time of conflict than we were expecting, our section was ordered to withdraw and get back into the transits. We were driven back out of Orgreave as swiftly as we had arrived, via the same route and without any explanation. We had no idea if other units would replace us, but we were all relieved and thankful to get out of there, relatively unscathed. We were told later on that we had been replaced by more local officers, who were nearer to home if they were injured. No wonder so many injuries occurred on both sides in that environment of aggression, hatred and mayhem, which left me with such negative thoughts of escalating and unnecessary conflict.

Someone mentioned that Arthur Scargill wore a hairnet! Maybe I'd read it somewhere. I doubted what I'd heard or read, until one day I was sitting at the back of a coach when he and his entourage walked past. He was directly beneath me. I looked down and saw the top of his head and I'd seen it for myself. Dark-coloured and very fine mesh.

Occasionally, we worked a whole night shift, from 10pm until 6am. One night nearing Christmas, we were at a colliery keeping guard with Inspector James as our shift inspector, a sergeant and 12 officers. We were billeted inside a warmly-heated green wooden colliery hut just inside the two main metal gates, and directly in front of the coal face entrance. The lads were doing what they usually did to amuse themselves – playing card games, reading or listening to the radio. Outside it was freezing cold, with snowflakes fluttering down like large white feathers and settling on the ground. The two big metal gates weren't locked but had to be kept closed and closely guarded. Only one of the gates was allowed to be opened if authorised personnel needed to go in or out. One of our police transits was strategically parked in the middle of the two gates on the other side, facing the hut effectively creating a barricade. The officer on guard duty was briefed, and was sitting in the driver's seat with instructions to check and log all authorised personnel going in or out. His job was also to open and close the gate. Inspector James instructed me to relieve the officer on gate guard duty from midnight until 4am. So, just before midnight I stepped out of the warm hut into the freezing cold air and signalled to my colleague in the Transit that I was replacing him. I undid the bottom bolt which secured the gate and opened it just wide enough for me to squeeze through to the other side. He got out and went through the gate the same way, back into the hut. I secured the gate and got into the driver's seat to take up my position. Fortunately, he'd left the engine running with the heater on and it was as warm as toast.

A couple of hours later, I heard PC Steve Perkins hammering on my driver's door window shouting, 'Bill, wake up!' I'd been asleep with my head and face across the steering wheel. 'I'm relieving you!' Great! You're early Steve, I thought? 'The inspector wants a word with you!' Oh, shit! I hurriedly squeezed myself through the gap in the gate and went into the little green hut, apparently still bearing some steering wheel indentation marks on one side of my face. When I went in, I was greeted by rounds of applause and laughter (this seemed to happen when I got in a spot of bother!) and reported to the inspector who told me how the south Yorkshire night-duty superintendent had visited him with his driver in a police Range Rover to carry out a spot-check. When they arrived at the gate the driver sounded the horn several times, trying to get my attention to open the gate for them to drive through, but without success. Evidently, no number of loud blasts on the horn could rouse me from the deep sleep I was in, so the superintendent's driver got out and reached through with one hand to lift the gate's security bolt. After opening the gate, he got back in the Range Rover and they drove slowly past with me still out-for-the-count across the steering wheel! The superintendent then introduced himself to our inspector. When they were about to leave, he told him, 'Oh, by the way inspector, you'd better send for some reinforcements outside.

Your scout Tonto has been shot in the back with an arrow!' (He was referring to the '60s cowboy television series the Lone Ranger.) Thankfully, for my sake, he had a sense of humour. They left in exactly the same way, closing and bolting the gate behind them. I was none the wiser and completely oblivious to everything that happened! Another lucky escape!

An effective tactic adopted by the police was to operate road blocks with turn-back points on the various approach roads to prevent protesters from reaching and congregating at the main picket lines to swell numbers. There were flying pickets and groups who travelled in their vehicles to join miners to cause as much disruption as possible. It was reported that university students were being paid cash to be there too. On one occasion our transit was parked up on the A15 at the end of the Humber Bridge on turn-back duties when PC Mark Herbert and myself picked a quiet time to ask if the crew could manage without us, so we could experience walking the full length of the bridge and back again, a total distance of 2.76 miles.

Some miners were tolerant of us when we met them in their groups, realising that we were just doing our jobs and following orders within a disciplined police service, but others refused to speak or communicate with us and would sometimes turn their backs and face the opposite way. I felt cut to the quick the first time it happened to me. One Sunday morning, Mark and I were dropped off to keep an eye on a group of just three pickets. Our brief was to inform control if they were joined by others. We had no idea how the three of them would react to our presence. It was bitterly cold and snowing again. After Mark and I were dropped off, we saw the three sitting inside an open-fronted wooden shelter, huddled around orange flames from a brazier, fuelled by wood from broken up pallets, to keep themselves warm while reading their Sunday newspapers. All headlines were dominated by the strike. Mark and I shivered and shook outside trying to keep ourselves warm with feet like blocks of ice. I thought I'd take my chance and speak with them to see if they were friendly or otherwise. At first, the conversation was a bit stilted and awkward but this eased until Mark and myself were invited inside to sit and share their newspapers. It felt like this was a small breakthrough, and an achievement for good common sense, and we gave them all of our sandwiches! It was almost a normal, peaceful moment, and it reminded me of the time during the First World War when the German and British troops came out from their trenches at Ypres to play football together, before going back behind enemy lines!

About half an hour passed before our convivial exchanges were interrupted by some silly halfwit who jumped in with two big feet. I heard a car pull up right in front of us and slowly lowered the tabloid newspaper I was reading and peered over the top page. As the driver's window lowered, I sensed danger. The driver had a pip and a crown on the lapel of his police uniform, denoting the rank of chief superintendent. Mark and I simultaneously dropped our newspapers to the floor, stood up and quickly moved outside the shelter standing side by side to attention. This was a high-ranking officer, who we had never clapped eyes on before and who was a completely different breed to the one who had joked about me being shot in the back with an arrow! We saluted his uniform in unison, but we were about to find out that he had no common sense nor manners either. If you pardon my expression, he was a complete knob-head, who appeared to want to take his anger and frustration out on me rather than Mark, who was younger than me. He had already made up his mind about what he'd seen and wrongly interpreted us as fraternising with the so-called enemy! 'Which police force are you from?' he angrily asked. 'West Mercia, Sir.' I respectfully replied. 'Well, you're nothing but a bloody disgrace, sitting inside there with them! I'll be sending you back to your force!' That's harsh I thought, given we were only pouring oil on troubled waters with three pickets we had just met, who we were beginning to get along with quite well. Turning redder in the face, he said, 'I'm going to report you to your duty inspector right now, what's his name?' Shit! Now I was feeling flustered, unjustifiably challenged and pressured by his harsh interrogation. His piercing, enraging stare and general demeanour only made matters worse for me! Our inspectors changed from week-to-week and for the life of me I couldn't remember who this week's inspector was. My mind went completely blank and I heard myself muttering the words, 'Er, um, gosh ... now let me think?' at the same time placing a hand across my forehead, searching for some flash of inspiration and desperately trying to remember the inspector's name. Although totally unintentional he thought I was taking the mickey, which had the effect of getting him even more irritated and bad tempered with me, but I just couldn't remember. Mark, who was still standing to attention next to me, came to my assistance and nervously piped up, 'Our inspector's name is Inspector James, Sir!' Whereupon he wound up his window and sped off, with wheels skidding like a boy racer. I remember thinking that we had landed ourselves in a bit of trouble. Both of us could soon be heading back to Herefordshire, perhaps to face disciplinary charges. Later, Inspector James saw me and calmly dismissed the incident as though it had never happened. 'Don't worry Bill, I've sorted it!' he said. After all, what did we do that was so wrong, other than being sociable and friendly under difficult circumstances? We were keeping the peace, and that was one of the reasons why I'd joined the police. Nevertheless, I was relieved. Then it struck Mark and myself how funny my temporary loss of memory must have looked and sounded, and how badly the superintendent, whoever he was, had overreacted! (I think this should probably be added to my list of lucky escapes!)

We needed some light relief during this time, as sheer boredom for a lot of the time would have driven us crazy. We were on standby duties at a police station that had a large car park, surrounded by a ten-foot red-brick wall. One of the lads brought along a cricket set and we split into two teams to play. It was fun and good-humoured until the ball got whacked for six and disappeared over the high wall into a private orchard next door. Our inspector, who I remember this time was Inspector Pritchard, accompanied by the sergeant, volunteered to go next door to apologise and to ask for our ball back. After ten minutes or so, we heard them talking with each other on the other side. Someone had the bright idea of turning on the fire hydrant and pointing the end of the hose over the wall to give them both a soaking. We heard the inspector shout, 'Oi, cut that out!' No one knew that the owners of the orchard, a man and his wife who lived next door, had kindly offered to help the inspector and sergeant search for our cricket ball, and were directly in the line of fire!

The miners' strike eventually ended and I continued working in uniform at Kington until I was temporarily transferred to Leominster CID as a detective constable. I then joined a small, specialist group of detectives, also based at Leominster, known as the Bumblebee Squad, which ran from October 1994 until March 1996.

HERE COMES MOSSY

IN 1981 Sergeant John Moss was posted to Kington from Hereford, replacing Kington's outgoing sergeant. John was altogether a very different character to his predecessor. He had an incredibly quick sense of humour, and would take risks. He and his family moved to live at the police house, which was next door to the police station in Market Hall Street. In the next few chapters, I will mention John and some events from when I and other colleagues worked with him. I shall never forget some of the close shaves he got himself into, though he always managed to get out of them again.

At around that time the police Mini vans were replaced by Vauxhall Astras, which were nippy and distinguishably decked out in reflective police livery with blue lights and sirens. Sergeant Moss or 'Mossy' as he became affectionately known, managed to scrape police vehicles and have numerous accidents. Len Bullock, the civilian police mechanic at Bath Street in Hereford, was often turning up at Kington with the police Land Rover and trailer to transport one of Mossy's Astras back for repair that he had somehow crashed, dented or broken-down in. Mossy was a quick thinker too, much preferring to drive everywhere than walk, and he was a much faster driver than any of us. When he first moved to Kington, I remember attending a burglary which was categorised as a high-class 'burglary dwelling', where property valued at many thousands of pounds was stolen from a house in a rural location. Our superintendent, the late Pete Parry, also attended because of the high value of the property taken. After leaving school and working at the Aeroparts factory in Hereford, Pete joined up and, among other postings, he quickly moved

185

into CID, where he became a very experienced detective in his early career and was later promoted through the ranks to become our uniformed superintendent in charge at Leominster sub-division. We all had the very highest regard and respect for him. He and I stood by the side of the driveway leading to the property that had been burgled and ransacked. Right in front of us was a perfect tyre mark impression, left behind in some soft mud by the vehicle the burglars had used. In those days, photos were taken and a plaster cast impression taken by a scenes of crime officer (SOCO) as evidence at court or for any forensic comparisons. Superintendent Parry was really pleased with himself as he'd spotted the tyre impression before any of us and had called SOCO to attend. While we were standing right by the tyre mark and waiting for SOCO to arrive, one of the new police Astras turned in and sped up the driveway right past us and straight over the top of this vital piece of forensic evidence, which was destroyed in an instant! 'Who the bloody hell was that?' Pete asked? 'Er, well, I don't think you've met him yet, Sir, but that was Sergeant Moss!'

Mossy was in charge of six police officers at Kington. There were four police houses in Llewellyn Road. Two were sold off to PC Paul Kirkham and PC Bill Button, and the other two were sold to the general public, as was Pembridge police station. PC Bob Hughes purchased the police house in Back Lane, Weobley, next door to me and Detective Sergeant Dave Gwynne purchased the police house and station at Mansel Lacy, after the late PC Paul Mason retired and moved to live in Hereford. Mossy bought the sergeant's police house in Market Hall Street next to the cattle market. Special constables stationed at Kington at that time were Brian Wright, Harvey Jones, Maureen Edwards from Byton, Merv Lewis from Titley,

Dierdre Leighton from Mansel Gamage and Terry Holden from Almeley. Before them, there were many more special constables in most villages. In 1973, when I came to Eardisley as the beat officer, there was Ray Greenhow (Eardisley), Godfrey Skyrme (Eardisley), Arthur Bowden (special sergeant at Lyonshall), Eric Holton from Weston, Harold Jones (special sergeant) of Lower House Farm, Huntington, Aubrey Price from Pentre Farm, Brilley and Jack Price from Hallaston Farm, Sarnesfield. When I met Jack, he still wore his high-neck police wartime tunic, which he had never had replaced!

In spite of how things were and how local policing was achieved, all of us took pride in our jobs – arresting criminals and attaining some really good results, which meant that the general public had confidence in us. When a local burglary or theft was reported, we would often sit down together in the police canteen to discuss the details over a mug of tea or coffee. We swapped information about who was seen when and where and who might be our prime suspect. We made telephone calls to informants, and to local people we knew who could help us find out who was responsible and if they were local. When we had a suspect and had evidence to suspect someone, then we went out and arrested them. With all due respect to modern policing methods, I doubt very much if this sort of approach happens anymore. Between us we knew a lot of people, and there were many more of us available to deal with the reports that came in. In general, this was how local crimes were solved, and why our crime detection percentages were extremely high. In my opinion, these days the public can't always be bothered to report some crimes because they know they will only be given a crime number to give to their insurance company so they can register a claim, even if that crime could, with a little more time and effort, be detected. Consequently, the increasing number of unreported crimes mean crime statistics show an overall reduction, which gives an entirely false picture but one that some politicians are happy to latch onto.

As the local beat bobby at Eardisley I remember a gentleman from Cheltenham who, like my mum, was an artist. He was on a painting holiday with his wife and family in accommodation at Upcott, Almeley, owned by Mr and Mrs Cripwell. He had just taken delivery of a brand-new Rover car and decided it would be reasonably safe to leave the keys in the ignition overnight. However, someone stole it, and he didn't discover it was missing until waking up on Sunday morning when he telephoned me to report it stolen. Soon after receiving the call, I received another call from a member of the public to say that they had seen a new Rover car abandoned on Brilley Mountain, parked in a particularly isolated location which seemed suspicious. It had to be the same car so I got a lift to Brilley. Luckily the keys were still in the ignition and the car was undamaged. I hopped in and drove it back to its owner at Upcott Cottage, which all happened in less than an hour. The owner was delighted that I had recovered his car so quickly, and that it was undamaged. A disco had been held at Almeley village hall the night before which had gone on late into the night. Putting two and two together, it was a fair assumption that whoever nicked the car had taken it to get themselves home. I had no proof but suspected that it might be someone who lived near to where the car was abandoned. On Monday morning I started to inform local people in the village about what had happened, and went to Burgoyne's garage to inform their staff. By chance, the late Rhona Jenkins, who worked in Harry Burgoyne's office, said that she'd seen the car speeding over the Tram Square junction from Almeley Road towards Woodseaves and Brilley, driven by a young male and she gave me his description. This was the link I needed, so I visited the suspect's address and arrested him on suspicion of TWOC (taking a vehicle without the owner's consent). He admitted to the offence, was charged and pleaded guilty at court. I rang the owner in Cheltenham who was very appreciative about how everything had been resolved so quickly. I received a personal thank you letter from him, as well as from the chief constable (who the owner had written to). This was how we responded to and dealt with local crimes. They were all fully investigated no matter how serious or minor they were. We were trusted in the community and always reminded ourselves that the public paid our wages. They supported us, and we depended on the information they gave us to do our jobs efficiently. Of course, we had more time, and there were many more of us locally than there are now. I don't know how on earth the police manage these days, with just one officer at Kington and no one at Hay-on-Wye. Surely this is an absurd situation if we are all to expect proper law and order with civil rest.

Although my time as a detective with the drugs squad ended, I continued to organise warrants and drug searches. Mossy was supportive and I think he appreciated and depended on my knowledge and experience. I must write about one example of Mossy's wit here. He was called in to work as custody officer in the charge room at Hereford police station because they were short staffed. The telephone rang and he answered it. 'Sergeant Moss'. 'Hello, John,' the caller said, 'This is the Chief Superintendent'. Thinking it was a wind up, John replied, 'Yea, yea, yea, yea!' 'John, this **is** the chief superintendent!' he repeated. Then another, 'Yea, yea, yea, yea!' Then the penny dropped as Mossy realised it really was who he said it was! Mossy replied, 'Oh, hello Sir, how can I help?'

As I've mentioned, John much preferred to drive rather than walk anywhere if he could. On one occasion, I'd organised a drugs raid which involved about six of us searching an isolated cottage for the cultivation of cannabis plants, with Mossy placed in charge. I briefed the team before setting out, but, because of no road access to the property, we had to face a three quarter of a mile trek to reach the target's address. Mossy kept harping on and moaning to me at every step. As we pushed through woods, tripping over undergrowth, and trekked along muddy tracks, he repeatedly quizzed me about the route I was taking them on. 'Surely, Billy, there's another shorter or different route?' But I'd convinced him that there wasn't. His constant whinging was exacerbated by us having to carry equipment, such as exhibit bags, boxes and labels etc. Mossy took up lead position as we trudged closer towards the target's address. Finally, we sauntered up and over the small brow of a hill. Mossy came to an abrupt stop in front of me and called me forwards to talk to him. He pointed at something in front of us, then said, 'Billy, look over there! What's that?' Right ahead and in front of us was a double-decker bus parked by the target's address! 'Now how the bloody hell did **that** get there?' I was stuck for an answer! It turned out there was a narrow lane with vehicular access over on the other side, which I admit I knew nothing about! After completing our search, we trekked the same route back to where we'd parked the police vehicles, accompanied by our prisoner who seemed rather baffled by the choice of route we (or I!) had chosen to get there. Mossy often recounted this story, adding a few derogatory remarks about my route-planning skills!

Entering premises by force needed to be carried out quickly in order to keep the element of surprise. This was not only to protect police teams, but also to prevent anyone inside from disposing of illegal drugs or other incriminating evidence, like drugs paraphernalia, syringes or tourniquets which could be flushed down a toilet. Police teams never knew quite what to expect until they were inside, when the situation could be properly assessed and contained. At one drug raid, we found a male occupant armed with a loaded crossbow, but, with the team's alacrity and his confusion, he was quickly and safely disarmed. Whole weights or blocks of cannabis resin (453 grams) were wrapped in thin, white, wet muslin cloth, to help prevent it from drying out, before being smuggled here and stamped with the country of origin, mostly Lebanon (Lebanese gold) or Afghanistan (Afghan black). Cannabis resin is a sticky brown or black pliable substance unless it has been left too long to dry out, then it becomes brittle but no less potent. It is produced by scraping, shaking and harvesting the female unfertilised buds and flowers of cannabis plants when they are sufficiently mature, with Afghanistan being the world's biggest producer of cannabis resin. We didn't have the sophisticated drug testing kits the police have now to analyse powders such as heroin or cocaine, so all seized samples were sent away to the home office forensic science laboratory to be analysed and identified. The results were returned with the substances identified, along with their quantities, purity and street values. Before sending off a very large quantity of what was thought to be cocaine, I opened up the top of the bag to show it to Mossy. I was gobsmacked, and couldn't quite believe my own eyes, when I saw what he did next: he stuck one finger into his mouth, moistened it, then dipped it into the bag of powder I was holding open! Then he put his finger into his mouth, and sucked it like a lollypop! I couldn't stop myself saying, 'You bloody idiot! You don't know what it is! What did you do that for?' He said, 'Billy, I've seen Kojak do it on the telly!' (Kojak is a '70s American TV cop series). Less than a couple of hours later, Mossy called me over, 'Billy, my mouth and lips have gone all numb!' Oh really?!

Mossy became a local legend, and is still talked about. He was very popular with colleagues, friends and the public. He was spontaneous, a quick-thinker and so funny, but never a push-over. He made our job more enjoyable when we worked with him, as none of us ever quite knew what to expect next. He certainly made us all laugh, and we enjoyed his quick witticisms. He made mistakes too, as we all did. Our senior officers liked him too, which kept them out of our hair. He once received some regular complaints in Kington about a well-known local elderly lady, who, if she spotted a traffic jam, would step off the pavement into the road to direct the traffic, which confused drivers and caused a number of minor collisions. Mossy asked her to refrain from doing this, which made not the slightest bit of difference, so he gave her a yellow reflective jacket to wear instead!

I was at the police station in Market Hall Street when Inspector P, from headquarters complaints and discipline department, came to interview all of us about a senior officer who was being investigated for alleged irregularities into mileage claims. We were asked to make witness statements about the dates and times we had seen him driving his car. My statement was written out for me by Inspector P in an upstairs interview room. On completion, I was asked to read through each page and sign it. The police station was a very old building with thick stone walls and wide window sills. When I was sitting down reading through my statement, I looked up and saw Inspector P had wandered over to look out the window, which had a lower-than-expected window sill. He hadn't realised just how close he was to it, or how thick the stone lintel was. When he bent down to peer outside, he accidentally banged his head really hard against the lintel, and started to rub and soothe his forehead with his hand. He was obviously embarrassed, and he looked over in my direction to see if I'd seen him do it. I quickly averted my stare from his, to save him any further embarrassment. After I'd signed my statement, I went downstairs, leaving Inspector P upstairs to finish off his paperwork. I related the story to Mossy, of how I'd seen him accidentally bang his head against the stone window sill, and how I'd decided to look away to save him being embarrassed, and we laughed about it. Minutes later, Inspector P appeared downstairs. The first thing Mossy said to him was, 'Oh hello, Sir. How's your head?'!

Dick and I were on duty outside the Burton Hotel in Mill Street, where discos were regularly held. After midnight, people were starting to spill out onto the street and we stood there to quell and prevent any trouble. I remember this particular night when the rain was pouring down on us like stair rods. In spite of always being told that a good policeman never gets wet, we were already soaked! Have you noticed how drivers are less likely to be stopped for speeding when it's hammering it down? As we stood a little apart from each other, I saw a young lad driving straight through a big puddle past Dick and he got soaked. This was, and still is, a road traffic offence. I stepped out in front of the car to stop the driver, but he failed to see me, or just decided not to stop. I wasn't sure. I jumped to one side and threw my long rubber torch at the car which hit its roof. My torch bounced off the car and somersaulted down the road, breaking up into separate pieces, but the throw had the desired effect because the young driver immediately pulled over and stopped. The driver waited patiently, watching me pick up all of my torch components and reassembling it before speaking with him. Remarkably it still worked. 'You've just soaked my colleague and failed to stop,' I informed the young driver before issuing him with an HORT1, which was a document requiring him to produce his driving documents within seven days at the police station. Providing young drivers were generally apologetic, which he was, I normally let them off with a telling-off, rather than booking them, as this would often prove to be more effective. I pointed out the offences he had committed under section 3 of the Road Traffic Act: (a) failing to stop for a police officer, and (b) driving through the puddle and splashing a pedestrian, in this case, Dick. The young driver was relieved that I hadn't booked him, but, when we looked at the roof of the car, there was a large dink right in the middle. I said, 'Well that's your fault for not stopping'. 'The trouble is,' he began, 'It's not my car, it's my dad's and he'll go nuts!' Oh shit! I went straight back to the police station to phone his dad at 2am in the morning. A sleepy man's voice answered the phone. After confirming who I was, I asked him if he was the driver's father, he said, 'Is he ok?' I reassured him that his son hadn't been involved in an accident, and explained why I had to throw my torch at the car to stop him, but, on this occasion, I decided to caution him rather than book him for the offences. 'Oh, thank you, officer', his dad said. 'The only problem,' I continued, 'is that there is a large dent in the roof of your car, where I had to throw my torch to get him to stop!' 'Oh, never mind about that, officer,' he replied, 'You just wait until the little bugger gets home!'

MEETING DIANA PRINCESS OF WALES

AFTER 22 years of uninterrupted police service, I was due to be presented with my Long Service and Good Conduct Medal when I received the following memorandum signed by Chief Superintendent Dalton at police headquarters. There was the chance that I would be introduced to HRH Diana, the Princess of Wales, and I was already thinking what an honour this would be.

I was truly moved by the presentation of medal ceremony which took place at police headquarters at Hindlip Hall on Tuesday 5 May 1992, and I felt so privileged to receive my medal from the late Princess Diana. Bless you Diana, and may you rest in God's eternal love and peace. It was one of the most unforgettable, special days in my life. A happy occasion and a uniquely precious moment meeting her for just a few minutes. I was aware too of her spiritual presence, and how unrushed she was, giving her time to talk with each of us individually. It was clear that she genuinely cared for others, from all walks of life and across the world. When she entered the room, I was struck not only by her incredible beauty, but by a bright aura around her. She was a unique spiritual lady who was graceful, sometimes shy, and dignified.

Skipping forwards 15 years after we had retired from the police, Dick and I travelled to London, after applying for two passes to march past the Cenotaph, with other retired police officers for the Armistice Day parade. We are NARPO members, which is the National Association of Retired Police Officers, and the parade was in the presence of Her Majesty the Queen. Dick was accompanied by his wife Jill, and my granddaughter Poppy came with me. We travelled by train from

All correspondence to be addressed to "THE CHIEF CONSTABLE"

A31
REV 5/91

Tel. No. 0905-723000
Telex No. 337429
Fax No. 0905 54226

Our Ref: MW

HINDLIP HALL
P.O. BOX 55
WORCESTER
WR3 8SP

20th March, 1992.

Dear B:ll,

I have been asked by the Chief Constable to inform you that your Long Service and Good Conduct Medal has now been received from the Home Office and arrangements are in hand for it to be presented to you and 32 of your colleagues.

It is a significant achievement to have completed twenty two years service to qualify for this award and I am sure you will agree that wives are also entitled to recognition for their encouragement and support over the years.

On behalf of the Chief Constable, it therefore gives me great pleasure to invite both you and your wife to our Force Headquarters for the occasion.

The ceremony will take place at approximately 1.30pm on Tuesday, 5th May, 1992 and the medals will be presented by Mr. T.R. Dunne, Lord Lieutenant of Hereford & Worcester, and I should be obliged therefore if you could arrive at Headquarters by no later than 1.00pm. A new car park has been opened at the back of the houses in The Drive which should provide adequate car parking facilities.

On the 5th May, H.R.H. The Princess of Wales is visiting the Worcester area and arrangements are being made for her to attend the medal presentation at Hindlip. The necessary arrangements have not yet been finalised, hence I cannot provide exact timings of events. If you confirm that you are able to attend, I will write again confirming the final arrangements.

I must stress the seating accommodation is limited, therefore you will only be entitled to be accompanied by your wife, <u>or alternatively</u>, a single guest.

After the presentation, a finger buffet lunch will be provided.

In order to assist with the necessary catering arrangements, etc., I should be obliged if you would inform me, by completing the attached slip, whether or not you will be attending. This should be returned to me by no later than the 11th April, 1992.

Yours sincerely,

W.H. DALTON,
Chief Superintendent,
Personnel.

P.C. 264 W.D. ROWLATT,
Kington.

(POLICING THE COUNTIES OF HEREFORD & WORCESTER AND SHROPSHIRE)

Hereford, staying at a London hotel for the weekend. During our stay, I managed to buy tickets to see a show with Poppy, and she and I visited Madame Tussauds. Poppy spotted the waxwork figure of Princess Diana and asked me to stand next to it so she could take a photo. Something happened, which I have decided to write about as it might help to reassure others too. I believe in an afterlife and that, when someone dies, their spirit moves to a higher spirit level, which none of us can completely imagine until we are there ourselves. My belief is that the spirit of someone who has passed away can return to our earthly life if they wish to, and may be here for a split second, or longer. My mind was focused on Poppy taking her photo when all at once and all around me felt spiritual and otherworldly. It felt like Diana's spirit and presence was there, and just as alive as she had

The presentation of my Long Service and Good Conduct Medal by Her Royal Highness The Princess of Wales

been when I met her in 1992. Some might suggest that it was a figment of my imagination. However, I was left with a word and that word was 'reassurance'. At the time, that word meant something very relevant to me, and it made complete sense. Many more people than we realise receive spiritual messages or signs in one form or another, but we rarely mention them or speak of them to anyone because the experience is personal to us, and carries with it our human fear of being disbelieved or ridiculed if we did. Any of us can feel, hear, touch, smell or sense something that comes to us from the spirit world, and it can be a simple but meaningful sign when the spirit of someone wishes to communicate with us. This has happened to me previously, and always when I least expect it, so I remain open-minded. I interpret the signs as them wanting to reassure us that they are being loved and cherished by God in a beautiful and completely safe place. After retiring from the police, I became a funeral director and, for more than 20 years, many families confided in me about their own spiritual experiences and signs, which they received after losing someone, usually someone close to them. So, I know I'm not alone in trying to explain how or why it happened like it did that day, but happen it did.

I cried, as millions did, when Diana died so tragically on 31 August 1997, and I vividly remember the day. After listening to the early morning news bulletins in my room at Kinnersley Castle, I made a special journey to Kington police station to hoist up the union jack flag at half-mast. Diana was loved by the nation and by the world. She adored, and was totally devoted to, her two sons, Harry and William, who share their mother's spirit, and her life's blood runs through them. I shall never forget being in her physical and, as I believe, her spiritual presence. I know that she will still be helping her boys and their families in this troublesome world from where she is now. Her heart was full of kindness and love, and now she is with God. May she rest in eternal peace.

FATHER CHRISTMAS FLIES IN

ALAN Edwards, who owns Kington Building Supplies, was also a helicopter pilot and he owned a four-seater helicopter. Christmas time was fast approaching when I thought about creating a special Christmas surprise for all the primary-school children in the Kington area. I had an idea and approached Alan with my plan – would he fly his helicopter into Eardisley, Kington, Almeley, Dilwyn, Weobley and Pembridge primary schools just before Christmas for me? Dick agreed to be dressed as Father Christmas to distribute sweets to the children, and I would be in my police uniform. Alan readily and generously agreed with the idea, which required a good deal of organising at short notice to make it all happen before the schools broke up for Christmas. I needed approval from the headteachers and their school governors. Local and national press would be informed, and Alan and I needed to check all the various safety aspects to ensure that it would be safe to fly to the schools. Last but not least, this could not happen without prior approval from my boss, Superintendent Pete Parry. As with all senior ranks we always addressed him as 'Sir'. He was a good man and was, as far as I was concerned, among those who were in the 'top drawer' of senior officers. I telephoned him, but omitted to let him know why I wanted to see him, just in case he dismissed the idea out of hand. I wanted to assess his initial response and, if necessary, fight my corner, so Dick and I met him in his office at Leominster police station. After explaining what we were planning to do and what we were wanting him to officially sanction, his initial response was, 'You're both bloody mad!' followed by, 'What happens if the bloody thing crashes and kills two of my most experienced officers?' Then Dick and I gave him, if you pardon the expression, buckets of bullshit, with all the excellent reasons why we wanted to do it, which was for the children, their parents and police/ public relations. He finally succumbed to the idea. Thanks Pete!

I dictated letters, with the help of our counter clerk and friend Jane Repton, which she posted to all six schools, and I sent out a press release. All the schools responded quickly and positively, posting back their signed approvals. I requested that none of the children be informed beforehand, just in case for any reason we couldn't get there and had to abandon the mission. I suggested that they be told about an hour before our arrival, which would give them time to wrap up warm to come outside to watch for Santa's helicopter to circle round and land at their school. The parents were sent out confidential letters from the schools giving them the opportunity to be there with their children, and to take photographs. I gave each school scheduled times for our ETA, including two nominated days in case of mechanical failure, snow or any other reason why we couldn't get there. Alan and I visited every school, making sure that the landing areas were safe and checking for overhead power cables that we might crash into, bringing to mind Superintendent Parry's warnings. Kington Lions Club would sponsor the supply of sweets and chocolates to fill Santa's giant sweetie bag, and the scene was set.

At 8am in the morning, Dick and I met Alan outside Kington Building Supplies at Sunset Yard in Kington, to push

Alan's four-seater Bell Jet Ranger helicopter out of its hanger, call sign GBLGV. The weather conditions were not too clever with ice and fog. Alan's decision was that we should just go for it, so I telephoned each school and placed them on standby. The Jet Ranger had two large glass windscreens giving all round front visibility and we climbed in. Dick, dressed as Father Christmas, sat next to Alan in the front seats. The plan was that the children would easily see Father Christmas through the helicopter's windscreen, and wave to him as we circled a couple of times before coming into land. I was sitting directly behind Dick in uniform, guarding Santa's large sweetie bag which was on the seat next to me. We fastened ourselves into our safety harnesses as the aircraft's rota blades slowly began to rotate. Then I heard the sound of its powerful turboshaft engine bursting into life. With headphones on, we established clear communication with each other, as well as hearing Alan radio in our position and destination to air control. Yippee! This was now actually about to happen and we were about to get airborne!

Our first scheduled visit was to Eardisley School. After take-off, we ascended then felt the aircraft shuddering as we hovered in mid-air like some bird of prey, reminding me of when I'd taken off from Shobdon airfield in the police helicopter. It was foggy and we were above the edge of town, going nowhere. Then Alan announced, 'Can you boys see anything? I can't!' then I whispered under my breath my most used expression, 'Oh Shit!' Minutes after taking off, the fog had got a lot thicker and we both reported back to Alan that we couldn't see a bloody thing either! Our lives in your hands, Alan, I thought? Then Alan announced that he would *try* to fly the helicopter by following the main A4111 road from Kington to Eardisley, and I quote:

'To give myself a better *feel* and a better sense of direction'. What!? What did he just say!? At that point, all communication between the three of us went eerily silent, as excitement turned to trepidation. Alan was obviously in full control, but there was this acute weather problem outside. None of us could see a thing beyond arm's length, above, below or on either side of us! Just this thick, dense wall of fog which we'd flown into! As Alan flew the aircraft cautiously and very slowly forwards, his next humdinger of an announcement was, 'Lads, I'm going to have to make an emergency landing! I can't see a ruddy thing and I have no idea where the hell we are!' Oh, really? At that point Superintendent Pete Parry's words came to the forefront of my mind to haunt me, 'What if the bloody thing crashes and I lose two of my most experienced officers?' We very slowly and cautiously descended and, as luck had it, missed any electricity pylons and cables that might have been lurking, until terra firma appeared just inches below us. Alan skilfully managed to land the aircraft safely in a field, but where? We hadn't a clue. It turned out that we were in the middle of a field at Lillwall Farm, Kingswood, just a couple of miles from Kington. We let ourselves out through the doors of the aircraft and were met by farmer Alan Pritchard, who we knew. Walking towards us, Alan recognised me in uniform and curiously asked me why we had landed in his field? 'Oh, it's you, Bill, what's going on?' 'We had to make an emergency landing, Alan. We've been trying to get to Eardisley School.' I said it like it was some sort of a police emergency, which it very nearly was! Dick lifted up his long white beard to reveal his real identity to Alan who said, 'Oh it's you, Dick!' and looked even more confused. Was it some sort of fancy-dress stunt, or was it official police business? While mulling it over, Alan kindly allowed us to use his car to drive ourselves back to Kington. The helicopter was abandoned in his field until the following day when we would attempt to do it all again! It snowed during the night, but the following day the fog cleared, giving clear visibility and brilliant sunshine, and thank God we were all very much upright and alive!

As we circled above and then came in to land at our first school 'fly in' at Eardisley School, I could see the joy and happiness on the children's faces. This, for them, was the real magic of Christmas, which I've never forgotten. This was where my two children went to school and, as the village policeman, the children knew me and were used to seeing me when I visited them to give talks. Dick, too, made a wonderful, and a very convincing, Father Christmas.

Dick, Alan and I repeated the same event for two more years, then our friend Steve Graham piloted a different helicopter,

Returning to Alan's helicopter the following morning after our emergency landing, then taking off from here to Eardisley Primary School

All waiting for our final approach!

And safely down ...

which was hired from Tiger helicopters at Shobdon. I am most grateful to Alan and Steve for agreeing to take part. I was also very grateful to our superintendent, the late Pete Parry, who, in spite of his dire warnings, gave our mission his blessing, and to Dick, who played his part really well.

INTRODUCTION TO THE 'WAYS AND MEANS ACT'

O NE very irritating case of criminal damage I investigated was at Almeley. The main suspect was a local resident who had recently moved to the area. The rotating arms of the village sewerage treatment plant were deliberately broken off, in spite of being repaired and replaced several times. These deliberate acts of vandalism were causing havoc because the village depended on the sewerage system functioning properly as an integral part of the village's infrastructure. Villagers suspected someone, but no one was in a position to prove anything. The suspect lived quite close by, but in those days there were no mobile phones and no sophisticated surveillance systems. Neither was there an electricity supply to set up a covert CCTV surveillance system. The locals were up in arms, frustrated and completely fed up with it all, and looked to me to sort it out for them. Much easier said than done. Everyone knows the tough, hard-hitting reputation of the SAS and that no one messed with them. I sought advice from Detective Inspector Rick Parry, who was very physically fit with a good physique and happened to have an SAS 'R' squaddies uniform. I asked him to wear it so we could spend time walking around the area together in our uniforms so we would be seen by the suspect. The SAS were now seemingly playing their part in assisting the police with their investigations and it worked! There were no more damage reports. This came to be known as our 'Police Ways and Means Act', or, shall we say, an alternative method to achieve a result.

Another example of the 'Ways and Means Act' was one Saturday morning after Dick and I arrested a local youth in Kington on suspicion of stealing a motor vehicle. We had reliable witnesses and overwhelming evidence to formulate a charge. Being a persistent offender, our prisoner had a string of convictions for various crimes he'd committed, including burglaries and thefts and we knew him and his family well. After arresting him, he was taken to the police station to be detained, interviewed and charged in the usual way, but because he had previously been in trouble many times already and was already on bail from court, he had effectively waved goodbye to any chance of being bailed again for our offence and would have to stay in custody. After we arrested him, we began completing all the necessary documentation, including fingerprints, photographs and custody record etc., which in those days was all handwritten. Just before charging him and keeping him in custody, he mentioned that his brother was getting married in the afternoon, and how he was disappointed that he couldn't go to his wedding as he had been asked to be his best man! Dick and I looked at each other and decided to be lenient and negotiate a compromise! He agreed that if we allowed him to attend his brother's wedding, then he would promise to return to the police station at six o'clock prompt and comply to the unofficial terms of our 'Ways and Means Act'. We de-arrested him, tore up the custody record and sent him away. True to his word, he returned on the dot of six to be arrested again! No one was the wiser and the job still got done. It was nice to be thanked by a prisoner for arresting him for a change!

So, there were times when it helped to show that we could be human too. I had to arrest a local man on a committal warrant issued by the court after he failed to pay his fines. The committal warrant was for a two-week prison sentence to be served at Gloucester prison, which would cancel out his debt. There was an added complication however because 'C' was the main carer for his sick elderly mum. Both of them lived in a small unmodernised cottage on my patch near Kinnersley and I knew them well. It happened in winter, in the middle of a bitterly cold spell. They were poor and their only form of heating was a small open coal fire in the living room, where C's mother spent all of her time, trying to keep herself warm in a bed by the fire. After taking C to HMP at Gloucester (no detours this time!), my conscience got the better of me. I was thinking about C's mum being left alone without enough coal to keep her fire burning, and which, more importantly, would keep her alive. I drove to Hedley Simcock's coal yard at Kington and loaded a few bags of house coal into the back of the police van to last her until 'C' was released, and informed a couple of caring neighbours who cooked and took her food during her son's incarceration. Fortunately, none of my bosses ever knew about this sort of thing, or the misuse of the police van to transport bags of coal and not logs this time! This was my patch and things like this just needed doing, though strictly speaking they were nothing whatsoever to do with official police business!

I often think of the many people I've written about in this book who have already passed away. I mentioned this just recently to my dear friend Jo, who said that their memory will live on in the book, which is a good thought and a good reason for continuing to write to the end. Thank you, Jo. My mum used to say, 'We're only here for the spit on the back of a hot shovel'. How true that is, as I swan into my 73rd year. Oh, shit! It feels like I'm on a conveyor belt that you can't switch off, watching others dropping off the end in front of me like a Wallace and Gromit sketch! Quick, jam a spanner in the mechanism!

By chance, following a heavy snow storm, we took delivery of a brand-new police Land Rover. Police headquarters decided that we needed a 4x4 vehicle to patrol Kington, as well as the outlying regions of the rural sections, in ice and snowy conditions. Mossy couldn't resist being the first person to take it out on a test drive to show everyone how impressive our new piece of kit was. He drove it through the busy town centre stopping to talk to locals on the way so they could see and admire it too. A report came in that a parachutist was in trouble after landing in a field that was covered with snow and ice. Mossy dutifully responded in what was now the most suitable vehicle we had for the job. Driving up snow-packed lanes and over level fields wasn't a problem, but when he drove over the top and down the other side of a steep-sided field, the Land Rover went into an uncontrollable skid, with Mossy clinging to the steering wheel, and skidding straight into some wire fencing at the bottom, which entangled itself around the Land Rover's front bumper. After reversing and tugging the wire fence backwards, the front bumper came off, so John tied it up with a piece of string (or Radnor belt – just checking you've read the rest!) before driving back through Kington High Street. Not only was the damage to the bumper clearly visible to bystanders and shoppers, but their attention was drawn to a dent in the front wing as well as a rasping noise coming from the front bumper being dragged down the street. Only 20 minutes earlier, they'd seen him proudly drive past them with it polished and brand new!

Why did so many incidents happen when it snowed? I was working a late shift at Kington when at about 3am, after even more heavy snow had settled on the roads, I was called to assist colleagues in Leominster and drove over in the now fully-repaired police Land Rover. I was responding, along with other officers, to a '999' call from the licensee of a pub in Leominster, who was woken by two intruders breaking into the public bar directly beneath his bedroom. It became another example of 'The Ways and Means Act', used to play down a situation without too much fuss! I arrived to find that SOCO were already there examining the scene. After chatting to the licensee, he showed me where the forced entry was made from the outside, through a back door into the bar. It was apparent that the two intruders left rather hurriedly by the same route when the licensee switched on his bedroom light. The point of entry and exit were identical, known in police jargon as 'egress as entry'. The licensee showed me to his bedroom and we looked through the window where, under the illumination of an outside light, he'd seen two silhouetted male figures beat a hasty retreat. He obviously wanted to tell me something more, but seemed a bit hesitant. He began by saying, 'I know I shouldn't have done what I did next, officer, but I wanted to frighten them a bit, so I took my shotgun and fired both barrels at them from my bedroom window.' 'Did you injure them?' I asked. 'I don't know,' he replied. 'But I think I put the frighteners up 'em a bit!' I went outside to look more closely at the two sets of footprints side-by-side in the snow. The track on the right, leading away from the pub, had some small droplets of blood in the snow. Both sets of prints appeared to show that the intruders had run away quickly, but the foot strides on the right, showing the blood, were noticeably more elongated, indicating that the licensee must have frightened him quite a lot! I contacted the local hospitals to see if they had treated anyone for shotgun pellet wounds, which drew negative results. Someone had learnt a harsh lesson that night, and they would probably think twice before breaking into anywhere ever again!

One of our jobs was to collect shotguns and firearms surrendered by the general public, which was becoming more common due to the increasing costs for shotgun and firearms certificate fees and more stringent gun-ownership restrictions. Surrendered shotguns were often handed in by farmers because they were either rusty, too old or completely unsafe. If someone wanted to hand in a shotgun, they were asked to sign a firearms' surrender form. The guns were then collected and sent up to police headquarters at Hindlip. Guns in a reasonable condition were sold off to firearms dealers, while unsafe guns were taken out into the North Sea and dumped. On one occasion, I took a surrendered double-barrel shotgun back to the police station in Market Hall Street after deciding to play a joke on Mossy and another couple of colleagues inside. The reception area had a sliding door leading to the public counter, which the station duty officer stood behind. Carrying the shotgun, I went through to the corridor's sliding door, slowly opening it until there was a small gap – just big enough to poke the end of the barrel through so they could see it! I heard various shouts of alarm as they ducked to take cover and I walked in with a beaming smile.

Plenty of First and Second World War guns, unexploded bombs and ammunition were being dug up by farmers ploughing fields, or unearthed on building sites, and we were called to deal with them. A gentleman from Lyonshall was digging in his back garden when his garden fork struck a metallic-looking object. Looking down at his feet, he saw that he had unearthed a Second World War hand grenade and went indoors to dial '999'. Mossy responded to the call and was shown through to the back garden. Picking up the rusty grenade, Mossy began to examine it by scraping some of the rusty bits off with the police car ignition key to see if the pin was still intact! Thankfully, it was! When he saw him do this, the gentleman gardener took a few precautionary steps backwards. Mossy carried the grenade back to the police vehicle and casually tossed it onto the back seat, before setting off to drive back to the police station. En route, he radioed in to give headquarters his all-important update: 'YK. YK. I've attended and can confirm it's a Second World War live hand grenade. I'm returning to Kington police station now, over.' After a short radio pause, the force headquarters control room inspector came online, 'Sergeant Moss, are you telling us that you have a live grenade with you in the police vehicle, which you are now driving in to Kington?' 'Affirmative!' Mossy replied. Another, shorter, pause was followed by the inspector calmly radioing back, but with a little more assertiveness and authority in his voice, 'Sergeant Moss, I want you to drive very slowly and cautiously back to Kington police station. When you get there, I want you to place all the sand bags you have around the grenade then stand back! We're calling the Hereford bomb disposal team right now!' 'Received,' came John's single-word acknowledgement. He never used many words, especially if he knew he was in a spot of bother. Bomb squad officers arrived at Kington and carefully examined the grenade, which John had cordoned off and encased in sandbags. Mossy asked the bomb squad commander if they were going to take it back to Hereford with them. 'Not likely mate! It's far too dangerous and unstable for that! We'll blow it up here and now in the cattle market car park!'

Dick had an enquiry to complete at a rather grand-looking, detached country house, lived in by an affluent, well-to-do family. Walking across their immaculately-manicured lawn to reach the back door, a little yappy, brown and white terrier appeared from nowhere and sunk its teeth into one of Dick's uniform trouser leg turn-ups and wouldn't let go! The terrier tugged, pulled and growled but held fast, in spite of Dick trying to shake the little dog off. A bedroom window opened and the lady of the house leaned out and shouted, 'Officer … kick his balls!' Oh, right, Dick thought to himself as he lined up his boot towards the terrier's backside. As he did so, another shout came from the bedroom window, 'No … not those, officer, the ones on the lawn!'

We had a good rapport with the general public and the large majority were very supportive of the job we did. It helped that we were living and working in the community, where we were all known. I was keenly interested and enthusiastic about Neighbourhood Watch and thought up an idea which would once again need to be approved by our divisional superintendent, Pete Parry, to stand any chance of success. Mobile phones were only just beginning to be introduced. At the time, we were hard-hit by burglaries and thefts in many of the rural areas and villages, and the public were crying out to assist us in as many ways as they could. In Eardisley, for example, there was a spate of house and commercial premises burglaries – at the village shop, the post office and the office of Peter Preece's butchers, where a heavy metal safe was taken out and trundled down the road to a more secluded spot about half a mile away before being forcibly opened. Burglars had chosen to take it to the old tram line just off the Almeley Road to force the back off it there and steal its contents. Older safes like this one were made of heavy thick steel and cemented into office walls making them more difficult to remove, but this one was left free-standing on the office floor, making it easier for them to shift. The backs of them were usually very thin and flimsy, as this one was, but little did they know that the safe in the office was there as a decoy. It was always locked by Anne Morris who paid out the wages to Peter's employees, but she never left anything inside it, so after all their efforts, they found it to be completely empty!

Police intelligence suggested that burglars who stole jewellery and cash were placing them inside self-addressed jiffy bags which were then posted through letterboxes and delivered to their safe-houses. If a suspect vehicle was stopped by the police and the jiffy bags had already been posted, then no incriminating evidence was found. Crimes committed then were no different from crimes committed now, except that the public's perception of the police has changed. We had more proactive roles investigating crimes because there were many more of us employed, and we were able to arrest the perpetrators, resulting in much more stolen property being recovered. Today, we should all take positive steps to protect our businesses and homes by installing CCTV and burglar alarms, which are a deterrent and give rise to greater peace of mind.

NEIGHBOURHOOD WATCH AND MEETING PRINCE CHARLES, OUR FUTURE KING

THE idea I'd been thinking about for a while was one which would allow our Neighbourhood Watch groups, who were members of the National Neighbourhood Watch Association, to become more proactive. My idea would authorise our

Neighbourhood Watch group volunteers to organise themselves on a rota system to go out on patrol, just like the police did. They would patrol their own areas, and would report anything they thought was suspicious to the police. I discussed the proposals with Superintendent Parry, who thought the idea was credible but needed it to be sanctioned at a higher level before giving his approval. And so it came into being. Neighbourhood Watch night-time volunteers went out on patrol, mainly during the small hours, between midnight and 4am. Up until then, burglars, largely speaking, were enjoying a free hand to commit night-time crimes virtually anywhere, unimpeded by the 'thin blue line'. I designed posters and metal discs bearing the national Neighbourhood Watch logo, adding words that volunteers were now actively patrolling. The discs and posters were displayed on telephone poles and lamp posts everywhere: 'Neighbourhood Watch night patrols operate in this area'. The main advantage was that the village Neighbourhood Watch groups knew who were local residents, their vehicles, their social habits and so on, so knew that something which looked out of place or suspicious would be worthy of reporting to the police. I kept the concept simple, purposefully trying to keep media attention away from the inevitable criticism that they were vigilante groups. The volunteers were armed only with notepaper, pen and mobile phone, if they were lucky enough to own one. They always patrolled in pairs and were given strict guidelines to adhere to. Each patrol had to telephone the police control room at police headquarters in Worcester before going out on patrol to let them know who they were, the vehicle and registration number they were in and which Neighbourhood Watch group they were affiliated with. Then, after finishing their stint, they were required to telephone headquarters again

12 THE HEREFORD TIMES, THURSDAY, MAY 13, 1993

Alert village in burglar watch

A HIGH-tech parish patrol, supervised and supported by police, is keeping a lookout for burglars preying on a picturesque Herefordshire village.

Organisers say the officially-backed initiative underway in Eardisley could become a model for other rural communities in the county.

The "Eardisley Observers", who regard themselves as a pro-active extension to the village's Neighbourhood Watch scheme, are using search beam torches, mobile telephones and other sophisticated equipment to combat a local crimewave.

But Peter Preece, the former county police officer in charge, dismisses suggestions of a "Magnificent Seven" syndrome saying the observers were vigilant, but not vigilantes.

"The observers are all mature blokes who will go out after dark to keep an eye out for anything that arouses suspicions. Information is passed on to the police and any action is left to them, we don't get involved in that side," he says.

The Observers grew out of local frustration at a recent series of village burglaries.

Raiders have looted the local store three times in succession and struck at both pubs.

The 12th century church and local school have also been attacked along with homes and business premises.

But a month after the Observers took to being out and about they can claim to have foiled at least one burglary. The number reported in the area has also dropped.

Both police and the observers believe similar initiatives, run under strict guidelines, could be adapted to many rural communities.

Other parishes in the Kington area have already tried such schemes with the approval of Superintendent Peter Parry, who heads the Leominster sub-division.

Kington eyes cut out crime

MORE than 200 people around Kington are regularly helping to cut crime by going out on Neighbourhood Watch night patrols.

PC Bill Rowlatt, liaison officer, said that of the 15 Neighbourhood Watch groups in the area, nine frequently went out between dusk and dawn to check their locality.

PC Rowlatt added that the indications were that the presence of the patrols had led to a reduction in crime in the areas.

Night patrols are observatory

■ **By** *EMMA HAWES*

bodies that inform the police of anything suspicious. They are not able to apprehend suspects themselves, but can provide vital information to Kington police force, and there are police guidelines to which the patrols must stick. PC Rowlatt added that at the moment it was too early to to tell if the patrols helped to lower crime rates, but that it was very likely they did.

Local news coverage of the Neighbourhood Watch initiative in 1993

215

to inform them that they were booking 'off duty' as it were. The system worked very efficiently and gained massive popularity, publicity and support. As a consequence, reports to the police came flooding in, resulting in many more arrests than usual. It was not only popular, but effective. Locally reported crimes, particularly burglaries, fell by as much as 50%, and our detection rates were even higher than that. I visited many of the Neighbourhood Watch groups in the county to explain how the system could be set up and by the mid-nineties there were almost 350 Neighbourhood Watch volunteers going out on regular, voluntary patrols covering North Herefordshire. Some

14   THE HEREFORD TIMES, THURSDAY, July 21, 1994

Villains 'get the message'

HEREFORDSHIRE'S "Heartbeat" bobbies, who work in one of the most isolated sub-divisions of the West Mercia police area, can count themselves among the force's top crime-busters.

But PCs patrolling the Kington patch are quick to praise public help in achieving their aims.

Crime in the rural region has dropped by 43 per cent with a detection rate that currently runs at 37 per cent – compared to the 18.4 per cent force average - and counts some notable successes within the figures.

PC Bill Rowlett, Neighbourhood Watch co-ordinator with Kington police, says that the pro-active patrols at work in its parishes have, despite recent controversy, proved their worth with the results .

"It appears our local villains have got the message that it's not safe for them to commit crime in our area anymore. Neighbourhood Watch volunteers will see them and report them," he said.

Observer patrols, which operate in Eardisley, Weobley, Lyonshall and Pembridge, involve local NW members out around their villages and its surrounds by night using mobile phones to alert police over any suspicious activity.

The initiative has been condemned as "coming close to vigilantism" by Brian Rowland, chairman of Herefordshire Neighbourhood Watch, but such comment is dismissed by backers.

"Night patrol groups are doing a tremendously worthwhile job and the results are quite clear to see," said PC Rowlett.

Each group receives a newsletter and plans are afoot for the patrols to take on an even higher profile.

"We have some yellow reflective jackets with the Neighbourhood Watch logo printed on them. A member may wear a jacket, but only when on foot patrol with a uniformed police officer," said PC Rowlett.

still go out on patrol today, 30 years later! The areas actively patrolled were Kington town and rural, Eardisley, Lyonshall, Staunton-on-Arrow, Pembridge, Dilwyn and Weobley. It captured media interest too, with TV coverage and press reports in local and national newspapers attracting attention, even as far away as New Zealand and Australia, and across to the Isle of Man where my friends David and Liz live. Consequently, many police forces across England and Wales contacted me for advice on how to set up similar schemes in their areas. The areas we policed quickly became 'no go' areas for criminal activity. One prisoner we dealt with openly admitted that the areas that had adopted the scheme were 'off limits' to criminals.

I became extremely pleased and proud of the general public's response to the scheme, and encouraged the growth of Neighbourhood Watch patrols by attending group meetings so that the scheme spread throughout the county of Herefordshire, the force area and nationally.

As a result of setting up the scheme, I received a memorandum from Sergeant Shayne Hancock at headquarters with details of a meeting and audience with the then HRH The Prince of Wales.

A small group of us assembled on 22 February 1995 to meet and speak with his Royal Highness, now King Charles III, who was interested in all aspects of community policing. Meeting him was such an honour.

On Remembrance Day 1995 outside Kinnersley Church, alongside our vicar, the late Reverend Ken Newbon

CHIEF CONSTABLE
D. C. BLAKEY, Q.P.M., M.B.A.

Tel. No. 0905-723000
Fax No. 0905 454226

Reference: *SH/AC*

Your Ref.:

16th February, 1995

Dear PC. Rowlatt

Arrangements have now been finalised for the visit of His Royal Highness The Prince of Wales to the Force Training School on Wednesday, 22nd February, 1995.

As you may be aware, His Royal Highness is a keen advocate of community policing initiatives and the Chief Constable has been advised, through the Prince's Private Secretary, that he may be interested in talking to a number of community based constables on the day of his visit. The Chief Constable chose to respond to this by inviting a representative from each Sub-Division. Dress for the day will be full uniform (no medals).

It would be helpful if you could arrive at Headquarters and be in the Social Club by 11.00 am, where refreshments will be available. You will be 'grouped' with your fellow community beat officers in order that you can be readily identified to His Royal Highness should he wish to speak to you.

Following the official opening of the Training School a buffet lunch will be served in the main canteen. Car parking spaces have been reserved in the South Car Park. A numbered car parking pass is enclosed which you are requested to display on the dashboard of your vehicle. Your co-operation in this area will obviously help considerably with security on the day.

For those of you unfamiliar with the new Training School complex a site plan is enclosed.

Yours sincerely

S. Hancock

S. Hancock
Sergeant
Chief Officers' Support Unit

PC. 264 Rowlatt
Leominster Sub-Division

West Mercia Headquarters, P.O. Box 55, Hindlip Hall, Worcester, WR3 8SP
(Counties of Hereford & Worcester and Shropshire)

Memorandum from headquarters about meeting HRH Prince Charles
(as he was then), February 1995

BUMBLEBEE SQUAD AND OUT OF OUR SHEDS

As mentioned earlier, during the mid-nineties I transferred back into plain clothes duty as a detective constable at Leominster, working alongside a small group of five detectives known as the 'bumblebee squad'. It was committed and dedicated police-work, headed by Detective Inspector Rick Parry, who was meticulous when it came to his team's efforts to solve crimes. During my time with the squad, I was asked by Chief Inspector B to assist with the planning and organisation of a covert police operation, which would culminate in dozens of morning raids taking place simultaneously on a specific date, throughout the sub-division and across the border into Shropshire, including the area in and around the market town of Ludlow. The early morning raids were based on intelligence gathered by bumblebee-squad detectives, and would focus on seizing drugs and stolen property. I was provided with an office, a budget and a time-frame of a couple of months to coordinate the information, documents and equipment needed for the operation's success. The operation involved 109 uniformed officers and plain clothes detectives from across the division, drafted in to execute search warrants. With that many officers and civilian staff involved, it was difficult for the operation (named Operation Bumblebee) to be kept covert until strike day, but it was. Part of my brief was to organise meals for all 109 police officers, who needed to be fed breakfast and one other cooked meal, provided at staggered intervals during the day. I negotiated terms with Walters trouser factory in Ludlow and Safeways in Leominster to provide the meals in their staff canteens. Officers were divided into individual teams and given numerically-marked boxes containing the equipment they'd need, with concise instructions inside each one to include forensic bags, labels, gloves, crowbar, sledge hammer, search warrants, maps, directions and the addresses they would search. On strike day, just a handful of senior officers and police civilian personnel had first-hand knowledge of what Operation Bumblebee involved, or the time it had taken to prepare and plan for it. All officers taking part had their duty rosters changed before strike day and were instructed to rendezvous at 4am at Russell Baldwin & Bright's saleroom, which at the time was located behind the police station in Ryelands Road, both of which have long since gone. The early morning gathering and briefings were led by senior officers and detectives, after which everyone left in dozens of police vehicles to travel to their various target destinations. At the end of the day, the operation made headlines in the local and national press, with coverage on local radio and TV.

I enjoyed live music and taught myself to play the drums at the age of 14. In the late seventies I bought myself a new Premier drum kit, complete with a full set of Paiste symbols and invited one or two musically-minded friends to form a band. We spent hours practising, hoping to achieve a reasonable standard before being brave enough to go out and perform at proper gigs. It was difficult to find somewhere local to practise so the sound of our rehearsals wouldn't disturb people. We started off in Steve Graham's garden shed at Almeley. After practising, we thought we were getting a lot better, when in fact we were probably just getting a lot louder! I hadn't given any thought about the local residential home in Almeley, run by Tim and Joyce Jones, until a complaint was received about the noise and disturbance to their residents by a live band practising nearby, and I had to lie low for a while. Fortunately, they didn't find

220

out that I was the noisy drummer until years later. Eventually, our first public performance happened one Saturday evening at the New Inn, now The New Strand, in Eardisley. We were all nervous, especially me, and we named the band 'Out of our Sheds' because of our early days practising in Steve Graham's shed. I advertised our very first gig in the local listings magazine *Broad Sheep*, and surprisingly quite a few people turned up. We had about 12 cover songs on our playlist but, due to nerves, our first two songs didn't sound too good. My friend Steve Graham kept apologising for making mistakes on his bass guitar but, having never picked one up in his life before, I think his apology wasn't all that necessary. He was keen. Sitting in the audience and listening to our first performance were two doctors who we hadn't met before, Doctors John Duffet and Pete Howard. After playing our first two songs, they came up to me to introduce themselves. They'd brought their electric guitars and amplifiers with them, and asked if they could plug them in and join in. Relief! I'm pretty sure they felt sorry for us, and were offering to dig us out of the musical doldrums, which frankly we desperately needed. They lifted the lids of their glossy guitar cases and took out their electric guitars, plugging them in. Before playing a single chord, I had a pretty good idea that they were accomplished musicians and we weren't disappointed. They knew all of our playlist and more, and we were soon up and playing again. It was like a musical magic wand had been waved over us. They lifted our spirits, and took us to a more professional-sounding level of rhythm and blues music, and 'Yippee', I was in a band!

'Out of our Sheds' or 'The Sheds', as we became known, became a popular rhythm and blues band, and gigs started to roll in. Our choice of music delighted audiences and we had so

221

much fun playing. Various band members came and left during the 12 years we were together. Gareth Phillpotts played blues harp, Don from Pembridge rhythm and lead, Francine from Kington, who was a student at the University of Oxford, played saxophone. The late Sam Spears, as guitarist and vocalist, was our front man and a teacher at Lady Hawkins school. Brother and sister vocalists were Helen and Martin. Jeremy Linguard, also a teacher at Lady Hawkins, sometimes stepped in to play keyboard for us. Cliff, son of my former boss Sergeant Ken Campbell, played bass guitar exceptionally well. Doctors Pete and John shared rhythm and lead guitar and stuck with us for the 12 years we were together, even after our first night's shaky performance! Martin from Burghill was another very talented and accomplished guitarist and a Jimmy Hendrix fanatic. We had a few excellent bass players who came and went: Nicky Davies from Eardisley (who's mum, Linda, cut my hair in double-quick time, getting me out of a spot of bother with the chief superintendent!); Martin Henning from Kinnersley Castle; and Colin, who owned a music shop in Hereford; then, latterly, Julian Greenway (who later became my gravedigger and a community police support officer). Julian's wife, Helen, was another vocalist. Len, who was licensee at the Tram Inn as well as Helen and Martin's dad, became our sound engineer, though being partially deaf in one ear presented a few sound-mixing difficulties! Have you ever noticed that no one likes to admit they've gone a bit deaf? My friend Steve Graham (one of Father Christmas's helicopter pilots) graciously bowed out from playing bass guitar in the early days after a couple of very courageous efforts. Thanks Steve, but at least you were there at the beginning. There were as many as ten of us in the line up at one gig we played, and our music was predominantly rhythm and blues covers, including songs by The Blues Brothers, Stevie Ray Vaughn, The Rolling Stones (Route 66, Walking the Dog, Jumpin Jack flash), Alanis Morrissette (Hand in my Pocket), John Mayall (Aint no Brakeman), Muddy Waters (Hoochie Coochie Man), Tina Turner (Addicted to Love), Bryan Adams, ZZ Top, The Beatles, Fleetwood Mac, Cream (Crossroads), Jimmy Hendrix (All Along the Watch Tower), Ry Cooder, Neil Young and so many more. We usually started each gig with Green Onions by Booker T. & the MG's. Someone said that if you know this song, then you have good musical taste. We once played at a private party for some doctors at Tarrington. Doctors and nurses were dancing with each other and enjoying our music so much that the girls started to take off their knickers and throw them at us. I found it difficult making one of the cymbals resonate properly when it was covered by a frilly black pair! (Don't try this at home!) I took responsibility for booking all the band's gigs and, apart from some expenses, our fees were all donated to local and national charities such as St Michael's Hospice or Cancer Research etc. During the 12 years we played, we raised many thousands of pounds for local charities and good causes. I'm really proud of our achievement. All of us had jobs, so we all unanimously agreed to give our fee to charity. We bought an old laundry van from Tim Hall at Kington laundry. Len fitted a row of bench seats in the back behind the front seats and behind them was just enough space to stack our musical instruments, drums and amplifiers. Sometimes, as many as eight of us would travel in the van, together with all of our equipment. We were illegally overloaded, but we never did get stopped or checked by the police, which is another lucky escape to add to my list. We painted our ex-laundry van with the 'Out of our Sheds' logo on both sides, and we enjoyed loads of laughs and good times together. One year, we were invited to the prestigious Bulldog Bash to compete in the annual battle of the bands competition. It took place somewhere in Wales, but its exact location was never announced until the very last moment. The Bulldog Bash was initiated in the '70s by the Hells Angels. We were honoured to be asked to take part at their summer gig, which lasted the whole weekend. When we arrived in our overloaded laundry van, there were literally hundreds of motorcycles lined up on either side of a long drive leading to the stage in a field; a bit like Glastonbury, with masses of people camping outside. Leaving the others in the van, I walked into a marquee to find one of the organisers to let them know we'd arrived. Walking back to the van I caught some whiffs of the all-too-familiar cannabis smoke from spliffs, and decided we should keep a low profile. All our musical instruments were unloaded for us by some heavily-tattooed, muscular men dressed in their Hells Angel leathers. Just before it was time for us to play, all our equipment was carried on stage and connected up. Their amplification systems were brilliant, as were their sound engineers. My drums were miked up, with the bass drum giving out the loudest resounding boom which echoed round the valley for miles. Although goodhearted, I don't think any of our hosts would have warmed to the idea that the drummer in the band was a police officer and an ex-drug squad officer, so I insisted that it would be far safer if none of us mentioned it! Just look at what happened in the Blues Brothers film when they pretended to be the Good Old Boys? It was a brilliant gig, and we finished playing at around 4am after being judged top live band of three. What an accolade!

For several years, we were invited by sisters Jane and Rose to the New Inn at Pembridge, where we played gigs during the

Out of Our Sheds playing at the New Inn, Pembridge. From left to right:
Dr John (lead/Rhythm guitar), Me (drums), Martin (vocalist), Colin (bass)
behind Helen (vocalist) and Dr Pete (lead /Rhythm guitar)

summer in the old market square outside. Other bands and
performers were invited to play or join us for a jam session,
giving anyone the opportunity to have a go. During
the winter, we played in the New Inn's basement room
downstairs. We also sold 'Out of our Sheds' printed
T-shirts and cassette tapes of songs we'd recorded at a
local recording studio in Leominster.

●BARBECUE — MORE than 200 people
supported a barbecue evening at the
New Inn, Pembridge, and helped raise
£600 for the St Michael's Hospice at
Bartestree. The organisers thank all
who supported the event, the local
Blues band 'Out of Our Sheds' for providing excellent live music, and the
New Inn for some superb food.

It's important to have interests outside of work – and the
band helped us to relax after the everyday stresses of being in
responsible jobs. It's a cliché but we worked hard and played
hard too.

RETURNING TO KINGTON
AND THE WAY WE DID THINGS

A FTER the bumblebee squad was disbanded, I returned to Kington to work back in uniform. On occasions, having a sense of humour was important when looking for a solution to tricky situations. We tried to deal with life's little difficulties sensitively and responsibly, using good old-fashioned policing methods and local knowledge, which this next story depicts. Dick and I were on duty together in the police Land Rover when we received the report that a local vulnerable lady was missing or 'misper', which is the police abbreviation for a missing person. We knew the family and the lady in question as they lived locally, so we set off to search for her, and quickly located this gentle, but quite determined, middle-aged lady who had learning disabilities. We found her perilously walking by the side of the main A4112 road towards Leominster. After stopping and talking with her, we found out that there had been a family disagreement, which was the reason she had decided to leave home. Our priority now was to reunite her with her family. However, no amount of gentle persuasion could coax her into the front seats of the Land Rover to come with us; though lots of patience and gentle persuasion was the only way. We tried, but we were hopelessly failing to persuade her until we remembered that she and her family occasionally attended church, so we started singing the first verse of the hymn We Plough the Fields and Scatter ... Her eyes immediately lit up and she gave us a big beaming smile, before bursting into song with us then immediately climbing up into the front seats. We sang the whole of the first hymn together (which Dick and I knew having both been church wardens), followed by another well-known hymn, How Great Thou Art, which we all sang at the top of our voices. It was magic, and lifted all of our spirits. We didn't hold back as we drove into Weobley high street on a scorching hot summer's day with the police Land Rover's windows wound down, though receiving some odd stares and puzzled expressions from people as we drove past them. Next up ... What a Friend We Have In Jesus! – a rip-roaring hymn written by a preacher living in Canada in the 1880s. After arriving outside the family's home, we stepped down from the front seats and walked up to the house, still singing the final verses of the third hymn. We were greeted by the lady's family who were very relieved and happy to see that she was safely home again, along with her police choir escort! I noticed an inquisitive group of neighbours huddled together gossiping and watching what we were doing, but that didn't matter because the job got done, albeit by our slightly unconventional 'Ways and Means Act' ... Alleluia!

One late afternoon, Mossy and Dick travelled to Hereford police station to deliver an urgent despatch, with Dick driving the police Astra. As they were driving along Whitecross Road on their way back to Kington from the police station, Mossy got caught short and urgently needed to find a gent's loo! Seeing a warehouse and business premises to his left, he asked Dick to pull over and park outside. Mossy ran into the building to ask someone if he could use their toilet facilities. He couldn't find anyone, but he saw the gent's loo sign above a door in the corner of the warehouse and made a dash for it. Moments later, with his uniform trousers down around his ankles, he heard the ratcheting sound of the roller shutter door outside. After feeling relieved, he walked aimlessly around inside trying to find someone when it dawned on him that it was after 5.30pm.

All the staff had finished work and gone home, leaving him locked inside and alone! Panic stations! Now, for entirely different reasons, he was just as desperate to get out as he was to get in! He walked through a door which led him into an office that had a large window overlooking the pavement and road outside. He could see Dick still patiently waiting for him in the police car, and he shouted and hammered on the office window, trying to attract his attention. Above the large office window was a smaller casement window which John opened to shout through to Dick, but the casement window was higher than he could reach. Turning the office metal waste paper bin upside down, he stood on it and shouted out loudly through the window, with his neck and head extended to one side, trying to raise the alarm. Luckily, this time Dick saw him and heard his desperate cry for help. 'Dick, Dick. I'm locked in!' No sooner had he shouted out, he completely lost his balance. Both feet slipped off the bin he was standing on so he fell sideways and shot forwards, and the whole of his body went crashing though the office window and onto the pavement outside. Walking past at the time was an elderly lady with her shopping trolley who had seen it happen, so she stopped and bent down to talk to him. Taking hold of his arm, she was surprised to see that she was helping up an able-bodied police sergeant but caringly asked him, 'Are you alright, dear?' By now, Dick, who had seen it all happen, went into raptures of laughter. After thanking the lady, Mossy brushed himself off and was relieved to find that he hadn't sustained a single cut or blemish after landing in the middle of all the jagged fragments of glass. 'Dick, we need to radio Hereford control room and ask them to contact the key-holder!' Mossy said, but Dick was in no fit state to speak or to send a radio message. After the police contacted the keyholder, the manager, who had been the last person to lock up and leave, arrived. 'I can't believe that someone's just tried to break in, sergeant,' he incorrectly assumed. 'I only left here about five minutes ago!' Mossy explained about his urgent call of nature, and insisted on paying for the damage so that none of his bosses would find out, especially the chief superintendent. In fact, no one ever did find out what happened, apart from Dick, the manager, the kind elderly lady, me and now all you readers!

There were certainly a few decisions we took then that would surely have got us into deep water these days. For example, we sometimes dealt with a few young local lads' drunkenness or high-spirited anti-social behaviour by some rather unorthodox methods rather than arresting them. Occasionally we resorted to our infamous 'Ways and Means Act'! Friday and Saturday nights were usually when trouble broke out in the town, often when there were just two of us on duty to deal with fights or incidents involving public disorder. Locals referred to Friday nights in Kington as 'Fighting Fridays'! A ploy we sometimes adopted was to get them to sit in the police vehicle so they thought they were being arrested, but then we took them on a magical mystery tour a couple of miles out of town on the Brilley road, and dropped them off somewhere between Hergest and the top of the Brilley mountain, depending on how drunk or argumentative they were. There they had plenty of time to walk back into town or to head home, which they usually did after sobering up!

One busy Saturday night in Kington nearly ended in a riot. It was a hot summer's evening and many young lads were drinking too much, causing tempers to run high and for fights to break out at several pubs and areas around the town. There were two of us on duty, but, on this particular evening, three

229

local bobbies had heard what was happening and had come in to volunteer to be on duty after realising that the situation was becoming too difficult for us to contain. We had just moved police stations, from the old police station in Market Hall Street to the new one in Churchill Road, opposite the fire station. The old police station had two cells, but presumably a critical design mistake meant that the new one only had a single cell. During the evening, a young lad, who was causing trouble and fighting, was arrested and taken to the new police station. In the absence of Sergeant Moss, who was off duty, I stepped in to act as custody officer. This meant writing out the young prisoner's name and details onto a custody record, then searching him, before locking him up inside the single cell. Soon after shutting and locking the cell door, two more prisoners arrived at the back door after being arrested. It was fair to say that bedlam had broken out in the town, with fights gaining momentum at lots of locations, and now our four bobbies were already finding it difficult to cope. After leaving the two prisoners with me, they went back into town to try to quell what was now a worsening public order situation. Just before they left, I had no alternative but to place the two prisoners into the same cell as the first prisoner, so all three of them were together. After locking the reinforced steel door, I placed the cell key in my pocket for safekeeping. About ten minutes later, PC Paul Kirkham came in through the back door, which is next to the cell, and shouted, 'Bill, there's a fire in the cell!' Oh Shit! I ran from the office to the cell and looked through the round glass spy hole in the cell door which revealed a bright orange glow, resembling the inside of a log burner, with the three prisoners locked inside! I fumbled in my pocket for the key to unlock it and we dived in with fire extinguishers. The smoke-filled cell was ablaze! The three had bundled up the single cell's mattress, pillows and blankets and placed them against the cell door, and set fire to the lot. All of them suffered from smoke inhalation, but they were all thankfully still alive – just. An urgent assistance call went out to the ambulance, fire and for police reinforcements from Hereford and Leominster. As I saw things, and if you pardon my expression, I was in the shit! We cleared the cell of the smouldering remnants, and I rang the duty inspector, Inspector S, to inform him, then typed out a full A.30 report outlining all the relevant facts and circumstances, and submitted it to the inspector. I felt certain that I would be severely reprimanded or disciplined by head-quarters, but I had no idea. It was indeed a miracle, or an angel at my shoulder, that none of them died. A week passed, then two weeks, then three. I hadn't heard anything, so I plucked up courage and rang Inspector S. 'Hello Sir, I was just ringing to ask you about the report I submitted to you regarding the incident at Kington?' 'What report? what incident?' he replied. I paused, 'Oh, OK, Sir, thank you!' That was how our conversation ended and I never heard another word. I was grateful for his wise and placid decision. My report had obviously gone nowhere other than into his waste paper bin which came as a relief. We were only trying to do our level best, under extreme and difficult circumstances. On the other hand, this was most definitely another very lucky escape, not just for me this time, but for the other three who came so near to death.

At the age of 45, I'd completed 26 happy and fulfilling years as a uniformed police constable and as a detective constable with the Criminal Investigation Department, drugs squad, and bumblebee squad. In order to retire with a pension, I needed to complete a further four years to reach the age of 49 but, even then, I wasn't sure whether I wanted to retire at that age or opt to continue working up to the maximum age of 55. I hadn't any idea what career or employment I would move into, if any, but the earliest age I could retire was 49, which has since changed.

The following year, in 1996, Superintendent Pete Parry called me to his office at Leominster, wanting to discuss something with me which I wasn't expecting, but I was pleasantly surprised when he told me. He said that he wanted to acknowledge the work and commitment I'd given in establishing the new Neighbourhood Watch initiative, and had decided to put my name forward to the chief constable for the force's national Community Police Officer of the Year Award, sponsored by the National Police Review. I was not only surprised, but astonished, to be told that my name was being added to other finalists from around the country. This auspicious occasion would be held at the law courts in Chancery Lane, London, where I would meet the Home Secretary, the Right Honourable Lord James Callaghan of Cardiff, who also became Chancellor of the Exchequer, Foreign Secretary and later Prime Minister. I travelled to London to receive the award, accompanied by my wife Janette and friends Brian and Diana Watkins from Weobley. Brian was a local veterinary surgeon, author and, at that time, chairman of the West Mercia police authority. In London, we were given five-star accommodation and enjoyed a lavish award ceremony dinner, followed by an after-dinner speech by the late Lord Callaghan, who in my opinion was a true gentleman and a very committed politician. I remember him delivering his jaw-dropping speech without referring to any notes.

After this, I continued to work at Kington before becoming, for a few months, a uniformed beat manager at Leominster.

I then moved back to Kington, where I was given responsibility for promoting all existing Neighbourhood Watch groups, as well as setting up new groups, assisted by local community beat officers around the county. I became recognised as an authority for all Neighbourhood Watch matters, and was provided with the police community relations mobile unit to attend village fêtes and shows, setting up displays

On being awarded the Community Police Officer of the Year Award, 1996

and drop-in centres at Ledbury, Ross, Ludlow and Hereford, so I could encourage and promote community policing and maintain good public/police relations.

MAKING MY MIND UP

A T about that time, my 25-year marriage ended in separation and divorce, though we continue to love and enjoy very special close relationships with our four, now grown-up, grandchildren, Josh, Poppy, Chloe and Adam. After separating, I had nowhere to live. I was on annual leave which gave me time to look around for somewhere to rent, but I didn't find anything immediately suitable. Then, what happened just happened. My belief in God has always been with me since I can remember

The police community relations mobile unit

and, as such, I knew that his love for me would help sustain me through this difficult period in my life. On the positive side, I was beginning to feel that I was being true to myself again and becoming my own person. I felt enormously grateful and receptive to God, and deep down I trusted that he would be there with me, helping me through some very harsh and difficult times. One afternoon, I was driving through Kinnersley, where Kate and her family live at Kinnersely Castle, and – this was entirely impromptu and I couldn't explain why or how it happened – I found myself turning right off the main road and driving up the drive to the castle, with the thought in my head to ask Kate if she would rent me a room for a couple of weeks until I could find alternative accommodation. Kate and her family are extremely kind and, after explaining my personal circumstances to them, they agreed to rent me a room. I moved into a small single room with practically none of my personal possessions or any plans, other than to stay there for a couple of weeks, when in fact I ended up staying with them for ten months. During this time, I was let down by a few people who

I mistakenly thought were my friends, but turned out not to be. And there were others, who I hadn't expected to be supportive but were. It's an odd life, and people never cease to amaze me. Kate and her family were all brilliantly caring, hospitable, kind and as close as any family could be, welcoming me into their home, which was exactly what I needed at that time. This happened during mid-summer so I busied myself by digging the castle's vegetable patch and helping John their gardener to mow the large castle lawns. I attended meetings at the Quaker meeting house in Almeley for some peace and tranquillity, and I joined yoga classes with my dear friend and yoga teacher, Jenny Matthews. I always tell her she is an angel. This was a pivotal time for spiritual thought and healing – I was now alone and starting out again for the rest of my life's journey. It was just beginning to feel like this part of my life was meant to be. I was invited to share meals with Kate and her family, and I joined in with various events taking place at the castle – French Bretton dancing, yoga, healing courses and singing etc. I shed two stone in weight having to adjust from how my life was, to how it was then, to what it might become.

Though I had no idea of it at the time, a knee injury sustained at work was to dramatically change my life's direction yet again. We were drafted in to assist at an Animal Liberation Front demonstration taking place at Ledbury. Myself, five other officers and a sergeant were ordered into an area that was at the back and out of sight of the main group of demonstrators as backup, if the group decided to change tactics and split up in different directions. Following in a line, we climbed up to the top of a high wire fence near the Ledbury viaduct. From the top was a sharp drop down to the other side. I climbed up and over the fence but accidentally fell onto the ground, landing awkwardly and injuring my knee which immediately became painful and swollen. I visited my GP to report sick for a week, to give time for it to heal before returning to work. After coming back to work, I was sent to deal with two violent incidents just weeks apart from each other. The first was a tussle with a drunken guest at an after-wedding reception at a pub in Leominster, and the second incident involved the disarming of a suspect carrying a knife at the Oxford Arms in Kington. Unfortunately, during these two arrests, it was sods law that the point of impact, after being thrown about a bit, should be the same knee, which was slammed down onto the hard ground. This added further complications to the existing injury, which then became painful to walk on. The prognosis was more serious than I thought – tests and x-rays showed that it was a permanent injury which needed to be assessed by the police surgeon. The police surgeon instructed me to report sick, and my request to be transferred to an office job was declined. It wasn't force policy at that particular time to allow that to happen, although the policy may now be different. I was pronounced medically unfit, along with being categorised as operationally unfit, and therefore would not be allowed to continue with any police duties. Effectively, it felt like I was being made redundant, after leading such an active, full-on police career. I was placed on permanent sick leave for ten months which nearly drove me crackers. After living in my room at Kinnersley Castle, I successfully applied to rent a small two-bedroom housing association house at Mountain View in Almeley, which was on a small newly-built estate. Among other interests, I became a volunteer driver for the community wheels organisation, which I hoped would relieve some of the boredom from suddenly not working. I'd already made up my mind that

I was going to build a positive future for myself, and I wasn't too old to begin a completely new career at the ripe old age of almost 49! The police had been my life-long ambition since I was at school, and I was fortunate because I'd thoroughly enjoyed my job. I remember my dad saying 'They take the best years of your life'. How right he was!

I'd been thinking about finding a job or a profession that I could follow after my retirement from the force, and my divorce. I needed to start focussing on something positive again, and I decided to set up my own business as a funeral director – I felt that this was a caring profession, and I knew how much I enjoyed caring for people, especially during difficult times and sad situations. I knew very little about the profession, so I contacted a couple of local funeral directors, who I knew and had met attending fatal accidents, suicides and sudden deaths, to learn as much as I could. I made effective use of my enforced sick leave to research and to prepare myself to become a funeral director, and I knew that my business had to be called 'Oak Tree Funeral Services'. Growing in John Mockler's field, on the other side of my garden fence in Mountain View, is the most perfectly shaped mature English oak tree (Quercus Roba). After moving into my house, the oak tree became a focal point in my thoughts. I truly revered the tree, continuously admiring and appreciating its magnificence, its beauty and strength. Something started to unravel, very gently and incrementally. My mind and body were linked to its energy, which I began to realise was this tree's natural store of healing energy, deep inside it, drawing up from its roots and trunk, and permeating out through its branches. This was extraordinary, but I felt that the oak was beginning to transfer energy over to me; something I would simply call 'tree healing', at a time when I really wanted to receive healing and was receptive to it. One afternoon, I was meditating and looking out at the oak tree through my open bedroom window when I started to receive what I would describe as compassionate ripples of gentle, soothing energy, which were emanating from the tree's central core and flowing into the depths of mine. This wholesome feeling and awesome experience ran through me, deep into my soul and heart centre, leaving me with what I would describe as a gift or a beautiful present. The 'tree healing' helped me to relax, while sending me gentle waves of affection, peace and love, which flowed right through me and which felt as natural as the blood running through my veins. I had no idea that this was possible or that it could happen, until it happened to me, and it was repeated several times. I instinctively knew how important it was for me to acknowledge my thanks each time, and I sent love and gratitude back in return. The tree healing energy helped me in such wonderful ways, and it has helped others too from the link that was formed. We are all connected with nature, and there is so much we don't know about how nature can help us, if we only empty our minds and open our hearts to nature's gifts. Oak trees are solid and dependable, and coffins are still made from them. Marriage ceremonies in ancient times took place beneath their splendid canopy of branches, and acorns were placed under children's cots to ward off illnesses and evil spirits.

I suspected rumours were circulating about me from a couple of individuals, perhaps fuelled by jealously. Gossip had reached the ears of some of the hierarchy at police headquarters that I was utilising my sick leave period to my own advantage, researching and sorting out a future for myself. I won't deny that this was exactly what was happening and I had no problem with it being known, but often jealousy and envy can take hold of some people, which is when we need to try and stay one step ahead. I've always had what I would describe as lucky alarm bells, which help me to differentiate between people who are genuinely friendly, honest and helpful with those who can't be. Consequently, one morning, I received a telephone call. 'Is that Oak Tree Funeral Services?' the male voice at the other end enquired in a strong Birmingham accent. 'It might be!' I replied. In an instant, my lucky alarm bells tinkled as I immediately recognised the caller's voice as that of Superintendent D, who I had worked with years before. His career path had taken him through promotion from constable to the dizzy heights of superintendent, whose job it was now to investigate complaints with the force's complaints and discipline department at headquarters. 'Bill,' he said, 'You can be a funeral director or a police officer, but you can't be both!' 'I'm not yet!' I remonstrated. 'You have a week to decide what you're going to do. The chief constable's going nuts.' 'Give me a fortnight?' I jested. 'No, Bill, a week and no longer,' D insisted. By that time, I'd completed my requisite 30 years' police service, so reluctantly I posted off my letter of retirement to the chief constable. It was such a disappointment that my retirement from the job I loved ended as it did, in this unsatisfactory way. The official date of my retirement was the 1 January 2000. I remember telling PC C, a young police officer who I'd worked with at Leominster for a short period, that I was retiring, and he said, 'We'll miss you, Bill'. I'm never comfortable receiving compliments, and retorted, 'Don't be so bloody silly!' He continued, 'No Bill, we will. You have the ability of bollocking the bosses with respect'. Now that meant so much more to me than a compliment. I arranged for my retirement party to take place on the evening of Friday 26 February 2000 at the Tram Inn. I put up posters around the area and invited everyone to come along and share a free buffet and round of drinks party evening. The pub was packed (must have been something to do with the free buffet and free round of drinks!) A couple of speeches took place. I was surrounded by friends, some family, colleagues and local people who came along to wish me well in retirement. My friend Clive Davies did a comedy half-hour stint mimicking the famous comedian Jethro to a tee, and 'Out of our Sheds' played well into the early hours. This was my final opportunity to say a fond farewell to a very genuine, close, caring community from in and around Eardisley, who I had the good fortune of knowing intimately since 1973. In all that time I was extremely proud to be there for them. Eardisley was and is a very special place to live, among many exceptionally genuine, good and honest people.

MY CAREER CHANGE

So now a brand-new chapter in my life was beginning, and I had no idea where it would take me. My dear daughter Lucy (who is so much on my mind at the moment and who I will mention later) drew a magnificent pencil drawing of the oak tree at Almeley which became my business logo. I had no business premises, no chapel of rest, no hearse and no staff, but I did have a plan and a dogged determination to succeed. I was hoping that I could rely on support from local people who knew me, and knew that I'd changed occupations from police officer to funeral director. My friend Len, who helped me to restore Ivy Cottage, was a former funeral director at Kington, with his father Ken. Len helped me and gave me lots of useful advice. Someone came up with nicknames for us. As a policeman, I was known locally as 'Bill the Bobby' and, as an undertaker, I was 'Bill the Box'! (Helping me was 'Len the Lid'!) 'Bill the Box' stuck with me for more than 20 years, though now it might be time for a final change to 'Bill the Book'! At the beginning, I worked with Abbey Funeral Services in Leominster as a bearer, then went on to arrange and direct funerals for the proprietor, Gabriel. The late Bob Hillstead had worked for decades, up until the 1960s, for local builder and funeral director Walter Howells in Eardisley, who built Eardisley police

Lucy's wonderful pencil drawing of the magnificent oak tree – my business logo for Oak Tree Funeral Services

station in the 1950s. Bob handed down to me several useful tips which he'd learnt from Walter. There was a lot to learn, from the practical aspect of dealing with a deceased's body to talking with families about funeral arrangements. Fortunately, I already had a wealth of experience dealing with the general public as a police officer, and a natural empathy for people. I wanted to give my personal best to each family, so they knew I could be relied upon to give advice and suggestions for how to make their loved one's funeral a unique and memorable celebration. I wanted to treat everyone as I would want to be treated myself, with respect and care. My written statement was: 'We care for you and for those you love from the moment you contact us'. These were not just words, but serious and honest intentions.

The next priority was to find a suitable building to be a chapel of rest, preferably renting rather than buying a building, as it would be foolhardy to buy somewhere when the business was not yet established. I started by turning my spare bedroom into an office. The council owned a redundant chapel of rest, known as the Cemetery Chapel, ideally sited in the middle of Kington's cemetery on the A4111 Eardisley road, just outside the town. The chapel, which was built in the early 1800s, had not been used as a chapel of rest for nearly 30 years after it was divided into two sections. The south-facing half was used for small funeral services where a deceased's body would stay in their coffin until the day of the funeral. This half of the chapel was used by families who were Christian – Roman Catholics, Baptists, Methodists or any other Christian denomination. The north-facing half was used by non-conformist, non-religious families. Whichever half was used, the funeral service was held there until the coffin was carried out and placed onto a wooden bier, which is still there and still used on occasions. The coffin was secured to the bier by leather straps, and pulled along like a hand cart from the chapel to the graveside for burial. The minister walked in front, followed by the funeral director with the coffin strapped to the bier, then finally by the mourners who followed behind. Traditional funerals have continued in this way since time immemorial. Other funeral services were held at St Mary's Church, the Methodist and Baptist churches or the Roman Catholic church in Kington, followed by burial at the cemetery, or cremation in Hereford. Cremations started in the late 1880s, but were formerly legalised in 1902, becoming more and more common since. Today, approximately 80% are cremations. I took the bull by the horns and telephoned a representative in the Herefordshire council offices to explain what

I was looking for, and to ask if they might consider renting the chapel to me. I then collected the key to look around the inside. The depth of dust and mass of cobwebs was unimaginable! Birds were flying in and out of the chapel through a gap in the bell tower, depositing droppings all over the Victorian pews and onto the now thread-bare crimson velvet altar cloth, which covered a solid oak altar table. It had been untouched since the two large oval chapel doors were closed and locked in the 1960s. Inside was a bit like Miss Havisham's! The exterior of the building was well maintained by the council, but the inside was a completely different picture – dirty and damp. The public toilets, built by the council, were still used by visitors to the cemetery and, if my plan succeeded, they would be a useful asset for visitors to the chapel, unlike Leominster cemetery chapel which had no mains electricity and no water supply. It would take a lot of work, expense and effort to bring Kington chapel up to a suitable standard, where bereaved families could sit quietly and comfortably with their loved ones. Being a council matter, it took an age to negotiate rental terms before a formal lease was prepared and finally exchanged. Paperwork and documents went back and forth from solicitors, and the town councillors needed to be consulted, and to approve my use for it following decades of closure. Once the lease was signed, I knew it would take several weeks to refurbish the inside. The majority of town councillors approved of my intended use for it, but just one or two were dead against it, if you pardon the pun! News that a new funeral business was setting up in the area quickly spread. To begin with, I shared facilities with Abbey Funeral Services in Leominster until our chapel of rest at Kington was finally ready to be used. I asked the late Reverend Jen Pollock, who was our vicar in Eardisley, if she would bless the chapel for me, which she did. I purchased an unreliable second-hand hearse from a dealer in Yorkshire, which was all that I could afford, and asked people I knew to be pallbearers for me if there were no family bearers available. Various equipment, including building materials and repairs to the chapel, were expensive. However, during my very first year in 2000, I completed 23 funerals at the average cost of £1,500 per funeral, and any profit was reinvested straight back into the business, which is my advice for anyone thinking of starting up a business themselves. Keep paying the bills!

It quickly dawned on me that I'd joined a very privileged profession and one which was respected and traditionally honoured. I supported families who were often completely devastated by the shock and grief of losing someone close and dear to them, especially if the death was unexpected. My role included personal bereavement counselling, which, for the most part, I'd learnt myself, as well as always being available for anyone who needed to contact me 24/7. What I found slightly surprising was that some bereaved families, who I'd previously dealt with in my former profession, began asking me to arrange funerals for their families too. There were a few setbacks, which is how life is, and some solemn occasions when a little bit of black humour kept us all from being too melancholy! I was learning all the time, and soon realised that there are never two funerals the same. I learnt valuable lessons, gaining much experience along the way, concentrating on attention to detail and being there for families who relied on me. This was just as important for them as it was for me. Funerals were slowly changing. Families were starting to choose the deceased's favourite music to play at their funeral, and were using their photographs in printed order of service booklets. This became more popular, as did non-religious ceremonies. Meaningful celebrations of a person's life, led by funeral celebrants like my good friend Mark Townsend, provided an alternative for families who were starting to drift away from the more traditional style of C of E funerals. In my experience, most families believed in something spiritual or in God, but with Mark, we respected all faiths or none. I was taught, and later practiced, spiritual hands-on healing, after attending different healing courses organised by the NFSH (National Federation of Spiritual Healers). For a couple of years, I joined Healing Earth in Hereford, who opened their doors as a drop-in centre where healers gave hands-on healing for people who came there asking for help. Sometimes I called on the power of healing energy from the universe, asking for it to come and be present to comfort and heal bereaved families when I visited them. Mark, who was a Church of England priest, left the church to become a funeral celebrant and he is so amazing at what he does! As well as being an author and a member of the magic circle, he conducts many funerals for us. I remember one particular funeral service I'd asked him to take at the crematorium in Hereford. A young dad tragically died after losing his battle with a long illness, leaving a widow and their two young sons aged around eight and ten. They came to the crematorium service with their mum, immaculately dressed in smart matching suits and ties, sitting together and close to their mum's side with Mark facing them. During the service, Mark took the lid off a small plastic container and started blowing lots of bubbles, from the soapy liquid inside, that floated all around them. He began by saying, 'Now I know you think I'm mad!' ... pausing to take a short breath before blowing lots more bigger bubbles. 'Do you like bubbles?' he asked the boys, but they were too mesmerised to answer. They obviously did.

He stopped momentarily as the boys were gazing intently at the spectrums of light that were passing through the floating bubbles like rainbows. Mark reached out and caught two bubbles which he magically turned into two clear glass balls. 'Now hold out a hand,' he said to them, as he lovingly placed the two glass balls into their palms, saying, 'Now hold onto these. Whenever you see a rainbow in the sky you can think of your dad because he's there too'. This was such a beautiful, gentle moment, and I am certain that they will never forget the message you gave them, Mark, on the day of their dad's funeral. Bless your heart!

I remember asking Bob Hillstead how long he thought it might take for my business to become fully established. He said about 10 to 12 years, and this was more or less correct. Bob, you were not only my mentor, but my hearse driver too. Although you have passed on, I want to say a great big 'thank you' to you for all your help and advice.

Mechanical diggers eventually replaced gravediggers, who used to dig graves by hand. Pete, who lived at Whitney-on-Wye and had recently retired from his army career, became our first gravedigger, which not only helped him to maintain his fitness levels but also kept him in good shape. An open grave had to achieve a high standard of appearance, with the soil neatly boxed in a square before being covered with green matting, pegged down to stop the wind blowing it away. Every job has its skills, and grave-digging is no exception. Sometimes, the grave sides would collapse just before a burial took place, or the water levels rose from heavy rainfall, which was always why I insisted that the gravedigger was present before, during and after each funeral service. Lots of these skills are never taught or handed down anymore, which is when things go wrong. There were so many details and traditional standards which I wanted to maintain. For example, dressing smartly – as I always did when I wore my police uniform (apart from the time when the chief superintendent caught me with long scruffy hair!). It's a tradition for funeral directors to carry a silver top black cane, a pair of black leather gloves, a top hat and to be dressed in formal funeral attire. Bob advised that I should never wear black gloves at the same time as directing a funeral. Gloves should only be carried in the left hand, or with only the left glove worn, leaving the right hand unfettered to greet and shake hands with the mourners. He showed me how to carry my top hat by cupping it into the palm of the left hand when it wasn't being worn. At times, I've seen shoddily-dressed funeral directors because they've not received any formal training and need to be dressed smartly to earn respect. Bob's advice was that a funeral director should always keep conversations with his or her staff to a minimum, because they should already know what they should be doing and only in exceptional circumstances should the director speak to a member of staff at a funeral, but I've noticed standards slipping! Often, I've heard unnecessary chit chat near the graveside or in church by pallbearers and funeral staff. On rare occasions, when this happened at one of my funerals, I would give them a disapproving look until they stopped talking, or I'd utter a sharp 'Shush!' Grieving families should never be distracted by anything like background chat, which is offensive and disrespectful. This is particularly the case for mourners from an older generation, or ex-servicemen and women who are used to discipline. Staff forgetting to button up their jackets or having crooked ties is another of my pet hates, and any attempt to wear a pair of dark glasses, like a member of the Mafia, would bring a searing response from me! I soon learnt that it's the funeral director's responsibility to quietly correct and keep an eye on the detail, always assessing and checking that everything is running smoothly. When coffins are shouldered into church, judging the distance between the lid of the coffin and the top of an archway is critical! I am pleased to say that it never happened on my watch, but there were times when flowers got jettisoned off the top of a coffin as they came into contact with a low archway or church entrance, something that is extremely unprofessional and completely avoidable. With high standards, Oak Tree Funeral Services would earn the reputation of being smart and dependable, giving us the edge over our competitors. When we were called to someone's house, nursing home or hospice to remove a body, I always left a small posy of freshly-picked flowers on the deceased's pillow. This little bit of kindness meant such a lot to grieving relatives and to care home staff too. The flower posy signified a level of care and compassion without having to say a word. The experience of losing someone we love can affect us all quite differently. Placing a small posy of flowers onto a deceased's pillow sent out a strong unspoken message that their loved one would continue to be cared for at our chapel of rest after being taken away. Often the way we feel can depend on the manner or the circumstances of the person's death, and of course how much they meant to us. We may experience feelings of anger as well as strong emotional turmoil inside, particularly if the death was unexpected. I have often heard families say, 'If only we had been allowed more time to share with them'. I compare our sad emotions and personal grief to tidal waves which ebb and flow. There were other courtesies I adopted. For example, when a person is about to be buried in the same grave as someone else (we call it reopening) and before the second burial takes place, I like to remove my top hat and bow to the open grave in acknowledgement of the person already buried there. Another thing we did was to stop outside the deceased's house for a few seconds, when we drove past in the hearse with the family following, as a mark of respect. These little details mean a great deal to the family.

After Bob retired, Chris from Almeley stepped in as my hearse driver, followed by Peter Bishop, and there were moments when we shared a bit of black humour together. At one funeral, before we travelled to the crematorium, Chris and I loaded the coffin into the hearse at our chapel of rest before driving to a large country house near Pembridge to meet the family, who wanted to follow us in their own cars to the crematorium. Just before we left the house and as a mark of respect, I removed my top hat and bowed to the front door of the gentleman's house to show that this would be his final farewell journey. As I was bowing, the family's pet dog scampered round from the side of the house and sat down inside the front porch to face me. As we drove slowly away, Chris asked me tongue-in-cheek, 'Were you bowing to the house or the dog!?'

In June 2000 I moved from my rented house in Mountain View and bought my own house in Eardisley. The house needed replacement windows, which my friend Colin Croose put in for me, ably assisted by his wife Tanya. Although Colin doesn't like to receive compliments, he is very clever and a talented craftsman. He trained as an apprentice in the traditional skills of carpentry and can turn his hand to almost any job and, like me, he had a good mentor. With a great sense of humour, he is also an accomplished guitar player and plays in a local band. I cannot thank him and Tanya enough for their friendship and for all the work which Colin has completed for me over so many years. Thank you both.

TWO CHAPELS OF REST
AND A FRENCH CONNECTION

I WAS permanently on call, with no inkling of what time of the day or night my phone would ring, to inform me that we were needed to attend a death somewhere. It was all part of the job I was committed to. As with the police, I was used to being called out on Christmas Day and bank holidays. As the business grew, it occurred to me that there was the opportunity to expand across to the Leominster area. Similar to Kington chapel there was a semi-redundant chapel at Leominster cemetery, larger than Kington's and owned by the council. I made enquiries in the hope that I could lease our second chapel of rest from them. The chapel had no mains services connected so I agreed with the council to connect the services at my expense, in return for a reduced yearly rent. So, with Leominster's chapel of rest, the business would reach further east into Leominster and the surrounding areas. Being a lot younger then, I had more energy and the enthusiasm to deal with practically anything, including any problems, more easily. We printed all our own orders of service from my office at home. By chance, two industrial units came up for sale at The Wharf in Eardisley. I used one of them for our office and garaging facilities for the funeral vehicles, and the other for my small collection of vintage cars and as storage space.

Quite a few of my part-time staff were retired from the police. They were either former special constables or retired police officers, and at one point I employed five. The late Phil Wilson was a retired army warrant officer who lived in Eardisley, and, after hearing that I was looking for a part-time assistant, he applied and worked with me from my office at home. He and I enjoyed walking together for regular exercise and became really good friends.

Kington chapel of rest, exterior and interior (left);
Leominster chapel of rest, exterior and interior (right)

I have known another friend, Vera Taylor, since she and her late ex-husband Gerry lived at Winforton Court. After divorcing, Vera went to live in France where she ran a successful property sales and antiques business. In 2002, I wrote to her asking whether she could find me a suitable small property to buy, and flew out to France with my sister Jane. With Vera's help, we looked at a few properties and I finally chose a two-bedroom apartment at No 3 Puits de la Roche in Richelieu, in the beautiful Loire Valley, as an investment and for holidays. Properties were generally far less expensive there than they were here. When I came home, Phil asked me about my visit to France, and I told him that I had been to look at, and agreed to buy, an apartment that was one of five in a block on the outskirts of the medieval town of Richelieu. I was taken aback when Phil expressed a keen interest to buy the other empty apartment directly above mine. A week later, I was back on a plane, this time flying with Phil from Stanstead to Tours airport. We hired a car from Tours to drive to Richelieu and stayed in a house that belonged to Vera, not far away at Descart. After looking at the apartment, Phil and Chris bought theirs almost at the same time as I bought mine. Our two, two-bedroom apartments were practically identical to each other – with the same layout, room sizes and balconies in the lounges overlooking the gardens below. Both bathrooms and kitchens needed a refit, with the kitchens only having a sink and drainer. After buying the apartments, we collected new and second-hand furniture and everything else needed to furnish them. We bought two identical flat-pack fitted kitchens from B&Q in Hereford, which we stored in my barn in Eardisley, and collected furniture, bedding, curtains and everything else needed to make our apartments homely and habitable again. We allowed ourselves six months to gather every single item needed, down to bath plugs and light bulbs, before we hired an articulated lorry and a driver to transport everything from Eardisley to Richelieu. We followed the lorry out to Richelieu, with Phil's stepson, Simon, coming with us to help. It was like a military operation, which of course Phil was very used to in his former career. Phil, Simon and I spent just ten days getting everything fitted in our apartments and fully furnishing them. This included fitting the two kitchens, with new plumbing and gas connections. We took masses of tools with us and every type of gas and water connector because, as you might imagine, the French fittings are different to ours. We worked hard every day and into the night. I don't know how we did it, but we just managed to complete all of the work by the time we had to leave for the ferry crossing from Caen to Portsmouth, and home again. Both apartments were now fully liveable in again. I spent many happy holidays there each year. Friends and family stayed there too, and any of my employees were welcome to visit and stay. I finally sold my apartment after Chris and Phil sold theirs, just before Brexit in December 2019. It came as a relief because, I find the older I am, the less I seem able to cope with the various responsibilities, especially the thought of owning and maintaining a property abroad. The local people in Richelieu were all so friendly and kind. I bought the apartment naively thinking that my family would want to take regular holidays there, as I did, but it was often more exciting, they told me, for them to holiday in different locations. I enjoyed the familiarity of returning to Richelieu year-on-year, visiting friends who lived there permanently, including Alf, Vera, Joseph and others, and always wanting to discover new places, especially French restaurants! I kept four bicycles there which friends and visitors were welcome to use.

After his retirement from the police, Dick became a police community support officer at Kington and also worked for me as a pallbearer and part-time funeral director, which was permitted by the force following a change in police regulations. I recruited Terry into the police years earlier, when he became a special constable, then he worked for Remenco, the animal feeds company,

The beautiful view of the gardens below from the balcony lounge doors

until his retirement. Terry and his wife Rene live in Almeley, and Terry went on to work for me, soon after I set up Oak Tree Funeral Services, as a pallbearer and funeral director. So, the three of us worked together. The way I set up my business was slightly different from most other funeral businesses. I decided that only one of us should have direct contact with a family, from the time a person died until the day of the funeral. This allowed continuity and individual support for the families. They had my office number as well as our home numbers and could contact any of us at any time. We provided details of various counselling and bereavement support organisations, and gave widowers and widows a leaflet called 'Moving On' which is a

Bowling club thrilled with new sponsorship

Kington bowlers show off their new gilets as club president Val Vaughan thanks Bill Rowlatt of Oak Tree Funeral Services which sponsored the new piece of kit

A KINGTON group has been bowled over after they received new gilets sponsored by a local funeral services company.

Kington Bowling Club, which currently has about 50 members, recently received 52 of the smart white and maroon gilets emblazoned with the club badge, from Bill Rowlatt of Oak Tree Funeral Services based at Eardisley, near Kington.

Mr Rowlatt visited the club's ground at Park Road last week to see all the members proudly wearing their gilets.

He said: "I am really pleased that you are happy with the gilets and that you are wearing them tonight.

"We have been in business for the last 18 years and we like to be involved with the local community and are proud to be able to offer our support to Kington Bowling

Club."

Club chairman David Walters said: "We thank Bill and Oak Tree Funeral Services for their most generous sponsorship. We will wear them for home and away matches, competitions and to visit other clubs."

Kington Bowling Club has been in existence since 1898 and it hosts a club night on Mondays and a practice session on Tuesdays between

2pm and 4pm.

The club plays in the Tarmac League which includes 14 clubs mainly in Herefordshire but the club also plays Hay, Talgarth, Knighton and Presteigne. They have a trip every year and also hold social nights at the club house.

They are keen to attract new members, and particularly want to encourage young people to try the sport.

Sponsorship of Kington bowling club

herefordtimes.com/news

Funeral boss doffs hat to youngest pallbearer

By Jess Childs

jess.childs@herefordtimes.com

A FUNERAL director believes his newest recruit could be the youngest pallbearer in the country.

Paul Davies got the job at Oak Tree Funeral Services at Eardisley by impressing boss Bill Rowlatt – despite being just 16.

The teenager, who lives in the village and finished at Lady Hawkins' School in Kington earlier this year, is a somewhat unusual appointment as most who do the job tend to be retired people looking for extra income.

Paul said: "I just came to Bill and asked him if he had any jobs for me and then I started cleaning the funeral vehicles, but then he asked what I would be like doing funerals and I said I'd give it a go.

"It keeps me out of mischief, I just like it as a job."

Bill, who runs the business at home in the village and through two chapels of rest at Kington and Leominster cemeteries, said some clients found having a young person on board helpful and that his protégé had broached some of the tougher elements of the job well.

"Some of the tasks aren't very pleasant and he's very good, he's really taken to it

very well and he's very respectful towards other people, which is important of course," Bill said.

"A lot of people have never seen him in a suit before either. He went into the village shop the other day and they said he had scrubbed up well."

Paul now hopes to achieve various related qualifications

and also pass his driving test to take charge of the various funeral vehicles – once he turns 17.

Working with the deceased has obviously been a steep learning curve for the teenager, but one he seems to be taking in his stride under Bill's supervision.

"The first case I experienced, I was a bit nervous,"

Paul explained. "But now I've just got used to it."

"It's just like they are asleep now to me, I found it weird at first but now I'm fine."

▲ Funeral director Bill Rowlatt thinks he may have found the county's, and possibly the country's, youngest pall bearer in 16-year-old Paul Davies. 103519-2

16-year-old Paul Davies – the youngest pallbearer in the country?

social support group based in Leominster. The group was set up and led by Barbara in Leominster, and it became a very popular and important lifeline for many. After Phil left my employment, Gill Layton, whose husband Andrew is a local farmer, worked with me from my office at home for a while before moving down to work at the industrial unit at the Wharf, while I remained working from home. Gill assisted with funerals and now directs funerals, as well as organising other office tasks such as the design and printing of orders of service and administration. Gill was later joined by Sally Lane, whose husband Tim is also a local farmer. Gill and Sally made huge personal contributions to my business, and together they are an exceptionally wonderful loyal team. I could not have wished for better, or more loyal and dedicated staff over the years.

There were a couple of times when funerals could have ended up differently to how they did. One harsh winter's day, we set off from our chapel of rest at Kington, giving ourselves plenty of time, to travel to St Peter's Church at Peterchurch, where a funeral I'd arranged would take place. The plan was to call in on the family at their address in Peterchurch to collect them on the way to the funeral service. It was bitterly cold, with snow showers forecast. The coffin was already in the hearse, which Chris was driving, with Dick following in the limousine. We drove over Bredwardine bridge, then turned right at the bottom of Dorstone hill to take us up and over the hill with a good 20 or 25 minutes to spare. At that point, large snowflakes began falling and settling on the ground as we cautiously ascended. Then it started snowing much more heavily, and I thought we might not make it to the top and over the other side. The higher we were, the worse the snowy conditions became. Chris turned the windscreen wipers on as heavy snow was beginning to settle on the windscreen, as well as the road and the grass verges. Just before reaching the top of the hill, the hearse wheels started to spin until we'd lost traction and could go no further. I knew we were in trouble, so came up with a plan! With hardly any time to think, my mind skipped back to Dick and the police driving training courses we'd been on and I asked Chris to change seats with me so I could drive. I got out of the hearse and told Dick to follow me back down to the bottom of Dorstone Hill, where we would

The above photo is of ex-serviceman Tom Carter's funeral procession at
Eardisley Church Lychgate on 24 June 2019. Tom was given military funeral
honours with three rifle volleys fired over his grave in recognition of his
service, duty and honour after single-handedly shooting down a German
Messerschmitt plane during the Second World War (see page 84). We wore
our medals and dropped poppies into his grave after the interment.

257

take the lower, circular route I was familiar with. This meant a nearly 14-mile detour, but, if we drove fast enough, we could get there just in the nick of time! 'Whatever happens, make sure you keep up with me!' I said. We turned around at the top and headed back down Dorstone hill to the bottom, where the weather had improved, and headed off towards Madley. To make up for lost time, we drove the hearse and limousine at speeds in excess of 70 miles an hour! After sweeping round a right- and a left-hand bend towards Peterchurch, I saw from the corner of my eye a sheep farmer leaning over his field gate facing our way. As we flew past him bumper-to-bumper I saw his shocked and puzzled expression. With less than two minutes to spare, we arrived outside the family home where I took a few deep breaths to compose myself before knocking at the door and informing the family that we had arrived. Chris got back into the driver's seat, after straightening up a flower arrangement on top of the coffin, so no one would know, apart from us and one very astonished sheep farmer!

There were one or two churches I'd never been to before, and St Bartholomew's at Thruxton was one, so I made a point of going there the day before the funeral to familiarise myself with the route and to estimate the time it would take us to travel there. The family wanted me to take the coffin and hearse, which Chris was driving, to the family home, where we would meet them so they could follow the hearse in their cars. We set off over Whitney toll bridge to go to the church, which was about 16 miles away. Chris was a bell-ringer who knew most churches in Herefordshire, but he had never rung bells at St Bartholomew's and was relying entirely on my directions. After about ten miles, I asked Chris to turn right, which he did, with the family cortège dutifully following us.

Suddenly I had a sinking feeling in the pit of my stomach as I realised that I had mistakenly told Chris to take the first right turn, when we should have taken the second right! We were now driving down the wrong road and completely lost, with all the family following and keeping up behind. Where the road ahead started to narrow, I was relieved to see a large tractor coming towards us. The driver slowed down and pulled in, to give us room for the hearse and our cortège to squeeze past. 'Chris, stop and put your window down!' I said, 'I'll ask him for directions'. Assuming that the tractor driver was a local farmer or farmworker, I leaned across to the driver's side to speak to him, 'Excuse me, could you tell us how we get to Thruxton Church please?' 'Haven't a clue, mate!' he replied. So, with no choice, we drove blindly on. After a couple of miles, we came to a crossroads, which had no signposts! Chris asked me the inevitable question, inferring that it was now entirely my fault for the mess we were in, which it was! 'Which way do you want me to go now?' he questioned. We were already totally lost, and I was feeling gutted that I'd let the family down so badly. I nervously spluttered, 'Er, don't know, turn left!' Half a mile further on, as luck had it, I spotted a small sign, practically hidden by the long grass, on the nearside verge, with a tiny black arrow pointing up to the right. Beneath it I read three very reassuring words: ST BARTHOLOMEW'S CHURCH! I can't tell you how relieved I was when we arrived right outside the main entrance to the church and, by some sheer fluke, exactly on time! The family mourners, who were still behind, were getting out of their cars when the closest relative came up to me and said, 'Bill, it would never have occurred to us to come that way. It is so pretty and mum would have loved it!'

AND FINALLY …

MY granddaughter Poppy once asked which half of my life had I enjoyed the best, the first or second? This is a thought-provoking question as I enter my seventy-third year and being honest, I'm not entirely sure! At the time I think I said the second half, but I am thankful for everything and have no regrets. I have some very treasured memories, otherwise I might not have written any of them down. The fact is that I feel extremely blessed, especially so, having survived cancer. I never use a capital c for cancer because I think it lessens the impact for the word. I've lived through a mixture of happy and challenging times, with disappointments too of course, as we all have in our lives. I've experienced very painful, personal grief too, so I know how it feels. I feel your pain too. I have always asked for a bit of God's help when I've needed it, and I am blessed to have a belief in God, spelled with a capital G! My darling daughter Lucy, who I love so much, became ill and in 2022 was diagnosed with terminal cancer. Her family, friends and carers did everything possible to help make the rest of her young life as comfortable and as tolerable as it could be. She was never frightened of dying, but sadly Lucy died on the 16 July 2022, aged just 48 years old. The family helped to arrange and carry out her funeral arrangements and it was all so beautiful, like she was. She loved horses and rode them in show jumping competitions when she was younger. Her cardboard coffin depicted photos of horses jumping over fences, and we, her family, joined hands around her coffin on the catafalque at the crematorium. We listened to special music and heard such moving personal tributes, from her daughter Poppy and son Josh, from her friends and from people who loved her. She helped many people who were less fortunate than herself during her career. She is still my little girl. It was, and still is, such a painful, emotional time for us, especially for Josh, Poppy and for Lucy's mum Janette. I made the decision to direct Lucy's funeral myself, spurred on by her love and by her words, which were running through my head, 'Dad, I want you to do it and no one else!' She will never be forgotten by all of us who loved you so very much. May you rest in God's eternal life, light, love and peace, until we meet again.

cancer is so limited.
It cannot cripple love
It cannot shatter hope
It cannot corrode faith
It cannot destroy peace
It cannot kill friendship
It cannot suppress memories
It cannot silence courage
It cannot invade the soul
It cannot steal eternal life
It cannot conquer the spirit.

Below are some wise words and readings that I am particularly fond of. The Desiderata are words for life, and were beautifully read at a funeral I directed a few years ago.

The Desiderata

Go placidly amid the noise and the haste, and remember what peace there may be in silence. As far as possible, without surrender, be on good terms with all persons.

Speak your truth quietly and clearly; and listen to others, even to the dull and the ignorant; they too have their story.

Avoid loud and aggressive persons; they are vexatious to the spirit. If you compare yourself with others, you may become vain or bitter, for always there will be greater and lesser persons than yourself.

Enjoy your achievements as well as your plans. Keep interested in your own career, however humble; it is a real possession in the changing fortunes of time.

Exercise caution in your business affairs, for the world is full of trickery. But let this not blind you to what virtue there is; many persons strive for high ideals, and everywhere life is full of heroism.

Be yourself. Especially do not feign affection. Neither be cynical about love; for in the face of all aridity and disenchantment, it is as perennial as the grass.

Take kindly the counsel of the years, gracefully surrendering the things of youth.

Nurture strength of spirit to shield you in sudden misfortune. But do not distress yourself with dark imaginings. Many fears are born of fatigue and loneliness.

Beyond a wholesome discipline, be gentle with yourself.

The Optimist Creed

Promise Yourself

To be so strong that nothing can disturb your peace of mind.

To talk health, happiness and prosperity to every person you meet.

To make all your friends feel that there is something in them.

To look at the sunny side of everything and make your optimism come true.

To think only of the best, to work only for the best and to expect only the best.

To be just as enthusiastic about the success of others as you are about your own.

To forget the mistakes of the past and press on to the greater achievements of the future.

To wear a cheerful countenance at all times and give every living creature you meet a smile.

To give so much time to the improvement of yourself that you have no time to criticize others.

To be too large for worry, too noble for anger, too strong for fear, and too happy to permit the presence of trouble.

Perhaps our emotions become more intense as we age because I've been finding it more difficult to maintain a funeral director's 'stiff upper lip' at funerals recently, which might be an accumulation of dealing with so many different, difficult and traumatic situations where people are suffering. In any case on the 6 May 2020, I decided to retire and my business, Oak Tree Funeral Services, was transferred to its new owners, carrying on our good name. My staff remained employed in the company, which is more than I could have hoped for. Following retirement, I am very occasionally asked to help at funerals, so I maintain some contact with the staff, who are also my friends, as well as seeing and meeting up with local families I've known for decades, both as a policeman and as a funeral director. The difference is that I no longer have the responsibility of running a business, which I think at my age was beginning to take its toll. Fortunately, I recognised this and am now moving in a different direction, perhaps helped by the very person whose name begins with a capital G! I know this was exactly the right moment in my life to step back, and I am so proud and thankful that I became a policeman and a funeral director, which were not only vocations but positions of huge privilege and trust. I remind myself of why I set out to write my memoirs, which was both for the benefit of family and for posterity. How interesting it would be to catch little snippets and glimpses of the lives and characters of my ancestral relatives, especially my grandfather John, who like so many soldiers fought so bravely for his country, and others like him who gave their lives for us in both World Wars.

So, what's mine is now yours!

There are many people, acquaintances, friends and family who I have not necessarily mentioned. I couldn't mention everyone, but you all figure so prominently in my thoughts and in my daily life, and you all know who you are and who you were. When I started both careers, I had no idea what lay ahead, but I was committed and I owe such a debt of gratitude to colleagues, staff, friends and family who supported me during my three years as a young police cadet, 30 years as a police officer and 20 years as a funeral director ... 'from bashes to ashes'!